Canadian History

A Captivating Guide to the History of Canada, French and Indian War, Klondike Gold Rush, and Quebec

Free Bonus from Captivating History (Available for a Limited time)

Hi History Lovers!

Now you have a chance to join our exclusive history list so you can get your first history ebook for free as well as discounts and a potential to get more history books for free! Simply visit the link below to join.

Captivatinghistory.com/ebook

Also, make sure to follow us on Facebook, Twitter and Youtube by searching for Captivating History.

Table of Contents

Part 1: History of Canada

A Captivating Guide to Canadian History

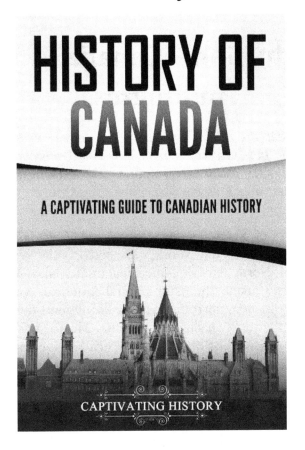

Introduction – Canada: A Work in Progress

"Human beings are works in progress that mistakenly think they're finished. The person you are right now is as transient, as fleeting and as temporary as all the people you've ever been. The one constant in our lives is change."

-Daniel Gilbert

The region of North America that we call "Canada" was at one time considered the New World's greatest frontier country. Yes, out of all of North America—meaning modern-day Mexico, the United States, Canada, the many Central American countries, and the various islands surrounding the continent—the Canadian frontier was the most challenging to settle. Mexico was the first of the three largest nations of North America to be colonized when Spanish conquistadors sailed from Europe to subdue the Aztecs, Maya, and Incas.

The midsection of the North American continent was then tackled by other western Europeans who slowly pushed west from the eastern seaboard. The northernmost section of North America, however—that great land of Canada—was the last to be subdued. Even today, there are sections of Canada in the far north that remain largely unexplored.

But as challenging as Canada was to settle, the attempts of doing so go back quite a ways. It has long been believed that even before those aforementioned Spanish conquistadors trailblazed through the Caribbean, Mexico, and Central America, the Scandinavian Vikings of the 11th century established a toehold on Canadian shores. The Vikings are said to have discovered the North American continent by accident, as they were lost and caught in a bad wind storm. As a result of this, a group of Viking navigators found themselves in Nova Scotia.

They did not know where they were, and they certainly did not grasp the significance of their landing. But neither did Christopher Columbus when he landed in the Caribbean. Columbus, after all, was seeking a water route to India, and he initially thought he had landed somewhere near the eastern Indian subcontinent. It's for this reason, of course, that he called the inhabitants he encountered "Indians."

Many incredible discoveries have indeed occurred as a result of mishaps and erroneous mistakes. And the discovery of the North American continent is most certainly one of them. The entrance of Europeans to the Americas would change both the Old World and the New World for good. Many staple crops and products that the rest of the world takes for granted were first discovered in the Americas.

Imagine, for example, a world without tobacco. From a man in Istanbul, Turkey, smoking a hookah to a teenager in Japan absentmindedly tossing a spent cigarette on the sidewalk, none of these things would have been possible without the discovery of the Americas and its indigenous tobacco crop. In fact, cigarette smoking is so ubiquitous and has been for centuries that it is hard for some to imagine life without it.

Yet, prior to retrieving tobacco from the Americas, such things were not known to exist in other parts of the world. And from the perspective of indigenous First Nations people roaming the lands that would one day become Canada, neither did the horse. Yes, as much as Native American warriors riding on horseback has become an ingrained image, horses themselves were not a part of their life until the Europeans reintroduced them to the continent. However, this is a debated topic amongst scholars, as some believe that the natives had access to their own horses during the wave of colonization. Most historians seem to believe that horses had gone extinct and that the European visitors suddenly flooded North America with horses, as well as guns and steel tools—all things that the indigenous residents of Canada came to desire.

As much as we might despair over the tragic outcomes that occurred as a result of contact, there were indeed benefits for both involved. And in at least the early days of Canadian settlement, trade between the original inhabitants and the newcomers was booming. In fact, the early Canadian economy was almost entirely built around the fur trade.

Local tribes knew that if they hunted animals and skinned them of their furs, they could turn around and trade them to European settlers for horses, guns, steel pots and pans, or whatever else they may have wanted. The locals had become so used to this routine that it was common for a ship just arriving on the North American shores to be greeted by excited residents raising their best furs on long wooden poles, indicating that they were ready to trade.

It was on this mutual beneficial understanding that much of early Canadian settlement would be built. As things progressed, however, it obviously did not end up going as well for the local tribes as it had in the beginning. But by then, it was too late. Their old ways of life had diminished, and they had become dependent on trade with the newcomers. They also began to be entangled in their own struggles and wars.

The French-Canadian settlers began to team up with Native American tribes in order to offset their small numbers against the more numerous British who began to encroach on Canadian territory. These happenings would eventually culminate in the French and Indian War, which France would ultimately lose, causing almost all of their Canadian holdings to be handed over to the British.

This would be the end of French overseas power in Canada, but the French Canadians would remain. Britain now had its hands full with trying to create some semblance of unity between the two distinct communities of English-speaking Canadians and French-speaking ones.

Although this union has become much closer through the years, it is a relationship that is still evolving. This was evidenced when Quebec citizens nearly voted to leave Canada altogether in a 1995 referendum. Canada is a wonderful place with room to grow, but it is definitely still a work in progress. This is the history of how that progress has been made.

Chapter 1 – The General Geology of Canada

"I grew up on the edge of a national park in Canada—Timberwolves, creeks, snow drifts. I really did have to walk home six miles through snow, like your grandparents used to complain."

-Dan Aykroyd

The Canadian landscape is about as diverse and dynamic as it gets. Canada clocks in at over three and a half million square miles, with Russia being the only country on the planet able to boast greater terrain. Canada is so large that it has full access to both the Atlantic and the Pacific, as well as the Arctic. The northernmost reaches of Canada, however, are a virtually uninhabitable wasteland of snow and ice, whereas southern Canada features immense forests and wildlife.

Canada boasts a wide variety of trees, with spruce, pine, and, of course, maple trees immediately coming to mind. These trees are hardy specimens that can survive cold spells as well as dry periods in which precipitation might be scarce. Canada also has rich farmland but not quite as much as its southern neighbor, the United States.

Only about 5 percent of Canada is farm-worthy, whereas about 40 percent of the United States is utilized for farming. Nevertheless, Canada makes use of that 5 percent, and with its lower population of just 38 million—compared to the United States of America's 330 million—Canadians have more than enough crops to make do.

Geologically speaking, the land of Canada was highly influenced by the last Ice Age. During the last full-blown Ice Age, Canada, at different periods, was almost completely covered in ice, as glaciers advanced all the way to the midwestern regions of what's now the modern-day United States. Canada experienced several cycles in which this glacial ice covered up most of its territory before it retreated back to the Arctic.

As the ice sheets retreated, they created great gouges in the land, which today make up Canada's numerous streams, rivers, and lakebeds. The site of great glacial retraction in the center of modern-day Canada is known as the Canadian Shield. After the ice left, an immense plateau of igneous rock was exposed. Such land is not so great for farming, but it is a real boom for miners seeking out precious minerals.

And here, in this abundant stretch of rocky land, plenty of copper, silver, nickel, and even gold can be found. This resulted in famous mining towns such as Ontario's "Sudbury" popping up, and these were centered almost entirely around the excavation of the precious minerals from the Canadian Shield. This sparsely settled region is just about as fantastic and remote to Canadians as it is to anyone else. This, of course, is due to the fact that the vast majority of Canada's population live just outside of the Canadian Shield in the coastal regions and southern Canada.

Of those aforementioned coastal enclaves, one of the greatest is on the west coast of Canada, and it makes up a geologic feature called the North American Cordillera, which reaches (at least geologically speaking) from Alaska all the way to Arizona, bristling with mountains of various heights. These mountains quite literally cast a shadow and result in plenty of cloudy precipitation along Canada's western coast. The mountains also keep the milder coastal air from reaching the interior, creating a pocket of warmer climate on the west coast of Canada that cannot be found after crossing these powerful and majestic mountain ranges. Most of the Canadian Province of British Columbia, as well as a section of the Yukon, can be found along the North American Cordillera.

Another major geological feature of Canada is the Great Plains. This is a stretch of flat steppe land that stretches from the Ontario region to the Rocky Mountains. It spans some 695,000 square miles of Canada's southern interior. This stretch of Canadian soil boasts a continental climate of rather chilly winters and hot but very brief summers. The powerful Saskatchewan and Mackenzie Rivers snake through this region for several thousand miles.

This land is great for prairie dogs and grazing animals, which roam fields that stretch as far as the eye can see. For human beings, though, it is the St. Lawrence Lowlands of southeastern Canada, nestled above the Great Lakes, that provides the most comfort. This region has a good climate, arable land, and a vast supply of water. In this region, one can find the populous eastern Canadian cities of Montreal, Quebec City, and Ottawa.

Just east of the lowlands, you get into Canada's branch of the Appalachians—a mountain range that stretches from Canada's Newfoundland all the way to Georgia in the United States. The whole mountain range is full of rivers, lakes, and streams in abundance, as well as some decent farmland to boot. However, the region is most known for its wooded terrain, as well as its rich mineral deposits.

Of course, the coldest and least populated portions of Canada are the north, and they make up the taiga and arctic climates of Canada. The taiga is a very cold region of northern Canada, and it is known for its harsh winters. The taiga, nevertheless, sports the great boreal forest, which is just a part of one massive forest system of the Northern Hemisphere that rings the entire planet. The boreal forest in northern Canada is connected to the same tree system in Russia and Scandinavia. Just imagine a ring of hardy, snow-covered coniferous trees circling some of the northernmost landmasses on the globe.

This northern region of Canada makes up a massive part of the country, but only a very small population of people can be found here. One of the main outposts in the taiga region is Yellowknife, a town that boasts a population of just under twenty thousand people.

Farther north, where the environment is even more extreme, one reaches the portion of Canada that is actually situated in the

Arctic. The Arctic region doesn't have trees as the taiga does, and it sports a landscape of uninterrupted ice and snow year-round. You might find some lichens and moss clinging to arctic rocks, but this climate is far too harsh to support even the hardiest of trees.

Nevertheless, the Arctic region does have some interesting wildlife, such as the Arctic fox, the snowy owl, and, of course, the polar bear. This is the general geology of Canada in a nutshell, although there is always more to discover.

Chapter 2 – Canada before the Arrival of the Europeans

"We owe the Aboriginal peoples a debt that is four centuries old. It is their turn to become full partners in developing an even greater Canada. And the reconciliation required may be less a matter of legal texts than of attitudes of the heart."

-Romeo LeBlanc

The part of the world we call Canada has a history that long predates the arrival of the Europeans. The name Canada itself is said to have been derived from a term that the Iroquois used: Kanata, which roughly translates as "settlement" or "meeting place." The Iroquois, of course, were just one of several Native American civilizations that inhabited the Canadian portion of North America.

The indigenous people groups that existed prior to European discovery were many and diverse. Some of the more ancient civilizations are believed to have already come and gone prior to the days of Christopher Columbus. Although some tribal leaders may tell you that their people have been a part of Canada since the dawn of time, it is generally believed that the first of what have been termed the First Nations of North America arrived around fifteen thousand years ago.

Much of what we know of these first residents of Canada comes from archaeology and oral legends since none of the Canadian tribes (as far as we know) had established a method of writing. Most mainstream archaeologists believe that the first Native American tribes arrived in North America and ultimately what we know today as Canada around fifteen thousand to perhaps even twenty thousand years ago at the end of the last Ice Age.

It is believed that these ancient explorers may have crossed over between continents on a land bridge that connected Eurasia to Alaska. Although the vast bulk of this land bridge is now submerged under water, the remnants of this bridge today can be seen in the form of Alaska's Aleutian Islands, which are a chain of islands that stretch toward Siberia.

The theory of a mass migration over a land bridge from Siberia has been greatly bolstered through DNA research, which has found a strong link between many Native American groups and the East Asians of the Mongolia and Manchurian regions of northeast Asia. However, there are those who have asked the question— could it be that this migration happened in the reverse of what archaeologists think?

It has been suggested that perhaps ancient indigenous Americans traveled to East Asia, where they set the foundations of the Mongolians and Manchurians and not the other way around. It is an interesting thought, but there is scant evidence that this was the case. On the other hand, there is very strong evidence that the ancient tribes of the aforementioned East Asian lands traveled across a land bridge to the Americas at the tail end of the last Ice Age.

During this period, much of the world was covered in glacial ice. The fact that much of the earth's water was frozen in pack ice resulted in a lower sea level and thus more dry land. It is believed that after all of this ice melted, the land bridge connecting Alaska with Eurasia was submerged under water. Perhaps the Native American tribe that bears the strongest evidence of this connection is the Inuit. The Inuit people are a "circumpolar" tribe, and they have an unbroken chain of settlements from Siberia to the North American Arctic to Greenland.

At any rate, the North American continent for these first people groups was much different than it is today. At the end of the last Ice Age, fifteen thousand years ago, North America was full of a wide variety of animals that simply no longer exist. Giant, fur-covered elephant creatures called wooly mammoths roamed the plains. There were also fearsome big canine critters called dire wolves. Another entirely unique animal inhabitant was the ground sloth.

The Native Americans interacted with and hunted these animals. In fact, there is evidence of the ground sloth having confrontations with humans shortly after humanity's first arrival. There are fossil records featuring several human footprints and sloth footprints imprinted together in a manner that suggests a struggle between human aggressors and a sloth, which appears to have been attempting to raise itself up and defend itself.

With indications such as these in the fossil records, it has been suggested that these sloths and other Ice Age-era animals may have actually been hunted by these early human settlers all the way to extinction. Other theories suggest that maybe they died off due to natural climate change or perhaps a combination of both climate change and overhunting.

Most of the new arrivals to America at the end of the last Ice Age eventually marched south, following the Cordillera Mountain range of Canada's west coast to the more temperate regions. As the ice began to retreat farther north toward the Arctic about ten thousand years ago, these Native American tribal groups began to move steadily north and east to settle most of what we have come to call Canada. This process is believed to have been completed about seven thousand years ago when the glaciers had fully retreated and when the temperatures were roughly equivalent to what we have today.

In the Yukon, one of the oldest Native American settlements was found. In a spot called Old Crow, we find a settlement that archaeologists date back to roughly fifteen thousand years ago. This is important since this coincides with the time period that most scholars believe the nomadic tribes first made their trek from Eurasia to North America.

These early settlers braved the elements and hunted large game such as deer, elk, and even the huge wooly mammoth. Such powerful beasts provided both warm fur coats and a large portion of meat, which enabled these early Americans to survive the harsh winters of the Canadian frontier. And there is archaeological evidence that tribal settlers were developing more complex communities and, along with hunting and gathering, began to regularly conduct fishing operations on the western coast by 8000 BCE. Then, as now, Canada's western shores have plenty of salmon for any would-be fishermen.

As tribal groups migrated east, there is evidence of the gradual advancement of tools. The earliest settlers used chipped stone tools. But soon there were tribes with better polished stone tools and weapons. Then, by 3000 BCE, there is evidence of tribes using copper as the main resource for crafting their various utensils.

Coinciding with these developments was the widespread use of canoes, which, in turn, led to the frequent trade of goods between various tribes. The use of pottery was also widespread by 1000 BCE, especially near the Great Lakes. Around Canada's portion of the Great Lakes, tribal groups began to transition away from a hunting culture to an agrarian one, causing widespread farming to become more prevalent.

It was here that signature crops such as maize were developed and widely distributed among local tribal groups. Maize, of course, is an important agricultural fixture, and it was first developed much farther south by the advanced indigenous civilizations of Mexico. The crop eventually spread from Mexico to the northernmost section of the North American continent (i.e., Canada). And yes, by 1000 BCE, maize was indeed a common enough crop, even in Ontario.

Complex religious beliefs also began to flourish during this period, as is evidenced by the vast burial mound complexes that began to dot the landscape. Archaeology can only tell us so much about why the locals buried their people in these mounds. But by the great lengths that they went to create and preserve them—well enough, in fact, that we can still see them to this very day—it is quite clear that these mounds were very important to their society. The most extensive of these mounts is the Manitou Mounds, which can be found in Ontario.

Many of these complex societies remained intact for thousands of years—some all the way until post-Columbian contact. It was around this time that the Iroquois tribe came to prominence around the Great Lakes region. The Iroquois, sometimes classified as a tribal confederacy, were a large group of indigenous tribes who all spoke the same Iroquois language and who had banded together to control a large swathe of the northeast. Their lands ranged from modern-day Virginia, Pennsylvania, and New York in the south to Ontario in the north. The political system of the Iroquois Confederacy was complex, consisting of local councils headed by village chiefs. They were independent states in themselves yet all bound together for mutual defense. This confederacy of the Iroquois is considered one of the most elaborate indigenous social structures present in North America.

Interestingly enough, it has even been recognized that the original Articles of Confederation, which banded the Thirteen Colonies together in their opposition to Great Britain, actually drew some inspiration from the Iroquois system. The tribes of the Iroquois brought together several tribal units into one common front, and they were united for defense and the general welfare of all members. The Thirteen Colonies initially united as a confederacy for much the same reason.

The most visible feature of Iroquois society was, no doubt, their famed longhouses. These long wooden structures, which were typically twenty feet in width and as much as two hundred feet in length, could be found all over the Great Lakes region. The longhouses were used for communal dwellings as well as a place for the local leaders to discuss the most pertinent political matters of the day.

Just imagine several local representatives of various tribes of the confederacy meeting in a longhouse to debate pressing matters affecting the tribal groups as a whole. Once the Europeans arrived on the scene, much of these debates would be in regards as to how the confederacy should handle these strange newcomers.

The Iroquois lived on both their crops and wild game, and these two labors were typically divided between males and females, with the men primarily being the hunters and the women primarily tending to the crops. The three main crops grown by the Iroquois are sometimes referred to as the "Three Sisters." These Three Sisters were the Iroquois staple crops of beans, squash, and maize. Supplementing the Iroquois diet was a steady number of fish, which were most abundant in the springtime.

Of course, the Iroquois were just one of many indigenous people groups in Canada, but their importance cannot be understated since they would eventually become the most important power players when the post-Columbian Europeans eventually made their way to Canada.

Chapter 3 – The Viking Attempt to Settle Canada

"Canada has always been there to help people who need it."

-Justin Trudeau

Brash explorers from the reaches of Scandinavia (northern Europe) known as the Vikings were making major inroads by the 9th century. Although they are perhaps better known for their bloodthirsty raids launched against Britain and continental Europe, the Vikings—despite their bloodlust—were also incredible sailors and navigators.

The Vikings are, indeed, an often-misunderstood group. For centuries, they have been stereotyped as belligerent pagan holdouts who suddenly swarmed down from their northern outposts on an unsuspecting Europe. They were described as bloodthirsty barbarians who ruthlessly raided villages and churches in places like Britain and France, thus leaving us today with one-dimensional characters at best.

But while it is true that the Vikings were capable of incredible violence, one of the main catalysts of this violence often goes unmentioned. The Vikings, you see, actually believed that they were at war with Christianity. And furthermore, they didn't feel that they were the ones who started the conflict. That credit went to Holy Roman Emperor Charlemagne (r. 800–814 CE), who began to forcibly convert the pagans of Denmark. This was conversion by the sword, plain and simple, and it sparked an armed conflict.

During the course of the conflict, Charlemagne's men actually set fire to a sacred tree of the Norse called the Irminsul, which was an earthly representation of Yggdrasil or the "tree of life" of Norse mythology. According to Norse prophecy, once Yggdrasil fell, Armageddon (or as the Norse called it "Ragnarök") would begin. Thus, the Vikings literally believed that Charlemagne had triggered Armageddon by cutting down their sacred tree, and it is really not much of a coincidence that they began descending upon Europe shortly thereafter.

The Vikings basically thought, "Well, if you burn my sacred tree, then I will burn your sacred church!" And that is what they did. It should be noted, however, that there are some scholars who contend the Vikings attacked places that seemed vulnerable, such as monasteries, as they would provide easy loot for little work.

The Vikings themselves, of course, would eventually find a peaceful means to convert to Christianity, with most of them becoming Christians by the 12th century. But in the meantime, there was a lot of fighting, as well as exploring, that the Vikings would take part in.

In around 825 CE, the Vikings left Norway to establish a settlement in the Faroe Islands, which lay in the waters north of Scotland and west of Norway. From this launching pad, the Vikings were then able to discover another sizeable island about four hundred miles west of the Faroe Islands. Settled by the Vikings in 860 CE, this new island was named "Iceland." It was a little over one hundred years later, around 980 CE, that the Vikings leapfrogged from Iceland and went even farther west, bumping into an even larger landmass—a place they called "Greenland."

According to the Norse sagas, Viking explorer Erik the Red was the champion of this cause. It has been said that he left Iceland and landed on the southwestern coast of Greenland. It was also Erik the Red who supposedly gave Greenland its name. He called it thus, thinking that such an appellation would serve as a great marketing tool for settlement since green pastures sound attractive. However, Greenland is not all that green; in fact, it is even more ice-covered than Iceland!

As an interesting aside, it was around the time that Greenland was founded that the Scandinavian equivalent of parliament—the Althing—was having vigorous debates about whether or not to leave the ancestral faith of the Norse religion for Christianity. With that in mind, it could be that some diehard Norse believers were seeking new lands such as Greenland and then maybe even North America for similar reasons that Protestant Christians would later come to the Americas—for religious freedom.

Even more fascinating to ponder as a possible motivating factor is the Norse legend of Valhalla. Many have the misconception that Valhalla was simply Viking heaven, a non-physical dimension that the souls of the slain Vikings passed on to. But this is not the case. The Vikings believed that Valhalla existed as a tangible piece of land far across the mysterious waters west of the traditional Norse lands of Scandinavia.

Taking that into consideration, one can better grasp what might have inspired some of these Vikings to make all of these dangerous westward journeys across uncharted waters. Some may have actually believed they were searching for Valhalla itself.

At any rate, once Greenland was tamed by the Vikings, they used it as a staging area to head even farther afield. According to Norse lore, a Viking merchant by the name of Bjarni Herjólfsson sailed into a bad storm on his way from Iceland to Greenland. He was knocked so far west that he ended up on the shores of a completely unknown landmass.

Bjarni had no idea where he was, but he quickly corrected his route to get to Greenland as planned. When a Norseman by the name of Leif Erikson heard of this account, he was intrigued enough to look into the matter himself. Leif Erikson was actually the son of the famed Erik the Red. It is for this reason, of course, that his name was Erikson, or Erik's son.

Leif Erickson and his fellow Viking mariners would use the clues given by Bjarni, and they would find their way to a place they called Vinland. Most scholars today believe that Vinland was actually the northeasternmost coast of North America. They also landed on a rocky island they called Helluland, which seems to correspond with present-day Baffin Island. Leif's group is said to have spent the winter of 1001 in what today is known as

Newfoundland.

It has been said that Leif spent the rest of the year at this outpost without much incident before heading back to Greenland. After Leif's return to Greenland, his brother Thorvald is said to have made his own trip to the newly discovered territory of Vinland in 1004. It is thought that Thorvald Erikson departed from Greenland with a group of some thirty men. This group landed in roughly the same location where Leif Erikson's encampment had been.

According to the Viking sagas, Thorvald was apparently a rather violent and aggressive fellow. They say that after stumbling upon a group of indigenous people resting under "three skin covered canoes," he launched an unprovoked attack against them. It remains unclear why he would do such a thing. Perhaps he considered it a preemptive strike, cutting down potential nearby aggressors before they could strike out against him and his followers.

If so, it was most certainly a cold-blooded calculation on his part, as he cared very little for the lives he took. But even if this was his aim, his efforts were a miserable failure. Thorvald and his men did indeed kill eight of the nine men they encountered, but one lone survivor managed to escape. And this was all it took to bring the wrath of a whole tribe down upon these Viking interlopers.

The Vikings hid behind some hastily constructed barricades put up around their settlement, and they managed to hold their assailants at bay, but Thorvald himself was killed in the process, making him the first European to die in the Americas. An arrow sailed through the fortifications and struck him down right where he stood. Nevertheless, the rest of the crew managed to survive the winter before heading back to Greenland in the spring.

The Norse sagas then speak of yet another ill-fated expedition in which a man by the name of Thorfinn (yes, quite a few Vikings had "Thor" in their name), along with his spouse Gudrid and several others, landed in North America. It was shortly after their arrival that Gudrid gave birth to a child named Snorri. If Norse legend is to be believed, this could be the first European baby born in the Americas.

Initially, the expedition went quite well for the group. And unlike their predecessors, these Vikings managed to set up some rather peaceful relations with the local tribes. Instead of fighting with the local inhabitants, these enterprising Norse began to trade with them. Trading food and furs were fine, but once the local tribes began to ask for steel weapons such as broadswords and heavy battleaxes, Thorfinn ordered his followers to deny them these trade goods.

His reasoning was understandable enough. Thorfinn feared that if he handed over their best weapons to the locals, the Vikings would lose any military advantage they might have had. It would be like the United States handing over its best stealth aircraft and nuclear submarines to China for the sake of "friendship." Most pragmatic military leaders would not do such a thing, and Thorfinn, no matter how friendly the locals were, was not about to do that either.

According to the sagas, the local tribes took offense to this, and they began to conspire against the Vikings. A group of them then apparently tried to steal from the Vikings what they would not trade, sparking an altercation that left one of the local tribesmen dead. In a virtual repeat of what had happened to Thorvald several years prior, this triggered a tribal avalanche of aggression, as a huge number of the natives descended upon the small Viking camp to avenge their fallen comrade.

Despite being outnumbered, the Vikings were able to hold off their attackers due to solid fortifications and—thanks to Thorfinn—their superior arms. Even so, they knew it was only a matter of time before they would be driven into the sea, so taking a hint, the Viking survivors loaded up their ships and headed off to Greenland once again.

The Viking experiment in North America didn't last very long. It is said to have taken place for just a few years—perhaps as brief as being from the year 1001 to the year 1007. The most concrete evidence of Viking habitation comes to us from Newfoundland, for it was in Newfoundland's L'Anse aux Meadows that intact Norse housing was uncovered, along with several other souvenirs of Viking settlement.

There was even evidence of iron smelting. Iron is not believed to have been known to the indigenous groups, but it is rather indicative of Norse settlement, as they had a penchant for fashioning mighty steel blades for their broadswords. This archaeological evidence seems to correspond to the Norse sagas that tell the tale of settlement in what is now Canada.

Chapter 4 – Early English and French Colonies

"If the national mental illness of the United States is megalomania, that of Canada is paranoid schizophrenia."

-Margaret Atwood

The story of how Christopher Columbus sailed to the New World of the Americas, reaching the Caribbean in 1492, is fairly well known. The much lesser-known expedition of John Cabot (the Italianized version of his name is actually Giovanni Caboto) on behalf of Britain took place in 1497. This Italian sailor was quite skilled, and the English monarch—King Henry VII—apparently had full confidence in him.

Good old King Henry had famously advised Cabot to "seek out, discover, and find, whatsoever isles and provinces" and claim them for England. Cabot sailed out of the British port of Bristol that year and ended up landing on the old stomping ground of the Vikings' Newfoundland. Cabot was authorized to claim any "newly" discovered land for England, and that is what he did, officially declaring Newfoundland to be the property of the British crown.

This, of course, was done no matter what any of the local tribes might have thought about the matter. The area was sparsely populated, and if any of the locals happened to catch a glimpse of the strange newcomers planting the British flag, they probably wouldn't have thought too much of the act itself besides being amazed by the alien nature of the visitors. For them, the lands of Newfoundland didn't have a single owner but were the ancestral homeland for all of the local tribes.

In truth, the British claim was largely a means of fending off other Europeans from attempting inroads in the region. The action was meant to notify their European peers that this little chunk of Canada was now in British hands. And even though Britain would not be able to develop any permanent settlements there for several years, just the notion that Britain had staked out a claim was considered to be of great national importance for the country.

Early on, one of the most bountiful resources to be discovered in Newfoundland was a rich supply of fish. The fish were so plentiful that mariners came back with tales of ships getting stuck in enormous swarms of them. At one point, Cabot is said to have had baskets dropped down under the waters only to have them pulled up absolutely loaded with these aquatic animals.

This part of the ocean was so full of fish that fishing wasn't even a challenge. The spot where Cabot's ship encountered this huge abundance of marine life was near the continental shelf in a particularly shallow section, which just so happened to be a breeding ground of cod. The fishing trade off the shores of Newfoundland would indeed become quite lucrative.

Besides finding new land for England, the English, like many Europeans, were still eager to find a westerly route to India. Even though both Columbus and Cabot had proven that there was a landmass between East Asia and western Europe, no one had yet figured out just how large this landmass was. At this point, it was anyone's guess, and it was commonly believed that the new land being discovered was much smaller than it turned out to be.

As such, explorers like Cabot figured that a quick expedition to the other side of this newfound land (well, it was called Newfoundland for a reason) would lead them right to East Asia. The land that lay between Europe and Asia was viewed as nothing more than a mere speedbump. Of course, we know that getting from the Atlantic coast of Canada to the Pacific coast is not a quick trip by any means.

Cabot, however, persisted in this pursuit. He led his expedition down into the Gulf of St. Lawrence, and he followed the waterway, hoping to find a direct passage to India or even China. Needless to say, he did not find what he was looking for. Cabot's explorations came to an end in 1498 when four out of five ships on his latest expedition were lost. One managed to limp back to Ireland, but nothing was ever heard of John Cabot again; to this day, it is not known what happened to the Italian explorer. King Henry VII himself perished shortly thereafter.

France, in the meantime, made its first forays into exploring North America in the year 1524. Like so many others, France was also interested in finding a quicker, westerly route to India. The French, just like the British—and consequently the Spanish via Christopher Columbus—utilized a skilled Italian navigator, a man known as Giovanni da Verrazzano.

By this time, Spain had leapfrogged from its discoveries in the Caribbean to settlements in Florida. John Cabot, in the meantime, had marked the outline of Newfoundland for the British. Interestingly enough, it was Giovanni Verrazzano who was convinced that there must be a water route between these two far-flung points. Giovanni obviously had no idea that both Newfoundland and Florida were part of the same continent.

Nevertheless, Giovanni persisted. He actually made his way to the spot where modern-day North Carolina is. There, his eyes played some tricks on him, convincing him that he saw a large "ocean-like body of water" just above where North Carolina would be. This was just a trick of the lighting, however, and just like Cabot, Giovanni would return to France with no new route to India.

Nevertheless, this trip added greatly to the knowledge of the correct contours (at least after Giovanni realized his mistake) of North America. French exploration would be put on hold shortly after this expedition, as wars erupted with the Hapsburg dynasty in continental Europe. France would not get back into the game until about a decade later, in 1534, when explorer Jacques Cartier sailed out of the port of Saint-Malo in the northwestern French region of Brittany.

His expedition consisted of sixty-one men, and they spread across two different ships. It took them a little over a month to reach Newfoundland. Jacques was not too thrilled with the ice and snow of the region, and he remarked that perhaps it was "the land God gave to Cain." He dubbed it thus in reference to the biblical narrative of Cain being exiled to the "Land of Nod." Just like John Cabot before him, Jacques sailed into the Gulf of St. Lawrence and then preceded to make his way to Prince Edward Island.

From here, he headed on up to Chaleur Bay, the body of water that separates the lands of Quebec from that of New Brunswick. While passing through this body of water, the expedition encountered some locals from the Mi'kmaq tribe, who were apparently waiting for them on the shore. It has been said that the locals became quite excited upon seeing them, and they held up furs on wooden poles, indicating that they would like to trade them for other goods.

This was a clear indication that these people had traded with visitors before and knew the routine. After this encounter, Cartier's expedition made its way to Gaspe, where they found more native inhabitants—this time members of the powerful Iroquois. It is said that the French readily handed out glass beads, knives, combs, and other trinkets to the Iroquois tribesmen. This was ostensibly done to win their friendship, which would then allow the explorers to use the locals to show them around.

But what happened next does not seem all that friendly. It has been said that the crew of Cartier's ship deliberately sought out and abducted a couple of the local chief's sons. These two Iroquois princes were then forcibly impressed into service for France and worked as regular scouts during subsequent missions. As brutal as this practice was, this was actually a recurring pattern with these voyages.

As well as forcing locals to serve as guides, the indigenous people were often brought back to the expedition's point of origin simply as living proof that the crew had traveled where they said they did. Yes, there was no denying that Jacques Cartier had landed in a strange new land when he had an Iroquois prince standing at his side upon returning to France. Cartier made his return trip to North America in 1535, landing off the shores of modern-day Quebec.

In fact, shortly after this landing, Canada got its name. At this time, one of Cartier's Iroquois guides made reference to the land as being Kanata, the Iroquois word for "meeting place" or "settlement." Cartier began using the word for the entirety of the land itself, and it stuck. From that point forward, the northernmost chunk of North America in its entirety would become known as "Canada." This expedition also named a cove St. Lawrence, and eventually, the aforementioned Gulf of St. Lawrence had acquired the very same name.

Despite the previous forceful taking of captives, the French actually maintained pretty good relations with the local Iroquois of Quebec. The Iroquois valued the French for the steel utensils that they were able to trade their furs for.

It was initially a fairly beneficial arrangement for both. The French were able to profit off of the fine furs, selling them back in Europe for great profit, and the Iroquois were able to get steel goods such as steel pots for cooking and steel knives for hunting and warfare—objects that they otherwise would not have had. Due to their solid relations with the Iroquois, the French were able to travel through their lands virtually unimpeded, and by that October, they had made their way farther north to the much larger Iroquois settlement of Hochelaga.

At the settlement, it is said that over one thousand locals greeted the explorers. It is quite obvious that word had already gotten around about their presence. You might think that these Frenchmen, who were greatly outnumbered and knee-deep in a foreign land, might have had some misgivings. But due to the friendly relations developed through trading, coupled with the far superior French arms—hardly any of the locals had guns at this point—the French were fairly assured they could handle almost anything.

The situation was obviously much different than what the Vikings supposedly encountered several centuries prior, as their one bad encounter was enough to drive them back to Greenland. Unlike the Norse, the French were quite confident in their efforts. Supposedly as Cartier confidently climbed up to the top of a huge hill, he named the spot Mount Royal. This is ultimately where the name of Quebec's future settlement of Montreal came from.

Interestingly enough, Cartier still had not given up on the old idea that a quick trip across this new frontier could possibly lead one to the shores of East Asia. He gazed toward the rapids of the St. Lawrence River, which was west of the settlement. Perhaps he thought that it just might somehow lead him to China. Whatever the case may be, he referred to them as the Lachine Rapids, or, in other words, the "China" rapids.

Cartier and his crew ended up spending the winter in Quebec. During this extended stay, the French apparently managed to overstay their welcome as far as the Iroquois were concerned. Growing suspicious of some of these expeditions upriver, the Laurentian branch of the Iroquois had become frustrated with the French. But a much greater threat than any local hostility for these French explorers was the elements. It was a brutally cold winter that year in Quebec, and by January, the French were dealing with ships nearly becoming encased in ice. And on the ground, their encampments were often covered in several feet of snow.

As they shivered in the cold, sickness broke out, especially bad cases of scurvy from a pronounced lack of vitamin C. It was only after learning to use a Native American cure of boiling bark and leaves of the white cedar tree and drinking the concoction that the crew's illness was alleviated. Upon recovering, the French expressed an interest in heading west to visit the land of the Saguenay tribes.

The Frenchmen had heard rumors that the Saguenay had copper deposits, and they wished to learn more. However, they ran out of time, and by the spring of 1536, they had to head back to France. Domestic turmoil and then a war with Spain ended up putting further expeditions on the backburner, and France would not return to the New World until 1541. On this return trip, Cartier would lead an expedition west of Quebec to check out that fabled land of the Saguenay, as well as take another stab at gaining access to the Northwest Passage (a sea route that connected the Atlantic and Pacific).

Upon their return to Canada, this French group of explorers split into two teams. Cartier led one team of explorers himself, and they headed upriver to the region of Cap-Rouge. They disembarked here, and some 150 crew members set up camp. They brought cattle, began an agriculture project, and constructed dwellings. They endured a rough winter, and they were occasionally attacked by local tribes. Some thirty-five of their number are said to have died. The results of this experiment were so dreadful that Cartier was ready to head back come springtime.

With a boat loaded up on quartz and pyrite (fake gold), Cartier returned to France. He was apparently under the false impression that he had diamonds and real gold in his possession. It has been said that he was so thoroughly ridiculed for his ignorance that the phrase "Faux comme un diamant du Canada," or, as it is in English, "fake as a Canadian diamond" became a widespread phrase in France.

After Cartier's return trip, the other half of the expedition arrived at the settlement of Cap-Rouge. This group consisted of two hundred colonists led by explorer Jean-François de La Rocque de Roberval. They tried their best to literally weather the storms of the Canadian winter, but fifty of them would die before it was through. Roberval would then return to France later that summer. Due to a lack of results and further turmoil on France's political front in Europe, further exploration was sidelined for the next few decades.

In the early 1600s, however, a new French explorer—Samuel de Champlain—began to pick up where all the others had left off. He took part in the Grave expedition, arriving at the St. Lawrence Valley in late 1603. They were accompanied by Pierre Dugua de Mons, a man who was leading the fur trade. This cast of characters sought to create a foothold in Canada's interior. Pierre eventually led his crew to what we now call Nova Scotia, which is just south of Newfoundland, setting up shop in the region in 1604. This led to the establishment of Port Royal and the beginnings of a long-term French-Canadian colony called Acadia.

It was a rough first winter, and it has been said that seventy-nine of these early French colonists perished prior to the first thaw. However, the French stayed, and by 1606, their condition had stabilized. Nevertheless, shortly thereafter, Pierre made the decision to move on due to what he viewed as a lack of profitable enterprise. During the French stay at Port Royal, much effort had been made to extract precious minerals, yet not much was gained. The ever-present side mission of finding the Northwest Passage had also failed to render any results. The port even seemed lacking as a trading post to trade furs since just about any European competitor could sail right through and take business from the French without ever having to put down any roots in the region at all. It was for all of these reasons that the expenditure of sustaining this outpost began to seem too costly to maintain.

Port Royal would ultimately be revied by Jean de Biencourt de Poutrincourt et de Saint-Just (yes, he had quite a long name) several years later as a self-sufficient farming community. And soon thereafter, the Jesuits would establish a Catholic base for French missionaries. Port Royal would ultimately be destroyed by the British in 1613 after a deadly skirmish erupted.

In the meantime, Champlain and company made their way back to the St. Lawrence Valley in 1608. Their goal was to create a solid foothold in the interior of Canada and to keep other European competitors out. Champlain oversaw the construction of a new settlement, which was situated around several fortified wooden structures. The fortifications were then further fortified by walling it off within a wooden stockade.

These colonists were far from home and could be waylaid by an outside force at any time without any additional recourse or aid to assist them. As such, they had to make sure that their settlement was as impregnable as possible. The narrow strait that surrounded the settlement was only crossable by a lowered bridge. It was this feature that inspired the French to name the settlement "Quebec," a French variation of the word Quebec, which was used by the local Algonquian tribe, which roughly translated meant "narrow passage."

But although the French were fairly safe in their fortress in the middle of the Canadian wilderness, they weren't immune to succumbing to sickness and the elements. And that winter would be another rough one, with some twenty-eight French colonists perishing.

The French managed to establish friendly relations with the local Montagnais tribe. The Montagnais were themselves looking for an ally since they were in a bitter war with the Iroquois. The Iroquois possessed the military advantage and were wreaking havoc on the Montagnais. The Montagnais wanted to use the French to regain the upper hand, which they hoped to do so through trade.

They sought steel tools as well as French muskets, which they could use against their adversaries. Pleased with the French trade, the Montagnais then went a step further and actually requested the French to actively join them in their fight against the Iroquois.

Eager to keep up the partnership, the French ultimately decided to take the Montagnais up on their proposal. Thus, in 1609, Champlain led a joint Montagnais/French force against the Iroquois. They ended up taking on a band of some two hundred Iroquois, and although the French and Montagnais were outnumbered, the French muskets proved decisive in cutting through the enemy positions and causing the Iroquois to retreat.

By aiding their tribal allies, the French were, in turn, aided by being given important information about the interior of the land, as well as unique tools and strategies to survive the elements. For example, the locals introduced the French to snowshoes and toboggans, which helped them get around even in the midst of bad winter storms. But perhaps most importantly, their resourceful tribal allies began to regularly supply the French with plenty of hunted game, which was more than enough to sustain them during long winter stretches.

The natives also taught the French colonists the fine art of making maple sugar, which would become a staple of the settlers' diet. Champlain soon sought to expand his alliances further by making contact with another powerful tribe. In 1610, he sent out feelers to the mighty Hurons. After contact was made, the French actually established a hostage exchange with the Hurons.

The practice sounds dreadful, but it was quite common in the ancient world, and it was a known practice among North American tribes. It involved one party sending one of their own in exchange for a member of the other party. So, in this case, the French sent one of their own young men, a man named Étienne Brûlé, to live with the Huron while the French took into their midst a young Huron called Savignon. It was through their special guest and further subsequent relations that the French settlers came to know the Huron people fairly well.

They discovered that this tribal group boasted quite a healthy population—it is said to have been thirty thousand strong—which was stationed around one of the Great Lakes, the one we now call

Lake Huron. The French also discovered that the Huron tribe was indeed powerful enough to take on the mighty Iroquois. The Huron had a mastery over trade in the Great Lakes region of Canada, dominating the trade from Lake Huron to Lake Superior and all the way up to James Bay. In fact, the Huron presence was so important that their native tongue had become the main lingua franca of the region simply as a means for the other tribes to conduct trade.

It was for all of these reasons and more that the French decided to establish formal relations with the Huron so that they could use them as a valuable cog in their own international wheel of trade networks. And by the 1620s, the Hurons supplied the French with the vast majority of the furs they received. Working as a local intermediary, the Huron gathered up as many as fifteen thousand fur pelts from surrounding tribes each year to trade to the French.

The fact that the Hurons became the primary intermediary in this trade network put them in a powerful position over their indigenous peers, as it meant that the other tribes were forced to trade their furs to the Hurons in exchange for valuable French goods, which the Hurons themselves had received from the French in the process of conducting trade. Once this "middleman" relationship was established, if the locals wanted French steel, they had to go to the Hurons to get it. And if the French wanted furs, they, too, also had to go to the Hurons.

Yet this strong alliance between the French and the Hurons had its downside since it meant that the French were obligated to engage in military operations against the Hurons' greatest threat—the Iroquois. This would set the stage for future confrontations with not just the Iroquois Confederacy but also with the British, for it was the British who would ultimately align with the Iroquois against their rivals—the French.

Chapter 5 – The Rise of New France

"Canada has a passive-aggressive culture, with a lot of sarcasm and righteousness. That went with my weird messianic complex. The ego is a fascinating monster. I was taught from a young age that I had to serve, so that turned into me thinking I had to save the planet."

-Alanis Morrissette

Although the British touched down in Canada as early as 1497 through the efforts of John Cabot, their real success story occurred in 1607 with the founding of Jamestown in what is modern-day Virginia. This colony had its ups and downs, but it gradually became strong. By the 1620s, it boasted a large population, and the people excelled in agriculture, making it highly attractive for more future colonists to settle there.

It was the success of Jamestown that made the French government realize that something was lacking with its own colonization project in the Canadian territory. It was decided that the French colony was far too dependent on the fur trade and that it needed to diversify its investments. With this in mind, King Louis XIII of France had his top court official—Cardinal Richelieu—send out the word that the Canadian colony of New France needed to wean itself off of its addiction to the fur trade.

It was made known that in order for the colony to stop being so dependent and become more competitive with the other European powers, it needed to develop its own strong farming and industrial base in Canada. It was through Cardinal Richelieu that a new colonial expedition was organized through the so-called "Company of One Hundred Associates."

This company was made up of one hundred investors who pooled their finances together behind efforts to maximize the profits of New France, as well as to spread religious missions. The Company of One Hundred Associates pledged to send around four thousand settlers to New France, as well as to promote missionary activity, over the course of a fifteen-year period. But it was right as this revamped colonial effort was gaining traction that war erupted between England and France.

Thus, in the backdrop of these colonization efforts, British pirates raided French settlements. In 1627, the British even managed to seize French vessels, which carried some four hundred would-be French colonists, interrupting their attempt to settle Canadian territory before they even managed to land. Under immense pressure, Champlain himself was defeated by the British in July of 1629 and forced out of Quebec.

It appeared that French Quebec was all but lost, but due to political intrigues between the British heads of state, an agreement was eventually hammered out to return the territory to France. As it so happens, the English king, Charles I, had actually wed French King Louis XIII's sister, and he used the capture of French territory as a bargaining chip to force the French king to pay for his sister's dowry. The French king did so in 1632, and that was enough for the British to relinquish the seized territory back to France.

Champlain returned to Quebec in 1634, where he returned to what he knew best—the fur trade. He established a new trading post for furs in the region of "Trois-Rivières in the year 1634. Samuel de Champlain passed away the following year, and with his passing, the stewardship of this outpost was handed over to the French Catholic missions, with the Jesuits taking a leading role.

The Jesuits, of course, had a primary mission of converting the native inhabitants to Christianity. This they did with varying degrees of success. The locals had a hard time understanding Christian concepts, and it could be furthermore argued that perhaps the Jesuits did not present the tenants of their faith in the most understandable of fashions. Without wading too deeply into the metaphysical realms of faith, the basic concept of Christianity is that humanity had fallen astray on a spiritual level, prompting God to manifest himself in a physical form through the person of Jesus Christ.

Yet if the Jesuits, like many preachers even today, just went around repeating key catchphrases without explanation, it might have been hard for the locals to follow. Without the proper metaphysical backing, they probably became confused with what the French preachers were talking about. And what might have otherwise been a powerful spiritual narrative about a creator God who loved his creation so much that he would take on a human form to rescue them had devolved into incomprehensible talk of blood and crucifixion.

To their credit, the Jesuits did eventually attempt to relate to their Huron audience on a more personal level and discovered similarities in their beliefs that could be used for some common ground. Both the Hurons and the Christians, for example, believed in the supernatural and its influence on everyday life. The Jesuits were able to use this natural inclination toward the supernatural that the Hurons already had and redirect it toward Christianity.

The Jesuits respected the Huron rituals of fasting and vision quests, recognizing it as being similar to Catholic fasting and communion. Also of importance was the fact that the Huron firmly believed in an afterlife, which gave the Jesuits familiar territory to develop upon by preaching on the Christian belief in heaven.

However, as the Jesuits were about to gain trust and make inroads, they managed to unwittingly shoot themselves in the foot. They unknowingly carried on their shoulders strains of viral infections from Europe to which they themselves were largely immune, yet the indigenous people had no immunity for. During the course of their missions, the Jesuits unknowingly spread smallpox to the local population. The disease absolutely devastated the Huron communities. Interestingly enough, the Huron were soon making the distinct connection between the visiting Jesuits and the arrival of the disease.

Always seeing things through a supernatural lens, the Hurons became convinced that the Jesuits were somehow using evil magic against them. They believed that the fact these priests were not getting sick while their presence seemed to sicken so many others was an indication that they had some kind of malignant, supernatural power. This led to the Hurons going from mostly confused and indifferent to the Jesuits preaching to becoming altogether intolerant.

Even so, the Hurons knew they could not expel the priests outright, as they would risk losing trade with the French, upon whom so much of their survival now depended. It was only when the Iroquois began to dip into the trade market as well, doing business with both English and Dutch traders, that the Huron situation seemed just about impossible. The Iroquois now had better and more plentiful guns than the Huron, giving the Huron leadership some serious doubts as to just how beneficial their relationship with the French remained.

In consideration of the aggressive conversion being forced upon them by the French Jesuits and their weakening position against their traditional rivals (the Iroquois), some Huron leaders were greatly concerned. One of them even went as far as to remark, "You tell us that God is full of goodness, and then, when we give ourselves up to him he massacres us. The Iroquois, our mortal enemies, do not believe in God, they do not love the prayers, they are more wicked than the Demons—and yet they prosper; and since we have forsaken the usages of our ancestors, they kill us, they massacre us, they burn us—they exterminate us, root and branch. What profit can there come to us from lending ear to the Gospel, since death and the faith nearly always march in company?"

Considering all of the misfortune that had befallen them, the Hurons were understandably enough at their wits' end with the tenuous position in which they had found themselves. In the end, however, they opted to continue to throw in their lot with the French, feeling that switching sides at this point would only bring more destruction to their community. This decision to stick with the French set the stage for a confrontation between the Hurons and the Iroquois in the spring of 1649.

For it was around this time that a huge Iroquois army attacked a major Huron settlement, killing or taking prisoner nearly four hundred Hurons. Those who were not killed were compelled to join the Iroquois as adopted members, and through them, further raids were led. Interestingly enough, these Huron turned Iroquois warriors carried an especial hatred for the Jesuit priests, and upon attacking French settlements, they captured many Jesuits and systematically tortured them in what was, in their eyes, revenge for all of the trouble they believed these priests had wrought upon their people.

The ultimate defeat of the Hurons led to a power vacuum in the region, which the Iroquois promptly sought to fill themselves. But the Iroquois did not set themselves up to become an ally of the French; instead, they began waging war against them. The French were now without their main native ally, so they were left to themselves to take on this resurgent threat. In the early 1650s, several skirmishes between French settlers and Iroquois ensued. The only good thing for New France during this period was that the actual French population had finally become substantial, reaching over three thousand by 1662.

In 1663, King Louis XIV of France decided to aid the stature of this growing colony. He declared the settlement to be an official royal province of France. This status enabled the colony to take on a much greater prerogative. Since it was now a province, New France would have its own governor, meaning a direct channel to the king of France. But most importantly, this distinction meant that more military troops could be deployed. And in 1665, one thousand troops were sent to the province of New France.

The province was also supplied with horses. This was a momentous occasion, for the colonists' native allies had never seen these animals before. Yes, as much as Native Americans came to be associated with horses in later years, the horse was not known to them at this time (although it is believed their ancestors once rode them). Horses were brought to various parts of North and South America by Europeans, and they rapidly multiplied from there.

The indigenous allies of the French were said to have greatly admired these majestic animals and referred to them as the

"French moose" since North America's homegrown moose was the closest thing that these indigenous tribesmen could associate with the horses being imported to their lands. The following year, the French took their growing army to take on an Iroquois Confederacy member, a tribe called the Mohawks.

The Mohawks were unable to handle this large force, and they ended up surrendering to the French in 1667. The Seneca, another tribe of the Iroquois Confederacy, bargained for peace just a few years later. These developments proved that the colony of New France could stand on its own. And by 1671, the French had taken control of the entire Great Lakes region. Their new native allies, the Algonquians, then moved down to take over the former territory of the Hurons.

The Iroquois, for a change, knew that they were beaten, and after the British entered into a peace treaty with the French in 1697, the Iroquois followed suit by forging a peace treaty in 1701. It has been said that the establishment of this treaty with New France's old foe was quite an affair, one that lasted for several days. During the signing itself, over a thousand representativeness from the Iroquois, who stood in for some forty different nations, had made their way to Montreal.

Rather than simply signing a piece of paper, these members of the Iroquois Confederacy made sure to give their own lengthy regards and words of wisdom. After these moments of reflection were through, several gifts, as well as former prisoners of war, were exchanged. It was only after all of this great festivity had run its course that the treaty was actually signed on August 4th, 1701.

However, the general peace and tranquility of New France would be shattered ten years later when the British decided to launch a major naval attack on France's holdings in Canada. First, an attack was launched against Acadia in 1710, which was followed up by an attack the following year on Quebec. This latest war with the British would last for a couple more years before the two parties signed the Peace of Utrecht in 1713.

This treaty allowed France to keep most of its territory, but the French had to agree to give the region of Acadia to the English. It was a tough price to pay, but this treaty would give France some thirty years of peace before the next round of fighting would begin.

Chapter 6 – The Next Round: France and England Compete for Dominance

"Canada has two emblems—the beaver and the maple."

-John W. Dawson

After the signing of the Peace of Utrecht in 1713, Canada was fairly evenly divided between the French and the British. The British were given the territories of Nova Scotia, Newfoundland, and sections of Rupert's Land in addition to what they already had. The British colonies now stretched all along the eastern seaboard of North America, from Newfoundland to the Florida border, with Florida still being controlled by Spain.

France, in the meantime, may have lost some territories, but the colonies it maintained began to prosper like never before. With less worry of fighting and dying in endless wars, the colonies' population exploded, and by the 1750s, New France boasted around fifty thousand settlers. This was a great improvement from the previous century, which saw numbers barely over one thousand.

These settlers were also much better provided for, as each man had his own piece of property complete with pigs, chickens, cows, and even some horses. The French Canadians became quite proficient at growing crops, such as wheat, for food, and they chopped firewood for warmth. There was also abundant wildlife to hunt, and fishing always produced stellar results.

Despite the cold winters, New France had become a land of plenty. As the settlers learned to better adapt, even the cold was not much of a hardship. They had learned how to build houses that were good at keeping in heat, as they were designed with a fireplace right in the center of the dwelling. The colonists also began making clothes that maximized heat retention, which eased their burden of having to move about on cold days. They even learned to pick up some fun pastimes in spite of the weather, such as ice skating and riding on sleds.

But not all was well for all of the French Canadians. For those who remained in lands that the British had seized, such as Nova Scotia, life was not always so easy. The English were naturally suspicious of their new French-Canadian subjects, and multiple times, they tried to get the French Canadians to sign an oath of loyalty.

Things came to a head in 1755 when it was demanded that they sign a pledge agreeing that they would take up arms and fight for Britain if war should ever break out. The French Canadians did not want to battle their own friends and relatives in nearby French-controlled territory should the two nations come to blows, and they flatly refused to sign.

The British authorities were not pleased, and they decided to evict the French outright. That August, it was announced to the French under British jurisdiction who refused to sign the oath that "Your lands and tenements, cattle of all kinds and livestock of all sorts are forfeited to the Crown with all other your effects, saving your money and household goods, and you yourselves to be removed from this province."

After being given this ultimatum, it is said that over the course of the next few years, some ten thousand French Canadians were kicked out of British-controlled territory. Of these, a sizeable chunk headed all the way down to the French-controlled Louisiana territory. The rest were pushed far and wide, with some settling in other British-controlled colonies, some in other French-controlled regions, and still others heading back to France itself.

War would once again erupt between Britain and France in 1756, as the Seven Years' War had begun to be waged on the European continent. By this point, the French and British colonies had already been fighting amongst themselves in what is known as the French and Indian War. Nevertheless, this war is often seen as one of the theaters of the Seven Years' War. This meant that the French stronghold of Quebec would become the main base for a buildup of troops, as well as additional French expatriates. The director of this military buildup was the governor of New France—the Marquis de Vaudreuil. The captain of the ground forces was a man named Louis-Joseph, also known as the Marquis de Montcalm.

Despite his name, the Marquis de Montcalm was not very calm. In fact, he was known for being agitated and short-tempered. And it was not long before he and the governor were butting heads. Most troubling for the French war effort was that these two men greatly disagreed on strategy. Montcalm wanted to use standard European battle tactics of simply marching an army in formation straight for the enemy. Vaudreuil, a man who was born and raised in North America, wanted to utilize the same kind of hit-and-run attacks that were so successful for the Native American tribes. Instead of charging headlong at the enemy, Vaudreuil wanted to use more cunning tactics to catch their British opponents off-guard. Nevertheless, despite the arguments over tactics, the war proceeded.

Initially, the French and their Native American allies did fairly well at repulsing the British from the interior of Canada. France was also beating the British on land in Europe. It was at this point that the British decided to pull out their trump card—the Royal Navy. Britain had the best navy at the time, and the British decided that if they couldn't best the French on land, they would do it by sea. They sent a powerful fleet to one of France's best Canadian ports—Louisbourg—and began to bombard it mercilessly in 1758.

Even so, the port held out for a couple of months, and despite the wreck and ruin all around them, the only thing that finally defeated the French defenders was their own hunger. When the besieged settlement's food began to run out, they realized that they had no choice but to surrender. It was not long after this victory that the British set their sights on their next main target in North

America—Quebec.

The British invasion of Quebec began in early 1759 when some twenty-nine warships bristling with artillery, along with fifteen thousand troops aboard various other attack craft, sailed up the St. Lawrence River and came face to face with the mighty fortifications of Quebec. Montcalm was in charge of Quebec's defense, and he tried a variety of tactics to fend off the intruders.

First, he sent a small group of fire ships toward the approaching British fleet. These were wooden craft purposefully set ablaze with the intention of sending them flying into an opponent's craft so that they might catch fire. However, the ships missed their mark, and to the delight of the British, they merely burned up some distance away. Montcalm desperately tried to get the French king to send reinforcements in the meantime, but France was too busy dealing with the war in Europe proper. He was only able to send a few hundred auxiliaries at most to bolster the defense of New France.

It is worth mentioning that such slights were not new for the French colonies, and many of the French subjects were already growing weary of their French overlords' seeming disregard for them. Considering the trajectory of this sentiment, one could only speculate that had the British not seized the French colonies in North America for themselves, the French colonists just might have staged a revolution of their own against mainland France.

At any rate, faced with an outright enemy invasion in 1759, such things were the least of these colonists' concerns. The British began to bombard Quebec on the night of July 12th. In the United States, the bombardment of the American Revolution is commemorated on the 4th of July with fireworks because, after enduring the worst that the British could dish out, with their "bombs bursting in air," the American revolutionaries' "flag was still there." However, for the French Canadians in Quebec, they were not as lucky, and this British bombardment on July 12th really took its toll. The British launched firebombs that tore through homes, churches, businesses, and military barracks alike, burning them to the ground in fiery explosions. They also launched repeated mortars and cannonballs that pounded Quebec's fortifications.

Although rubble and ruin lay all around them, the French held on for a few more months. But when their food supply began to run low, they seemed to be in for a repeat of the last defeat at the hands of the British. The British then dealt the final blow on September 12th when a British force of around three hundred men made landfall at L'Anse-au-Foulon. They found a wilderness path that allowed them to sneak around the coastal fortifications. After walking some 150 feet up to the clifftops, they were able to easily overpower the French defenders, who were unprepared for an all-out assault.

At the time of this breach, the main bulk of the French-Canadian forces were about an hour away. As soon as they received word of what was happening, they immediately rushed over as fast as they could. The armies met shortly thereafter, and a climactic land battle ensued. Just as the British and French were fighting to the death on the European continent, they were now fighting to the death in North America.

The battle didn't go well for the French. Montcalm himself died in the melee, and the French forces were forced to retreat into the cover of the wilderness. Rather than the French flag surviving this onslaught, on September 18th, the British flag was seen flying high in Quebec. The British were now in control of Quebec, and their most immediate problem was now what they were going to do with it.

After all, they were now the stewards of a wrecked and ruined city, which contained a frightened populace of foreign civilians. There was also the threat of disease, with outbreaks among these huddled masses not at all uncommon. The British also had to contend with French fighters from Montreal. This fortified city had not yet fallen, and a French force was being sent to try to retake the ground that had been lost to the British. This French contingent collided with the British out on the open plains in April of 1760.

The British had trouble with their artillery since it sank in the springtime mud, becoming relatively useless. The battle was pitched, but there was no clear winner. The French and British were both in need of reinforcements, so when a ship was seen arriving by way of the St. Lawrence River, both hoped that more of their countrymen had arrived. It was only when the craft unfurled a British flag that the French knew that all hope was lost. The French troops were now outnumbered, so they retreated back to Montreal.

The British pursued them, and Montreal surrendered shortly thereafter.

In the aftermath of their defeat, the French were primarily concerned with the religion of the French citizens who would remain under British occupation. It was for this reason that the so-called "Articles of Capitulation" were to have a religious clause. The clause declared, "The free exercise of the Catholic, Apostolic and Roman Religion, shall subsist entire, in such manner that all the states and the people of the towns and countries, places and distant posts, shall continue to assemble in the churches, and to frequent the sacraments as heretofore, without being molested in any manner, directly or indirectly."

And with that, Canada was in the hands of the British, and this situation was made official by the Treaty of Paris in 1763, which also ended the Seven Years' War. But although the French had been defeated, there was still the matter of what to do with their Native American allies. Several local tribes had alliances with the French Canadians, and the British had to contend with those First Nations peoples who remained. Not all of them were friendly to these European newcomers.

This was evidenced by the words of an Ojibwe chief, who remarked, "Englishmen, although you have conquered the French, you have not conquered us!" And as it pertained to Pontiac—the famed chief of the Ottawa—as far as he was concerned, the war was still indeed on.

The Ottawa dreaded the arrival of the British because they tended to settle more densely than their French allies had, and they also cleared and used up more land. In addition, the Ottawa had no trade relations with the newcomers, so it makes sense that they might pine for their close relationship with their old French partners. Pontiac was not willing to negotiate with the British, and he took the fight directly to them.

He ended up launching several assaults, one of the most devastating being the one he launched against Fort Detroit, which had only recently been taken over by the British. Here, countless British troops and civilians alike met a grisly end. Pontiac's initial onslaught was quite terrifying, but he was unable to keep up the enthusiasm among his troops. Due to a variety of factors, including the outbreak of smallpox, as well as fighters losing interest and dropping out of the fight to get back to their old stomping grounds, the offensive began to stall.

Pontiac realized that he could not sustain a large enough army to drive the British out, so he finally agreed to enter into a peace treaty with them in 1766. This was the end of the fighting, and it would soon be the end of Pontiac, as one of his own disillusioned people killed him in a fit of rage over what was perceived as their defeat.

However, the British did develop an understanding with the remaining indigenous people. This understanding led the British government to forbid their subjects from establishing any unauthorized settlements in the interior (west of the Appalachian Mountains), which was traditionally considered Native American territory. With this line drawn in the sand, British Canada could have peace—at least for the moment—with its newfound neighbors.

In French Canada, in the meantime, decisions were made to ease the French Canadians' load. In stark contrast to what had happened to previous French settlers who found themselves under the dominion of the British, it was decided to give these French Canadians significant leeway. It was determined that they could keep not only their religion but also their own French civil law and even a form of governance, as they could have their own elected officials. Although they would speak French and have their own religion and customs, these citizens would be granted the same rights as all other Canadians under British rule.

These measures were finalized in 1774 in what would become known as the Quebec Act. Little did the British know that these newfound freedoms for the French Canadians would provoke unsuspected yearnings from thirteen of their American colonies just a little farther to the south.

Chapter 7 – An American Revolution and the War of 1812

"But what do we mean by the American Revolution? Do we mean the American war? The Revolution was effected before the war commenced. The Revolution was in the minds and hearts of the people; a change in their religious sentiments, of their duties and obligations. This radical change in the principles, opinions, sentiments, and affections of the people was the real American Revolution."

-John Adams

In 1775, although Britain had made peace with both France and its own French subjects, the descendants of British colonists in the Thirteen Colonies that would one day become the United States of America were seething with discontent. The Quebec Act of the previous year was seen as an insult to them since they believed it gave a small population in Quebec special treatment over the much larger population of the American (as in the original Thirteen Colonies) settlers in the Northeast. They also resented the fact that their own heavy tax burden had helped to pave the way for England's victory against France, yet they didn't feel that they received many benefits in return.

The Canadian neighbors in Boston, Massachusetts, were particularly incensed, and they staged the Boston Tea Party to show their displeasure in 1773. They dressed up as Iroquois, stormed a ship, and dumped tea into the waters in order to protest excessive taxation without proper representation.

These tensions ultimately led to the Thirteen Colonies making the fateful decision to break with Britain, and the colonists launched the American Revolution in 1775. After the war was launched, it was suddenly a "you're with us or against us" kind of moment, and many of those who wished to remain loyal to the British fled north to Canada.

The French Canadians, in the meantime, wished to stay neutral. They had only just recently patched things up with the British, and they did not have much sympathy for the rebellious Americans to their south—certainly not enough to join them in a war against what was then arguably the greatest military power on the planet. However, the general of the revolutionary forces, George Washington, could not stomach this neutrality, sensing the French posed a potentially grave threat to the revolution should the British coerce them into marching south to the Thirteen Colonies.

It was with all of this in mind that Washington rolled the dice and decided to send American forces up to Quebec to see if Canada could be taken by force. In the fall of 1775, Washington led troops over Lake Champlain and across Maine. The Americans were initially quite successful, and by the end of the year, Montreal was in their hands. The defenders, however, were able to rally, and the American siege of nearby Quebec City was not quite as successful.

One of the men leading the charge against Quebec City was perhaps the most infamous American of all time—Benedict Arnold. This man's very name would become synonymous with the word "traitor." But even though Benedict Arnold would famously turn traitor and flip to the British side, at the outset of the war, he was a formidable figure for the revolutionary cause.

Along with Arnold, another general leading the siege was General Richard Montgomery, who had arrived just in time from Montreal to add some seven hundred additional troops to the group that Arnold was leading. After the victory over Montreal, Montgomery was feeling bold. In fact, he was bold enough to declare that he would "eat Christmas dinner in Quebec City or in hell." Well, if he somehow managed to eat Christmas dinner that year, it certainly was not in Quebec City. Montgomery and his troops were still outside the walls of the city after Christmas had come and gone.

On December 30th, braving white-out conditions, Montgomery and his men managed to storm into the city, but it did not go well at all. General Montgomery passed right by a gunner's nest, and his head was blown apart as powerful muskets opened upon him. He most likely died from the terrible head wound he suffered, but even so, the shots kept coming, literally riddling the American general with bullets as his body crumpled in a bloody heap on the snow. The sight of their commander brutally dispatched like this sent a shockwave of fear through General Richard's now leaderless troops, and they immediately fled out of the city.

Benedict Arnold was now left to try and salvage the disaster. His army, like General Montgomery's, managed to enter the city, but they did not get very far after that. Arnold would get hit by gunfire, with a bullet blasting through his leg, pulverizing flesh and bone. Unable to walk, Benedict Arnold had to be taken off the field. The revolutionaries would struggle on without him, but due to a lack of supplies, the outbreak of disease, and mounting casualties, they became bogged down in street fighting.

Matters would get even worse when on May 6th, 1776, British reinforcements arrived on the scene. Unable to deal with thousands of fresh British troops, the revolutionaries were forced to retreat. In the end, Benedict Arnold, who was replaced in April of 1776, had nothing to show for his troubles but a bad leg injury and perhaps a growing disillusion with the capabilities of his fellow revolutionaries against the British.

With Quebec firmly under their control, the British would use it as a future staging ground for attacking the rebellious American colonies. France, in the meantime, officially declared itself to be allied with the Thirteen Colonies of America. The French king wished to take full advantage of the situation in a wide variety of ways. First and foremost, the French wanted to strike at their old foe by supporting the Americans. France wished to weaken and humiliate the British by aiding the Thirteen Colonies in breaking away, but it did not want to push out the British completely. It served French interests to leave Britain in control of Canada in order to be a buffer to the upstart Thirteen Colonies should they outgrow their usefulness to France.

At any rate, the Americans ultimately bested the British, and another Treaty of Paris was created in 1783, ending the war and recognizing the independence of the newly formed United States of America. As for the British holdings in Canadian North America? They would indeed remain in British hands.

Interestingly enough, after the war was over, a call went out from the British asking anyone wishing to remain loyal to the crown to come to Canada. Several did so, seeking a better life and a little plot of their own to settle in underpopulated Canada. This group of post-revolutionary immigrants is sometimes referred to as "Late Loyalists" since they only professed loyalty to Britain after the war was already over.

Many of these later arrivals ended up in a section of what was then Nova Scotia, located above the Bay of Fundy. In 1784, this settlement was turned into its own colony called New Brunswick. Just north of Maine, the boundary of this new colonial province was the St. Croix River. Since it was so close to the former Thirteen Colonies, many feared an invasion from the Americans. As such, British garrisons at New Brunswick's capital of Fredericton were always at the ready.

More big changes were on the way in 1791 when Britain divided Quebec into what it termed Upper Canada and Lower Canada. Known as the Canada Act, this act of the British Parliament divided Quebec by way of the Ottawa River, with Upper Canada being the portion upriver and Lower Canada being the piece that was downriver.

By the early 1800s, the situation had mostly stabilized, and the younger generations of Canadians and Americans had, for the most part, come to accept the status quo and were more likely to trade goods with each other and conduct commerce than to fight. In the meantime, Britain had problems of its own after the French Revolution of 1789 and the Napoleonic Wars that followed.

Britain was at war with France off and on from 1803 to 1815. In the midst of this struggle, the actions of the British began to rub the Americans the wrong way. The British supposedly sought naval deserters, and they developed a habit of randomly stopping and searching American craft just in case British deserters were on board. This "stop and frisk" of the high seas was very insulting to the Americans who had to go through it.

The so-called "Chesapeake-Leopard affair" demonstrated just how volatile and potentially explosive this situation had become. In 1807, an American freighter called the Chesapeake got the bad end of the stick from the British. The British naval craft, the Leopard, came across the American sailors near the shores of Virginia and demanded that they be allowed to board and conduct a search on their craft.

These sailors were perhaps a bit bolder than most. Despite the fact that they were staring down the barrels of British guns, they denied the British access to their craft. This prompted the indignant British military men to take over the ship by force. Without any apparent regard to the damage they might do, the British opened fire on the civilians, killing three in the process. Several more were wounded.

Even worse, after searching the craft, the British grabbed four men on board in order to force them into impressment. For those unfamiliar with the term, impressment was when a civilian was forced against their will to serve someone else's cause. Things did not end well for at least one of these impressed American civilians, as the British eventually had him killed.

The United States was understandably outraged by all of this, yet at the same time, American leaders were not confident that they would be able to win another war with the British. As such, the sitting president, Thomas Jefferson, tried his hand at diplomacy in order to avert a cataclysmic confrontation with Great Britain. Even so, Jefferson understood the anger of the American public. In the midst of this ordeal, he is said to have remarked, "Never since the Battle of Lexington have I seen the country in such a state of exasperation."

Americans today would no doubt be just as frustrated if they were put under similar circumstances. Just imagine a foreign power seizing an American craft in American waters and then killing and injuring several and taking hostages. It would not be viewed upon favorably, that's for sure! Yet, since this took place just a few decades after the American Revolution, no one was quite ready to pull the trigger as it pertained to British aggression. Perhaps the British had already called this bluff.

However, once James Madison became president, he decided that enough was finally enough. He spoke of the tough position he was in, of how he essentially had to choose "between war and degradation." Rather than have America be bullied and pushed around any further, he chose war. This led to a formal proclamation of war against the British Empire (Canada included) on June 18th, 1812. The War of 1812 had begun.

At the very outset, striking at Canada was seen at striking at the British. Since Canada was not as heavily populated as the United States, it was also considered an easy target. Even the previously hesitant former President Thomas Jefferson believed this to be the case. On the eve of war, he had remarked, "The acquisition of Canada this year, as far as the neighborhood of Quebec, will be a mere matter of marching, and will give us the experience for the attack on Halifax, the next and final expulsion of England from the American continent."

But neither the Canadians nor the British would be that easy to overcome. As evidenced by Jefferson's words, many at this time believed that it was in America's interest to push the British right off of the American continent. The former Thirteen Colonies were indeed destined to push out farther west, but as the young nation of the United States of America would soon learn, pushing north into Canada was not going to be a walk in the park.

The greatest advantage that the Americans had was the fact that Britain was quite distracted with its war against Napoleonic France. French dictator Napoleon Bonaparte had proved to be a thorn in Britain's side. Bonaparte had seized much of the European continent, and Britain was doing all it could to contain the threat of Napoleonic France. With Britain's hands tied in Europe, it was indeed a nuisance for the British then to have to double back to the Americas in order to prevent the United States from taking over Canada.

But the British Empire was massive in those days, and it would soon find enough reserve troops to take the war to the Americans all the same. Just like the United States was later able to fight both the Japanese in the Pacific and the Germans in Europe during

World War Two, the mighty British Empire of 1812 was able to simultaneously fight a war on several fronts as well.

Britain mustered up some six thousand troops for the defense of Canada. The Americans pulled together about twelve thousand total troops from their various militias, but getting them all in an organized fighting condition was difficult. Many states that bordered Canada on the East Coast, for example, were against sending their militias to fight. They wished to remain neutral, thereby limiting the total number of troops that could be cobbled together.

Today, the United States has a federally operated standing military; back then, however, the US Army was a patchwork of state-based militias. And if certain states refused to cooperate, there was not enough centralized control back then to do too much about it.

As it pertains to Canada, the man in charge of Canadian defense was Major General Isaac Brock. Due to limited manpower and resources, Brock was ordered by his British taskmasters to maintain a defensive posture. However, Brock had other plans; he felt that rather than wait for the fight to come to him, he would take the fight to the Americans. He marched south to Fort Detroit. Fort Detroit had a few thousand troops and should have been able to fend off the smaller Canadian force fielded by Brock, which was just over one thousand in number.

Brock's group, in fact, was said to have consisted of three hundred British soldiers and four hundred Canadian troops, along with six hundred Native American fighters who were allied with the British. But what this Canadian attack force lacked in numbers, they made up for in sheer cunning.

The Native American division of the forces was led by a daring Shawnee commander by the name of Tecumseh. Tecumseh was famed for his fighting prowess and superb use of military tactics. As soon as Tecumseh and his men arrived at the gates of Fort Detroit, he decided to employ some psychological warfare. With all of his men emblazoned with terrifying war paint, he had them march right outside the fort's walls in full view of the defenders. He then had them double back a couple more times, creating the illusion that the group was much larger than it actually was. In the meantime, General Brock used some subterfuge of his own by making sure to dress his motley Canadian militia in British uniforms, making it seem that there was a large force of elite British soldiers backing up this fearsome assembly of indigenous warriors.

After this frightening display was made to the defenders of Fort Detroit, Brock sent a message to the American commander, requesting for him to surrender. Brock laid it on thick in this missive, being sure to mention that if they came to blows, he would be unable to hold his ferocious Native American allies back. Or, as Brock actually stated, "It is far from my inclination to join in a war of extermination, but you must be aware that the numerous body of Indians who have attached themselves to my troops will be beyond my control the moment the contest commences."

Brock's scheme worked. Fort Detroit was not only the home of American men at arms but also women and children. And fearing for their safety, the commander of the fort—General William Hull—caved into doubt and fear. The very next day, he ordered the fort to surrender. Without having to fire a shot, Fort Detroit was in Canadian hands.

One has to wonder if the defenders of Fort Detroit regretted their decision after realizing just how small of a group they had surrendered to. The defenders were almost twice in number as the attackers, yet they handed the keys over to these enterprising Canadians in short order.

Along with the two thousand American prisoners of war now under their charge, Brock's Canadian contingent also acquired a huge stockpile of guns and artillery. But perhaps most important for Brock was the stash of cold hard cash he acquired, as he could use it to pay his restless band of soldiers.

The United States was understandably alarmed at these happenings. Seeking to immediately recoup from the loss, they sent a regiment up to Queenston Heights and began to open fire with long-range cannons from the other side of the Niagara River. Even though it was a tough crossing, the US troops crossed the choppy Niagara and laid siege to Queenston Heights. The Canadians put up a brave fight, and Brock himself died during the exchange. The defenders were temporarily overrun, but the rest of the Canadian army rallied and were able to drive the Americans out, retaking Queenston Heights once again as their own.

After this exchange, 250 Americans were killed, and 925 were made prisoners of war in Canada. In all, the first phase of the war had gone in favor of the British and their Canadian allies. But by 1813, however, the situation had begun to change. American forces were able to occupy York (modern-day Toronto), and they caused British troops to retreat from the Niagara Peninsula, with the Brits running all the way to Burlington Heights.

It was only after the British launched a sudden assault on American positions at nearby Stoney Creek that they were able to boot the American forces out. This was followed by a skirmish at Beaver Dams near Montreal, in which members of the Iroquois Confederacy participated in a surprise attack on American positions. The Americans were soundly defeated and forced to flee from the Niagara Peninsula altogether.

The major blow to the British, however, would occur not on land but at sea when Admiral Oliver Perry was able to successfully orchestrate victory over the British during the onslaught of Put-in-Bay over the waters of Lake Erie. This was a devastating blow for the British because they were using the lake to ferry supplies.

But perhaps a worse defeat occurred when the leader of Britain's Native American allies—Tecumseh—was killed and his warriors defeated at the Battle of Moraviantown (also known as the Battle of the Thames) on October 5th, 1813. With Tecumseh's death, Britain's Native American allies were essentially knocked out of the war since no other indigenous leader rose up to lead them.

British fortunes improved in 1814 with the defeat of Napoleon (his first defeat prior to his ultimate end at Waterloo). With France subdued, Britain was able to redirect its forces to the war in America. Things then came to a head on July 25th, 1814, when British forces once again collided with the US Army on the Niagara Peninsula in a region called Lundy's Lane.

Now known as the Battle of Lundy's Lane, this fight took place with the Niagara Falls as a backdrop. Since the fighting was often hand to hand, to say that they "duked it out" is actually fairly close to what happened. In these close-quarter conditions, one of the greatest threats they faced was getting on the receiving end of friendly fire.

At any rate, the Americans got the worst end of this brutal contest and were forced to flee, leaving almost two hundred dead soldiers behind as they ran. This was a terrible defeat, and the worst was yet to come. In August of 1814, the British marched on Washington, DC, and set the capital ablaze. Both the White House and the Library of Congress were burned to the ground. The president was fortunately evacuated to Virginia, but the psychological blow was immense.

In September, the British also seized part of the eastern portion of Maine, where they created their own base of operations right on American soil. Nevertheless, the Americans were able to make a comeback, delivering a decisive defeat to the British on Lake Champlain in the Battle of Plattsburgh.

The British, at this point, were quite frankly tired of fighting. They had just finished a terrible war with France, and it was determined that fighting the Americans further was just not worth the effort. As such, overtures for peace were made, and on December 24th, the two parties entered into the Treaty of Ghent, officially ending the war. It should be noted that neither side won the war, although if a "loser" had to be named, it would have to be the indigenous people, as they lost their land and the trade they had established with the British.

Interestingly enough, even though the War of 1812 was over, General (and future president) Andrew Jackson apparently did not get the message since he would famously fight the British to a standstill in New Orleans in January of 1815. Nevertheless, the Treaty of Ghent was a milestone in North American history. The British, for the first time, recognized the USA, and they finally gave up the idea of seizing territory in Canada.

Chapter 8 – From the 19th to the Early 20th Century

"Canada was built around a very simple premise. A promise that you can work hard and succeed and build a future for yourselves and your kids, and that future for your kids would be better than the one you had."

-Justin Trudeau

Immediately after the War of 1812, Canada experienced major growth in population as well as an increase in prosperity. Some subsequent historians would attribute this phenomenon as a "postwar boon," but more recent scholars have called the notion that the war had anything to do with these developments into doubt. Besides the war, the biggest development in Canada in the first half of the 19th century was the end of the fur trade.

Since its inception, the fur trade had played a major part in the establishment of Canada and its growth. The fur trade was such a big industry that its end would have been equivalent to the end of the oil industry today. Just to give you an idea of how important the fur trade really was for Canada's economy—it is said that in the 1770s, the fur trade made up over 75 percent of Canada's export products. Yet, by 1810, that number had dropped dramatically to just 10 percent.

Needless to say, that was quite a big drop. At this point, many fur traders had no choice but to put their eggs into more than one basket. Some got into the timber business, some in railroad development, and others became shipbuilders. The timber industry proved to be the driving force that would lead Canada away from its dependence on a fur-trade-based economy.

Canada has always had plentiful lumber due to its vast forests. This dates all the way back to the Vikings, in fact. The Vikings may have very well left treeless Greenland in order to bring back timber from Canada. Having said that, timber was still a readily available resource in the 19th century, and it was ready to take the place of the fur trade. And by that same year of 1810, it was actually the lumber industry—not fur—that made up 75 percent of all of Canada's exports.

The St. Lawrence River was also bustling with shipbuilding activity, with Great Britain being the biggest client when it came to Canadian ships. Further industrialization in Canada led to a boom in textile industries, sawmills, flour mills, and a wide variety of other industrial-based manufactured goods. Much of this production, however, took place in the English-speaking settlements, leaving French Canadians out of the loop.

This naturally led to some resentment and sparked renewed interest in their independence. The Lower Canada region of French Canadians had asked for several reforms in the spring of 1837, but they were denied. This led to widespread discontent, and public protests began to mount. By summer, these protests began to turn violent, and the destruction of both public and private property took place.

As tensions mounted, the French Canadians began to form their own militia groups as they prepared for the inevitable backlash from the British and their loyalist colonial collaborators. An all-out confrontation between the two erupted on November 23rd, 1837, in what became known as the Battle of Saint-Denis.

On the British colonial side, a certain Lieutenant-Colonel, Charles Stephen Gore, led a group of men to root out the insurrection and arrest the rebel leaders in the Richelieu River valley region of Lower Canada. The rebels were found holed up in a stone house that had a good view of the open street right in front of it. This enabled the group to easily take potshots at the authorities as they approached.

In the meantime, Gore and company tried to blow the house apart with a cannon but proved unable to do so. The house stood, and their antagonists continued to fire upon them. At this point, Gore's ill-equipped bunch actually ran out of bullets and were forced to flee. This meant that the Battle of Saint-Denis was a technical victory for the rebels. However, their winning streak would be a short one since just a couple of days later, on November 25th, 1837, the colonial authorities struck back with a vengeance.

The next encounter between the two sides of this conflict occurred near Saint-Charles. This time, more British military might was added to the picture, and a contingent led by Lieutenant-Colonel George Wetherall was able to make short work of the rebels positioned around Saint-Charles. Wetherall unleashed an infantry of over four hundred troops, with an auxiliary militia cavalry said to number around twenty, along with two powerful cannon pieces.

This well-armed group faced off against approximately 250 rebels. This group was soundly defeated, with fifty-six being killed during the conflict and several more being taken as prisoners of war. This rebel defeat was followed by an even more decisive one when the British tore through rebel positions at Saint-Eustache a short time later, effectively ending the rebellion of Lower Canada in December of 1837.

The rebels' will to fight had been broken, and those who did not surrender fled as refugees to the United States. This was not quite the end of the story, however, since these rebel refugees managed to regroup and make a comeback approximately a year later. In November 1838, they crossed back into Canada and were able to stir up yet another revolt.

However, this one was quashed even quicker than the last one. After the revolt was put down, the British authorities did not dispense punishments with any sense of mercy or leniency—they had twenty-five of the rebels summarily executed and another fifty-eight exiled to British Australia. Canada's British taskmasters were obviously not taking any chances, and they sought to yank the sentiment of rebellion out by its roots so that it would not be able to grow and fester once again.

But a more permanent political solution was needed, and so, it was decided to bring Lower and Upper Canada together with the Act of Union, which was enacted in 1840. By creating a United Province of Canada, it was hoped that the loyal English majority, which resided primarily in Lower Canada, would be able to prevent further outbreaks of rebellion. By uniting the English dominant Lower Canada to Upper Canada, it was also hoped that the English ways and sentiment would rub off on the French Canadians. The British generally believed that it was the isolation of the French Canadians that allowed thoughts of rebellion to foment.

Further adjustments occurred a few years later for Canada as a whole when the Oregon boundary dispute erupted in 1846. The British and the Americans were arguing over a region of territory that would ultimately become the Northwest of the United States. Some in the US claimed a much larger portion should be annexed to American territory at the fifty-fourth parallel, which would bring American land in the Northwest all the way up to Alaska (a region still administered by Russia at the time).

However, the British were not going to go for this, and US President James K. Polk did not wish to provoke the British at a time when tensions with Mexico over the recent acquisition of Texas were already bad enough. Polk, therefore, sought a compromise and scrapped the idea of staking a claim as far north as the fifty-fourth parallel. Instead, he sought to negotiate with the British for a claim at the forty-ninth parallel. In the end, the British decided that a war over this small portion of land would not be worth their while, and they agreed on the American compromise of establishing Canada's westernmost border at the forty-ninth parallel.

The recently United Province of Canada, in the meantime, began to strengthen its trade ties with the United States. And by the time the American Civil War erupted in the US in 1861, Canada was in a good position to benefit from it. The US federal government was suddenly looking to Canada to supply much-needed goods during the course of the conflict.

Before the Civil War broke out, Canada had experienced a push to its western frontiers. This had been the case ever since the gold rush of 1848, with settlers slowly inhabiting lands that had previously remained wild and largely deserted. Just as Canadians were expanding to the farthest reaches of western Canada, Britain sought to create a firmer, federalized union of the Canadian territory. These efforts would forge the Dominion of Canada. This was established with the Constitution Act of 1867 (also known as the British North America Act). Within this act of British Parliament, we find the statement that Canada is to be "one Dominion," which will have "a constitution similar in principle to that of the United Kingdom."

This act, although not severing direct ties to Great Britain, sought to create one united Canadian body and to give the citizens of Canada roughly the same rights as British citizens. This act linked all Canadian lands into one dominion, and it saw the largely unsettled Northwest Territories and Rupert's Land get merged with the already established provinces. Britain would have the final say over things such as foreign policy, but Canadians would control their own destiny on the local level.

This, of course, also meant that Canada would get its own prime minister. Canada's first prime minister was a man whose name comes down to us as Sir John Alexander Macdonald. Macdonald was a conservative, and he ran against a liberal adversary, whose name was George Brown.

After Canada reached its dominion status, one of the greatest efforts of localized government was to improve Canada's infrastructure. A major part of this entailed the creation of railways that stretched across Canada from east to west. Canada received another boon when Prince Edward Island joined the dominion in 1873.

The biggest problem that the Canadian government of Prime Minister Macdonald faced was the Red River Rebellion. The tumult was in regard to a large settlement of Métis, a distinct people group that had developed from a long history of intermarriage between Europeans and local tribes. The Métis had their own large piece of territory carved out in Rupert's Land, situated around the Red River Valley and in the vicinity of the Hudson's Bay Company outpost of Fort Garry. When settlers from the eastern Canadian provinces began to settle in this region, trouble began to emerge. Not wishing to be swallowed up in the Canadian dominion, a local Métis leader, Louis Riel, rose to prominence and created what was termed a provisional government of their own.

Prime Minister Macdonald was surprised by these developments, but he took a highly pragmatic approach. He did not try to push the issue any further and consulted with the British instead. The British sent in troops, and a large British/Canadian army was assembled. They were sent some one thousand miles to the Red River region. In the meantime, Macdonald and Riel seemed to make good progress in their negotiations, and it seemed that perhaps a peaceful settlement could be arranged.

But as this was going on, Canadian settlers from the east began to cause trouble. This led Riel to take matters into his own hands and have people arrested. These actions led to him actually authorizing the execution of a man named Thomas Scott. Prime Minister Macdonald was appalled that Riel would attempt to assume such power over the region and become a one-man judge, jury, and executioner. So, Macdonald threw down the gauntlet and decided to dismantle Riel's provisional government by force.

As the large army approached, Riel's resistance all but collapsed. Riel himself took off over the border to hide in the United States. Even so, Prime Minister Macdonald was fairly benevolent when it came to the Métis who remained, providing generous tracts of land that were set aside specifically for the Métis.

The whole region, in the meantime, would become the Province of Manitoba with the Manitoba Act of July 15th, 1870. This was followed a year later by the joining of British Columbia to Canada proper in 1871. Prince Edward Island would also join the fold in the east in 1873. It seemed that Canada's own manifest destiny of reaching out from east to west was becoming a reality.

Prime Minister Macdonald seemed to have a lot of success stories to tell about his young nation. But average Canadians at the ballot box were ready for change all the same. And in 1873, the Macdonald government was replaced by the Liberal Party of Canada. Beyond simply being "against the conservatives," the Liberal Party did not seem to be too unified, and their agenda began to stall. Making matters worse, by 1874, Canada entered into a recession. This paved the way for Macdonald and his conservative government's return in the very next election. Macdonald ended up serving a second non-consecutive term in 1878.

One of the first things Macdonald's government did to change course was to enact high tariffs on imports, a move that began in 1879. These efforts managed to attract attention from overseas competitors, and they also created more industrial output at home. The populace was grateful for Macdonald's efforts, and he easily retained his prime minister post in 1882, 1887, and 1891.

Macdonald actually died in June of 1891, right after coming out on top in what would turn out to be his final successful election. His party would then have a succession of four different prime ministers at the helm of Canada's government before they lost their majority position in the election of 1896. That year, the liberal wing of Canadian politics was once again ushered into power with Prime Minister Wilfrid Laurier at its head.

Laurier was himself a milestone in that he was the first French Canadian to rise to the role of prime minister. Laurier was a stylish, neat, and trim man who impressed his peers with his impeccable English as well as his impeccable French. Laurier was a man who looked to the future and often proudly proclaimed that the "twentieth century belongs to Canada."

But the 20th century would bring things that neither Laurier nor many other Canadians could have imagined at the time. Once the year 1900 rolled around, Britain was still a power that spanned the globe, but cracks in this great empire were already beginning to emerge. War had broken out in South Africa between the British and the Dutch, leading to great disdain from the international community.

Nevertheless, the Canadians were tapped to join forces with the British in this struggle, and the British ultimately won in 1902. However, the empire was mired in controversy afterward. Many around the world questioned the tactics of the British in this engagement, and the victory itself was at least somewhat Pyrrhic in the sense that the British Empire racked up a huge number of casualties in order to achieve it. The British side, in fact, sustained nearly 100,000 casualties, twice as much as their opponents that they supposedly bested in the war.

Nevertheless, after the war, Canada entered into a boom period in which immigration from both the US and Europe increased. There was also a push into underpopulated territories, and by 1905, Canada had gained a couple more provinces with the establishment of Alberta and Saskatchewan. Interestingly enough, most of the settlers to converge onto these new provinces were not Canadian-born citizens but mostly immigrants from eastern Europe, such as Poles, Russians, and Ukrainians.

Canada would enter into a relatively productive and beneficial period, with its population rising to seven million. Life was good, but there were those who were disenchanted with the high price of some of the staple goods that Canada routinely imported. To alleviate this concern, in 1911, Laurier made an agreement with US President William Howard Taft to enter into a mutual tariff reduction.

Laurier and his party were confident that this accomplishment would ensure the continuation of their government through the next election cycle. They were wrong. Instead, many Canadians were put off by what they felt were policies that were too pro-American. And instead of riding on a tide of victory, Laurier and company were cast out on a tide of electoral defeat.

Politics can indeed be unpredictable at times, and as much as politicians think they can manipulate their constituents, they are occasionally thrown curveballs that they did not quite anticipate. Laurier's successor, the conservative Prime Minister Sir Robert Borden, would be thrown just such a curveball when the war to end all wars—World War One—took up most of his time in office.

Chapter 9 – Canada, Two World Wars, and a Cold One

"After two world wars, the collapse of fascism, Nazism, communism and colonialism and the end of the cold war, humanity has entered a new phase of its history."

-Hans Kung

The war to end all wars—as World War One (or the Great War) would come to be called—had been long in the making, but it was sparked by a single incident. A Serbian nationalist had assassinated the visiting archduke of Austria, Franz Ferdinand, and his wife in June 1914. This led to Austria seeking damages against Serbia. Eventually, Austria issued several demands, but one of them was so draconian that the Serbs knew to give in would essentially mean giving up their own autonomy. They refused to meet the unrealistic demands, and Austria prepared for war.

Austria's ally of Germany also made it clear that it, too, would fight. Even the Ottoman Empire—the sick man of Europe—sided with the Central Powers against Serbia. Serbia was not alone in this struggle, though, as it was able to rely on the might of its powerful ally Russia. After Russia joined, so did France and Great Britain. And with Britain drawn into World War One, the Canadians were brought along for the ride by default.

Even though Canada was basically an autonomous dominion, the one thing out of their control was major foreign policy decisions, and with a snap of their fingers, the British could have Canadians running to war. Fortunately for the British, the Canadians were fairly enthusiastic about the prospects of participating in this conflict. In all, some 425,000 Canadians would don military uniforms and join the fight in Europe.

Some of the most brutal fights would take place on the Western Front in Belgium and France, and one of the first major operations that the Canadian troops would take part in occurred in Ypres, Belgium, in the spring of 1915. One of the most thrilling moments for the Canadian troops occurred in April of 1917 when Canadian forces broke through a solid German line of defense at Vimy Ridge, leading the way for the Allied Forces.

However, as well as the Canadian deployments were doing, by 1917, the recruitment efforts in Canada proper had slowed down considerably. Fighting in the war had become a polarizing subject, and it was primarily the French Canadians who did not wish to be involved. It must be said that French Canadians have been somewhat notorious in their desire to remain neutral.

During both the American Revolution and the War of 1812, French Canadians sought to distance themselves from taking a side. The same can be said of World War One. And even when some tried to use their French heritage as a reason to join the war effort, they would not budge. Even though France was being invaded by Germany, it did not seem to mean too much for the average French Canadian, as they had become completely disconnected from their ancestral France centuries ago.

Nevertheless, among the segment of Canadians who did wish to serve, they served with distinction. The Canadians were also there for the climactic Battle of Mons in November of 1918, which saw the German military's most decisive defeat. One of the top Canadian leaders during this struggle was a certain general named Sir Arthur Currie.

Interestingly enough, prior to the breakout of World War One, Currie was actually a real estate agent who happened to participate with a local Canadian militia in his off-time. But while his real estate career was lackluster at best, Currie's service as a military commander was absolutely outstanding. Currie led his troops during a time when the British and German forces were locked in a stalemate, literally dug into the trenches and popping up to fire at one another. Neither side was making any real progress.

It was up to Currie and his Canadian regiment to break through this stalemate. And after the Canadians broke through the German lines at Vimy Ridge, Currie was promoted to the position of "Inspector-General" for the Canadian Armed Forces.

Along with directly providing troops, Canada also contributed to the war effort on a monetary level, and it actually paid for British munitions in the final years of the conflict. Britain itself was put under great financial stress during the war, and as a result of Canada's role in aiding the British with money, the Canadians managed to rise from a junior partner to more of an equal on the world stage. When peace talks were carried out in Paris in 1919, Canada was treated as an equal, and it was even made a member of the newly established League of Nations.

After the war, Canada had grown considerably, both in its political stature and in its population, which had reached eight and a half million at this time. Its infrastructure had also greatly improved, with efficient railways connecting one side of the country to the other, as well as streetcars being readily available on the local level in cities. Roads for cars were also in development, as Canadian interest in automobiles began to increase.

In fact, Henry Ford (the founder of Ford Motor Company) set up shop right in Windsor, Ontario, and since Detroit was not far away, vehicles were not hard to find, at least for those with enough money to buy them. As good as things were going in Canada, the early 1920s saw yet another recession. It is important to note that this downturn in Canada occurred several years before the stock market crash of 1929, which would send shockwaves all over the globe.

Yes, even before the crash, Canada was still very much a country in transition, and Canadians were having financial difficulties. Many average Canadians who had left rural farms for the industrialized cities were suddenly having a hard time even finding a job. Canada's welfare system, which was put in place to help support those in need, was not up to capacity for the need that was present, and the Canadian government at this time was hesitant to expand social programs.

This sudden recession was over quickly, though, and postwar economic conditions quickly improved. Canadian products such as wheat and wood pulp were in demand, and Americans, in particular, were paying large sums of money for a steady supply of them. Canadian manufacturing, such as the aforementioned Ford plant in Windsor, also began to pick up steam, hiring droves of local factory workers in order to meet the demand for the steady production of goods.

Canadian cities also saw a construction boom, during which some of the earliest Canadian skyscrapers were built. These were not quite as massive as the ones that had sprouted up in American cities such as New York and Chicago, but the Canadian skylines of Montreal and Toronto featured towering buildings in the 1920s all the same. Mining in the Canadian Shield, which was far from the cities, was also highly profitable. With proceeds from projects such as these, Canada's government was finally able to decrease taxation on its people and begin to set aside funds to pay lingering debts from the war.

The prime minister during this boom period was a man by the name of William Lyon Mackenzie King. King was a charismatic firebrand of Canadian politics, and he was able to reach out to Anglo-Canadians and French Canadians alike. Being able to bridge this divide was important for King since he felt that the best way to have a strong and prosperous Canada was by healing the divisions of the past—primarily the historical division between French- and English-speaking Canadians.

King was sharp-witted, but he was ultimately a pragmatist, one who played for the long game rather than short-term success. King would maintain leadership throughout the rest of the 1920s, seeking stability above all else. Canadian stability would be severely challenged just like much of the rest of the world after the stock market crash of 1929 and the ensuing Great Depression of the early 1930s.

For Canada, the first and most immediate effect of the Depression was a drastic decline in one of the nation's staple agricultural crops—wheat. Canada had long made money through its wheat, which was primarily grown in the western provinces of Alberta, Saskatchewan, and Manitoba. Yet, at the start of the Great

Depression, there was a wheat surplus, and people just were not buying as they had been. With this drop in demand for wheat, the price rapidly dropped until farmers could not make enough money to justify all the hard work they put into growing this heavily involved crop.

The next domino to fall was the wood pulp industry. Canada had long been supplying American cities with wood pulp for the production of paper. However, paper purchases also went into decline during the Depression, and soon the prices—and ultimately the profits—of pulp sank like a rock. This trend continued to affect all of Canada's industrial sectors.

The year 1930 had seen a return of the conservatives to power, with Prime Minister R. B. Bennett at the helm. Bennett sought to use the tariffs to break through Canada's stagnation. Or, as Bennett himself put it at the time, he would utilize tariffs "to blast a way into the markets of the world." Although tariffs might have worked under normal circumstances, the global Great Depression did not make for normal times, so his tariffs had very little effect.

Canada's saving grace came in 1932 when Britain agreed to lower rates of duty on all commerce conducted between members of the British Empire. These measures helped keep the Canadian economy afloat during these tough times.

The previous year, in 1931, Britain had also enacted the Statute of Westminster, which served to solidify Canada's independent status in the commonwealth. The statute, however, left one thin thread of coercive power on Britain's part, as it allowed the British Parliament the ability to amend the Canadian constitution. However, this could only be done with the consent of Canada's own parliament.

So, in some sense, full autonomy was a fine line in Canada at this point since, if, for whatever reason, the Canadian Parliament agreed on it, Britain could still intervene. Such a scenario, however, would seem highly unlikely. The statute also further cemented the dominion status of Newfoundland, which at this point was still being treated as a separate colony.

At any rate, independent or not, there was still the problem of widespread unemployment, and the Canadian government had to take action to try and put all of these suddenly idle hands to work.

This was done largely through industrial projects, such as the construction of roads, railways, and other infrastructure. And if all else failed, some were even given the monotonous task of simply mowing grass in local city parks.

The situation was much different in rural communities, where farmers struggled both with poor economic conditions and poor soil due to bad droughts that occurred in 1936 and again in 1937. Making matters even worse, the drought came paired with a bad infestation of locusts, making the situation seem like a true tribulation for those who experienced it.

One of the most peculiar phenomena for rural folk during these days was the rise of Bennett buggies. Just what exactly was a Bennett buggy? Well, since gas prices were sky-high, folks had resorted to putting their cars in neutral and hitching horses to the otherwise useless vehicle to pull them into town! This was both an inventive and ironic fixture of the times. Most of these cars were purchased during the prosperous 1920s under Prime Minister Mackenzie King, yet in the 1930s, under Prime Minister Bennett, these once proud automobile owners had to pull a page from the past and transform their autos into horse-drawn buggies.

Bennett himself had his reckoning in the election of 1935, in which he and his party were thrown out almost entirely. Bennett was humiliated, and he left Canada altogether, heading to Great Britain to lick his wounds. Returning to lead the nation in his place was the former Prime Minister William Lyon Mackenzie King. The slogan during King's campaign was "It's King or Chaos." And many, remembering how successful King's steady hand was in the 1920s, believed it and chose King over what they perceived as absolute economic chaos in the land.

In truth, Bennett was partially a victim of circumstances out of his control. Bennett, of course, had no control over the stock market crash and the ensuing Great Depression, but his policies were certainly not as helpful as they could have been. And it was this perceived failure to respond to the pressing needs of Canadians that gave the Liberal Party all the opening they needed to surge once again to the top of Canadian politics.

However, once King was in office, he realized just what kind of trouble he had inherited. He had run on a platform of fixing what ailed the Canadian government, yet once in power, he struggled to find the right approach. And as he was stumbling to figure out what to do, international affairs proved to be a rather convenient distraction from troubles at home.

During the 1930s, dictators had come to prominence in many parts of the world. Germany was being led by Adolf Hitler and his Nazi Party. Japan was being run by a pro-military faction led by Japanese Prime Minister Hideki Tojo. And Italy had been in the grip of Italian fascists, with dictator Benito Mussolini at the head. The world community was intensely worried (and rightly so) about these developments, yet Mackenzie King, just like his British peer at the time—the infamous appeaser Neville Chamberlain—took a hands-off approach.

As early as 1935, when the League of Nations sanctioned Italy in condemnation of its invasion of Ethiopia, Canada refused to cooperate. And in 1937, while visiting London, King expressed Canada's lack of interest in foreign entanglements. From here, he actually went on to visit Hitler himself in Germany. Damningly enough, Canadian Prime Minister Mackenzie King even wrote about the Nazi leader in glowing terms, making him out to be a humble servant of the people or, as he put it, "a simple German peasant." At one point, King even referred to Hitler as being a kind of German version of Joan of Arc.

Of course, these musings of Mackenzie King would not age well, as this man whom he perceived as a champion of the common people would not only lead the world to war but would also be the principal architect and director of the worst atrocities ever committed in world history. Yet, at the same time, he did manage to tell Hitler that if war really did erupt, Canada would most certainly be backing the British.

King, in truth, was totally for British Prime Minister Neville Chamberlain's policies of appeasement. Like many others, King desperately wished to avoid war, and he was willing to appease the bullying tactics of fascist dictators in order to do so. As such, King fully approved when Neville went above and beyond to bend over backward for Hitler and all of his many demands as long as if it meant that bloodshed could be avoided. Along with visiting European heads of state, King also crafted a close relationship with

US President Franklin Delano Roosevelt.

President Roosevelt—often simply referred to as F. D. R.—came into office at the height of the Great Depression just like Mackenzie King, and he quickly presented himself as the champion of the working class. He did this by using the power of the federal government to create major projects to get people back to work and to create safety nets for those who had fallen on hard times.

F. D. R. and King hit it off well enough, and the forward-thinking Roosevelt, who was already worried of a future world war, consciously considered close ties with Canada to be paramount for the sake of mutual defense of the North American continent. And in 1938, just on the eve of World War Two, the United States and Canada did indeed forge a mutual defense pact should they face an assault from an outside aggressor. The following year, in the fall of 1939, Germany launched a merciless attack, not on the US or Canada but on neighboring Poland.

Although Poland is far from the coasts of North America, this assault kickstarted what would quickly come to be called the Second World War. Britain, which had tried so hard to appease Hitler, was now forced to declare war on Germany. Britain's ally of France did so as well. Canada then came to the fold, officially declaring war on Germany on September 10th.

Even so, the United States did not feel obligated to do so. Yes, the US pledged to defend Canada if it were attacked, but the United States was not ready to declare war on a foreign power simply because Britain had. It would take a couple more years and a Japanese attack on American soil to finally get the United States to declare war on the Axis Powers of Germany, Italy, and Japan.

Mackenzie King, in the meantime, won the right to lead the government once again in the election of 1940, positioning him to be Canada's wartime leader. As would similarly be the case in the United States, once Canada was at war, its economic circumstances would change. Droves of Canadians were being hired to work in industrial plants and factories in order to supply the war effort. Canada would produce everything from bullets to aircraft for the Allied war machine. To further safeguard the wartime economy, Prime Minister King also made sure to establish wage and price controls to prevent any chance of inflation. The Canadians also had to commit themselves to a bit of sacrifice on the home front, as important goods for the war, such as rubber, coal, and even coffee, were being reduced to ration levels for the average Canadian citizen.

Nevertheless, due to the industry boom, Canadians were suddenly in a much better position economically speaking, with most of them being fully employed and making more money than ever before. And when the United States of America finally joined the conflict in late 1941, Canada was in a prime position to rev up the American war engine as well. The US, as it turns out, was a bit behind in armaments, so it was agreed to essentially bring the US and Canadian armament programs together in order to bring the United States better up to speed.

And as it pertains to the actual war overseas, Canada was indeed a valuable player, sending over a million troops to fight in both the European and Pacific theaters. Of this number, it is said that approximately 131,000 served in the Royal Canadian Air Force, fighting alongside the British and other Allies in daring air raids over Nazi-occupied Europe.

However, as intense as the fighting was in Europe, some of the most brutal engagements that the Canadian forces experienced were in the Pacific theater. In fact, around the same time that the United States was being attacked by Japan at Pearl Harbor, Hawaii, Canadians were desperately trying to fend off an invasion of Hong Kong. Although the city of Hong Kong is situated on the mainland of China, it was a British colony at that time.

Japan had been waging war with China since the early 1930s (since the 1931 Mukden Incident or Manchurian Incident, in fact), and after declaring war on Britain, all bets were off. The Canadian force in Hong Kong was a small one, and they were quickly overwhelmed by the Japanese invasion force. The Canadians stationed in Hong Kong ultimately ended up surrendering to the Japanese on December 25th, 1941—Christmas Day, no less.

Needless to say, it would not be a very good Christmas for these Canadian prisoners of war, and for the next four years, they would be at the mercy (or lack thereof) of the Japanese. But it was the Japanese attack at Pearl Harbor that would be the ultimate game-changer since it brought the previously hesitant United States into the war on the side of the Allies. Both Britain and Canada were immensely pleased that they could now rely upon the industrial juggernaut of the United States to back them in the war.

The Americans largely led the war from here on out, with Canadians and the British playing a backing role. A massive US invasion force landed in North Africa, leapfrogged to Sicily, and then invaded Italy. This rapid invasion prompted the Italians to surrender, knocking out the first of the three Axis Powers. The Canadians also served alongside the Americans when they took the fight directly to the Germans on D-Day, landing off the shores of Normandy, France, in June of 1944. These courageous Canadians braved machine gun nests in order to create a beachhead in continental Europe.

Germany would ultimately be defeated in May of 1945. The last holdout of the Axis would be Japan, which would not give up until the late summer of 1945. And they only did so after having two nuclear bombs dropped on them and after a very late-stage declaration of war by the Soviet Union. Yes, the Soviets, who had been fighting a desperate war against the Germans since 1941, did not actually declare war against the Japanese until August 9th, 1945. Japan officially surrendered on September 2nd.

Interestingly enough, the nuclear weapons deployed on Japan were the beneficiaries of uranium developed in Canada. The dropping of the atomic bombs on the Japanese cities of Nagasaki and Hiroshima still remains controversial to this day, but most historians believe that their use did indeed shorten what would have otherwise been a prolonged quagmire of guerilla warfare and ferocious battles if the Allies had attempted a conventional land invasion of Japan.

Regardless, the world was shocked by their use, and soon, with the development of the far more powerful hydrogen grade nuclear weapons, fear would grip both the US and Canada, as hydrogen bombs could suddenly fall on North America. Canada, which had worked closely with its US partner in the development of nuclear weapons, would have front row seats for the ensuing Cold War that followed.

Although the Soviet Union was ostensibly an ally of the United States, Canada, Britain, and the other Allied Powers during the war, shortly after their common enemies had been defeated, the relations between the Soviet Bloc and the Western powers began to frost over. There were almost immediate disagreements over what role the Soviets should play in postwar Europe, and after several land grabs by the Russians, British Prime Minister Winston Churchill famously stated that an "Iron Curtain" had descended across Europe.

These were prophetic words from a world power that soon saw a great decline. Yes, the fighting of World War Two took a terrible toll on Britain, and soon, it would be bereft of much of its empire. In the meantime, the United States, as well as Canada, took on a leading role. Canada was a leading member of the newly established United Nations, and it played a major part in the Cold War discussions over the dangers of nuclear weapons. In 1949, the Soviet Union exploded an atomic bomb of their own, thereby raising the stakes significantly.

The world was now dominated by two superpowers—the US and the USSR (the Union of Soviet Socialist Republics)—which both had nuclear weapons. As the arms race between these two nations commenced, the possibility of ending all human life on Earth became a possibility. This is exactly the sort of thing that the United Nations was (and still is) supposed to prevent. A commission, of which Canada was a part, had looked into a means of peaceful disarmament, but neither the US nor the USSR could agree on any feasible way of doing this.

As the Cold War gripped the world, heads of state in Canada realized they would have to work outside of the United Nations in order to find meaningful solutions. Thus, Canada joined the North Atlantic Treaty Organization (otherwise known as NATO). By grouping itself in a strategic alliance with both the United States and Britain, Canada was hoping to strengthen its military capabilities, as well as deter any would-be belligerence by the Soviets in the North Atlantic.

NATO made Canada puts its money where its mouth was since the treaty pledged that both Canada and the United States would immediately aid any NATO ally should they come into conflict with the Russians. This called for a massive military buildup on Canada's part, and by 1953, the Canadians were spending 45 percent of their budget on their military. The most important investment, however, would be in the complex early warning systems—radar installations—that would serve to warn not just Canada but also all of North America of an impending nuclear strike.

Canada would have three main installations—the Distant Early Warning Line located in the Arctic, the Mid-Canada Line, and the Pinetree Line, which was situated at Canada's forty-ninth parallel. These installations stood as silent sentinels during the Cold War to tip off Canada and, more importantly from a military sense, the nuclear-bomb-wielding United States that immediate action was necessary.

In reality, however, if the Soviets had lobbed nuclear missiles at North America, there was not a whole lot Canada or the US could do to prevent them from hitting their targets. The most that could be done in the brief amount of time that the early warning systems provided was simply to lob nuclear missiles right back at them. Since both parts of the world would be catastrophically destroyed in the process, such a thing seemed pointless—perhaps even a bit mad.

But "mutually assured destruction" (MAD), as they called it, was actually the name of the game. It was theorized that if the Soviets knew ahead of time that their attack would receive an equally devastating counterattack, they would be deterred from launching an attack in the first place. Yes, it seems crazy, but during the Cold War, it was crazy enough to work. This is demonstrated by the fact that nuclear war did not occur, and we are still here.

Chapter 10 – Canada at the Dawning of a New Millennium

"The northern border is a different problem set than our southern border. We're not going to put a fence between America and Canada, across Glacier Park. I grew up there. We can use some technological controls. We work with the Canadians more, and there's a lot of property we share, along with tribal lands."

-Ryan Zinke

By the late 1960s, Canada had truly come into its own. Not only was Canada independent of Great Britain and equipped with both a strong economy and military, but it had also forged its own unique national culture. This was—at least symbolically—demonstrated in 1965 when Canada established its own national flag, marked with the now-iconic red maple leaf.

Just about everyone born after 1965 can readily recognize the Canadian maple leaf flag. Yet, prior to this date, Canada had had a variety of flags, which all, in one way or another, paid homage to Britain's Union Jack. But the maple leaf, as unique and quirky as it might be, was something that Canada could finally call its own.

Another Canadian milestone that occurred in 1965 was the national implementation of Canada as a bilingual country. No longer would French speakers have to feel like second-class citizens. Nevertheless, it was in French-speaking Quebec that a movement toward Quebec independence began to take root. In

1967, with the Canadian centennial anniversary celebration of the 1867 independence through the British North America Act as a backdrop, some serious questions as to whether Quebec should hang on to the rest of Canada were being asked.

To mark the centennial, many heads of state from abroad arrived on Canadian soil, such as then US President Lyndon B. Johnson, Queen Elizabeth II of Britain, and President Charles de Gaulle of France. The most greatly anticipated among them was, no doubt, Charles de Gaulle, especially in light of the Quebec question.

De Gaulle visited Quebec, and rather than simply celebrating the centennial, he courted controversy by appearing to support Quebec's independence from Canada. De Gaulle gave a speech in French to an admiring crowd of French Canadians, in which he was heard to declare, "Vive le Québec libre!" These were not just words to wish the Quebec people well; it was a specific phrase that was used by Quebec residents who wished to separate from Canada. This was considered to be particularly troubling because France was a member of NATO and ostensibly a partner with Canada. Yet, de Gaulle's actions were little more than bluster since France was a weakening power and had very little clout on the world stage at this time.

Still, it was a hard pill for Canadian unionists to swallow. They could not believe that de Gaulle had, well, the gall to do such a thing. De Gaulle was subsequently condemned by Canadian authorities, and the brash French prime minister left shortly thereafter. However, some would wonder if the damage was already done.

In the late 1960s, radical separatist movements began to grow. And by 1970, a particularly nasty Quebec nationalist group, which called themselves Front de libération du Québec, or FLQ for short, was established. Although it is unclear what socialist or communist ties the FLQ may have had, it is worth noting that throughout the late 1960s and early 1970s, several communist-backed or inspired groups appeared all over the globe with similar names. For example, in the northern Ethiopian region of Tigray around this time, the TPLF, which stands for Tigray People's Liberation Front, was formed. Also, in the Middle East, Palestinian radicals formed the PLO or Palestinian Liberation Organization. Sudan also had a group called SPLM, which stood for Sudan People's Liberation Movement. These are just a few examples of the countless groups from this time period that have the words "people," "liberation," and "front" in their clumsy, unwieldy acronyms, and many had ties to the communist bloc, in one way or another.

At any rate, the French-Canadian radicals known as the FLQ were bad news for the federal government of Canada, and in the fall of 1970, they kicked off what was known as the October Crisis by inflicting several terrorist attacks against the Canadian government during that month.

During their rampage, the group actually abducted the British trade commissioner for Montreal. They ended up holding this man hostage and vowed not to free him until some of their own separatist colleagues who had been previously arrested were released. The Canadian government, of course, was not about to do any such thing. They had their hands full as it was; the last thing they needed was to set free even more radical separatists.

The group also strangely demanded that the Canadian government read their manifesto to the nation across broadcast media, as if such a thing would help their struggle. On top of this, there was also a request for a large amount of cash and an escort to a "friendly country." Predictably enough, the federal government of Canada declined to do any of these things.

Once the FLQ radicals knew that Canadian officials would not negotiate with terrorists, the separatists tried to do even more damage by taking Quebec's labor minister—Pierre Laporte—hostage. This time, it was the provincial government of Canada that became distressed enough to invite more draconian tactics to be used by the federal government. The local Quebec government requested Prime Minister Pierre Elliott Trudeau to intervene by sending in troops.

An alarmed Trudeau, fearing that Quebec's provincial government just might disintegrate in the chaos, obliged this request. Both the military and police worked together to capture the terrorists, but unfortunately for the abducted labor minister, his fate was already sealed—he was killed by his captors. The British trade commissioner fared much better, gaining his freedom from his captors in December of 1970, just in time for Christmas.

Although the threat of the October Crisis was waged by a relatively small group of people, their tactics were so devastating that this incident ranks as one of the greatest threats to Canadian sovereignty of all time. Canadian officials afterward learned to play hardball with terrorists, and future would-be agitators seemed to get the message. For the rest of the 1970s, Canada's domestic affairs remained relatively quiet and stable.

This stability came just in time since Montreal was scheduled to host the Olympics in 1976. The show went on without much of a hitch, except for the faulty design of Montreal's stadium, which boasted a retractable roof that did not seem to work all too well.

But that same year, a movement for separatism was once again beginning to take up steam; at least it did so quietly this time around. This movement was not a violent radical terrorist group of French Canadians but rather a provincial political party that sought reform and possibly future separation, not through bullets but rather ballots. The group, which called itself the Parti Québécois, gained power in Quebec in November of 1976. One of the first things that the Parti Québécois did was institute mandatory French in public institutions in Quebec. Street signs were in French, emergency services required French, and so on and so forth.

The most immediate result of this legislation was an exodus of English-speaking Canadians out of Quebec. Rather than taking the time to learn some French, these English-speaking Canadians decided to move to another province where English still reigned supreme. This was not good for Quebec in the long run since Quebec was sparsely inhabited and still struggling to bolster a decent-sized population.

But the greatest development of the Parti Québécois was the creation of a referendum in which residents of Quebec could actually vote on whether or not to leave Canada proper. This referendum was ultimately held in 1980. The referendum failed, with only 40 percent voting to leave Canada and the other 60 percent voting to stay. Nevertheless, the very fact that Quebec would vote on secession sent shockwaves throughout the rest of Canada.

Besides this referendum, the next most consequential moment for Canada in the 1980s came with the introduction of the Canada Act in the year 1982. This act served as the final step in Canada's long march to full independence. This act formally ended the ability of the British government to amend the Canadian constitution at the "request and consent" of the Canadian Parliament. Now—no matter what—the only ones who could change the Canadian constitution were Canadians.

The only connection to Britain left intact was the fact that Queen Elizabeth II was still recognized as the monarch. But as is the case in Britain itself, this role is primarily a ceremonial one, with the true power of government laying in the parliament. The queen ultimately came to Canada herself to sign off on the act, which was made official on April 17th, 1982.

By 1985, a new Canadian prime minister—a conservative—by the name of Brian Mulroney was actively courting powerful new trade agreements with US President Ronald Reagan. Reagan also liked the idea, and he sought to establish a better trade deal between the United States and both Canada and Mexico. The first step of this new partnership with Canada was made in October of 1987 when tariffs between the United States and Canada were removed for what was slated to be a ten-year time period. They also established a bilateral panel in which the two partners could oversee the whole process to make sure it was being conducted appropriately.

As many readers may very well guess, it was these measures that began the push toward what would become NAFTA (the North American Free Trade Agreement). It might surprise many, but Prime Minister Mulroney initially received some severe pushback from the idea of an economic trade union with the United States, with some suggesting that this was only the beginning of a more permanent political union. The concept might almost sound absurd, but for Canadians who long feared being annexed by the United States, their suspicions were real. Nevertheless, Brian Mulroney and Ronald Reagan formalized the deal on January 1st, 1989.

Prime Minister Mulroney began to lose favor, and he stepped down from politics in 1993, paving the way for Kim Campbell—Canada's first female prime minister—to take the helm in his place.

Mulroney and Campbell's party would lose power in the election that took place later that fall, and the new government would be led by the liberal Jean Chrétien.

The rise of Jean Chrétien coincided with the rise of President Bill Clinton in the United States. Clinton would turn out to be a big supporter of free trade between the US and Canada, and he made sure that NAFTA was the law of the land, signing off on it on December 8ᵗʰ, 1993.

After putting NAFTA to bed, the next major political upheaval in Canada involved a second referendum on Quebec. Consequentially enough, many in Quebec were unhappy with NAFTA, thinking that the economic controls of the deal would have an adverse effect on local Quebec business. This referendum was held in 1995, and it managed to produce a startlingly much closer verdict. The campaign for this referendum touted as "Oui ou Non?" asked a simple question of Quebec residents—do you wish to stay in Canada? Yes, or no? It was a nail-biter—50.6 percent chose to stay part of Canada, while 49.4 percent of voters in Quebec voted to leave.

Prime Minister Jean Chrétien's party would manage to come out on top in the 2000 election, ensuring that his agenda would make it into the next millennium. Jean Chrétien would be prime minister when the United States was struck by the horrific terrorist attacks of September 11ᵗʰ, 2001. These attacks were launched by the terror group Al-Qaeda, who were being protected and given a safe haven by the Taliban of Afghanistan.

This attack sparked a US-led invasion of Afghanistan, and the subsequent occupation would last for twenty years before the US withdrew in August of 2021. Canadian troops were sent right alongside Americans to participate in this conflict. However, Canadians would not participate when the United States decided to go to war with Iraq under the false pretenses that Saddam Hussein had weapons of mass destruction (WMDs).

The case for WMDs in Iraq was famously made by George W. Bush's Secretary of State Colin Powell, who claimed that it was just a matter of time before Iraq had the capacity to attack the US with its WMDs. These claims were thought to be ludicrous by some at the time, and they were ultimately proven to be so. Canada, for one, was not buying it, and it declined to participate in the US invasion the Americans called Operation Iraqi Freedom.

However, Canadians did participate in NATO efforts to intervene in the Libyan Civil War. This is something that many Canadians now view as a mistake, perhaps of similar proportions to the misguided invasion of Iraq. After all, it was disruptions in the governments in Libya, Egypt, Iraq, and Syria that helped to pave the way for the rise of ISIS (Islamic State of Iraq and Syria).

ISIS, a group that has been condemned by none other than Al-Qaeda for being "too extreme," unleashed abuses upon civilian populations that have not been seen since the Middle Ages. ISIS members proved how intolerant they were by rampaging through much of the Middle East and killing and enslaving anyone who was not exactly like them. Even Muslims were slaughtered if the members of ISIS believed them not to be "their brand of Muslim."

Canada, like much of the rest of the world, saw the pure evil of ISIS for what it was. Canada readily supplied its troops to help combat this menace.

In the meantime, Canada entered into a new era in 2015 with the rise of Justin Trudeau as the new prime minister and the face of the Liberal Party of Canada. Trudeau is also the son of former Prime Minister Pierre Elliott Trudeau, establishing what many see as a Canadian political dynasty. Justin Trudeau was ushered into office with a pledge to decrease the tax burden on middle-class Canadian families while simultaneously increasing the tax responsibilities of the richest taxpayers in Canada. With the extra tax revenue from Canada's wealthiest earners, Trudeau was able to increase social programs for the average Canadian citizen.

Another major pledge of Prime Minister Justin Trudeau's government was to improve the situation of Canada's First Nations residents. Another highlight of his first term was the introduction of the controversial medically assisted dying provisions of 2016. This bit of legislation essentially allowed for assisted suicide for those who were suffering from incurable, terminal conditions.

In 2018, Prime Minister Trudeau also made waves when he made marijuana use completely legal throughout Canada with the passing of the Cannabis Act. This made Canada the second nation—after Uruguay—and the first G7 country to officially legalize the use of marijuana.

In 2020, Justin Trudeau participated in the forging of a revised and updated NAFTA-styled trade agreement called the United States-Mexico-Canada Agreement, or USMCA for short. It was around the time of this milestone that Canada—like much of the rest of the world—was being rocked by a global pandemic.

Justin Trudeau's party went on to retain their majority in Canada's election in 2021, but it was an uphill climb. The election took place in the midst of the botched US withdrawal from Afghanistan. The centralized government of Afghanistan, which had long been propped by the US and its British and Canadian allies, collapsed in stunning fashion, as the Taliban soon took it over. Prime Minister Justin Trudeau, just like US President Joe Biden, was criticized for how these things transpired under his watch. Critics and supporters of Justin Trudeau, of course, greatly differ on just how much blame Trudeau should take. But nevertheless, Justin Trudeau and his party prevailed. Prime Minister Justin Trudeau—as of this writing—continues to lead Canada to this very day.

Conclusion – O Canada! O Canada!

Canada has an incredible history, yet it is a history that often goes unnoticed. Canada, of course, has long lived in the shadow of other great powers. First, Canada was overshadowed by its early French colonizers. Once the British subdued the land of Canada, it would be the might of the British Empire that would obscure our view of true Canadian history.

Once Britain subsided in influence during the Cold War, the United States, as the dominant military and political force in North America, took the front seat, and Canada continued to remain in the background to much of the rest of the outside world. But while these juggernauts strode the world stage, Canadians have lived a rich and unique history all their own.

Canada can recount its history from the first of the First Nations people to cross the Bering Strait some fifteen thousand years ago, to the French fur trappers who dared to call early, icy settlements such as Port Royal home, and to the Canadians who immigrated from Britain and ended up becoming true trailblazers as they pushed westward through wild and rugged terrain to reach the western shores of the North American continent.

The story of Canada is not just the story of one group of people but of many. Those who live in Canada have a deep ancestry that traces to all over the globe, yet they have come together to forge something truly unique. The living standards and resources of Canada continue to rival much of the rest of the world; in fact, Canada is consistently listed as one of the best places to live. In April of 2021, in the annual "Best Countries Report," Canada was actually ranked as the number one country in which to live. If you are a resident of Canada, you most likely have excellent work opportunities and a top-notch quality of "life and social purpose." Canada was also seen as being a leader in social justice, something that has become increasingly important to many all over the world.

So having said that, if you can handle some lower temperatures, Canada is indeed a nice place to lay your head! O Canada! O Canada! It is a country with a great history and a great place to live!

Part 2: The French and Indian War

A Captivating Guide to the North American Conflict between Great Britain and France along with Its Impact on the History of Canada, the US, and the Seven Years' War

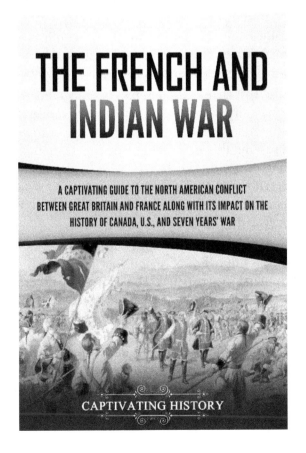

Introduction

Two great empires, Britain and France, had a long-standing struggle for supremacy dating back to medieval times. The numerous battles and centuries' worth of conflicts caused bad blood to form between the powers, and aggressions began spilling over into colonial North America.

By 1756, the British and French had been fighting over imperial interests for two years. It caused plenty of tension over who had the rights to commercial trade, with many in government having a financial interest in the new land. But it was not just over the coveted trading of goods like beaver pelts. They also fought over alliances with native tribes. Each nation worked to woo allies away from the other. Threats flew from both sides, telling the other to back down or face dire consequences.

Native tribal leaders promised the British that they could build an outpost in the Ohio Forks region, but the French did not like this encroachment on what they considered their territory. They already held posts in Canada, New York, and Pennsylvania. Ohio was a strategic region for them, as it gave them a straight shot into their Louisiana territories. It would also serve to keep the British contained to the East Coast, making them unable to spread their armies and empire any farther west. The French worried that if a formidable British presence was allowed to grow on the continent, all of their colonies would fall. They were not wrong.

Tribal chiefs saw the trouble brewing between the British and French. For nearly a century, they managed to pit the two empires against each other and stay hidden in the shadows of war, coming out occasionally to fight. Despite having been able to maintain neutrality in the "white man's war" for so long, they now began to feel pressured to take sides. With more colonists arriving every year and the Europeans' hot ambition for land and its resources, they believed the survival of their people depended on it.

Some sided with the British, feeling that they were the greater military strength. However, most tribal leaders allied themselves with the French, as they appeared less land-hungry. The French also proactively wooed them with promises of "exotic" goods, liquors, and other luxuries, which they more often than not delivered on.

In addition to white settlers moving westward and pushing the Native Americans from their lands, tribes of the Iroquois Confederacy faced problems from within and from other indigenous nations. There were often conflicting interests, agendas, and allegiances, sometimes even within the same tribe. Western tribes moved into the Ohio Valley and farther eastward, trying to get closer to the white settlers with whom they could trade. This hemmed in the Iroquois tribes, like the Delaware and Shawnee, giving them few options.

The tribes were not the only ones caught between the two empires. Colonists, who were struggling to find freedom and survive in this new land, faced increasing difficulties as they were inevitably drawn into the conflict. This gave rise to bitter feelings about their home country.

This epic struggle between two empires would last from 1754 to 1763, but it stemmed from a larger war that began in 1756. The Seven Years' War would spread across the globe. Though the French and Indian War was fought on North American soil, the conflict would have far-reaching consequences for many people. It would create new nations and change the course of world history forever.

Chapter 1 – First Confrontation

The major and his party had just ridden their horses fifteen miles on the cold morning of December 4th, 1753, the dampness of the rain the day before still hanging in the air. The log cabin he had so eagerly been riding toward now appeared, a white flag with a fleur-de-lis waving above. Major George Washington had finally arrived at the place where he would deliver an important message from Virginia Governor Robert Dinwiddie. It was his first mission of this kind, and his heartbeat quickened in anticipation.

The cabin, once a business and a home, had been fortified for defense by the trader John Fraser before he had been ousted by the French the year before. Leaving his native escorts to stay back, Washington took his translator and his field guide to the entrance of the cabin. There, three French officers and Captain Philippe-Thomas Chabert de Joncaire politely greeted the gentlemen and invited them in. He had heard much about the man on his journey, and now he stood in front of him, courteous to a fault toward sworn enemies.

Joncaire was born to a Seneca mother and a French father. He easily stood between the two worlds and held as much sway and influence in the region as any governor. He held a military position with the French, and he was also the chief interpreter for the Six Nations.[1]

---

[1] An Iroquois confederation council of fifty sachems (chiefs) from the Mohawk, Oneida,

Major Washington was eager to deliver his message from Dinwiddie. It was a letter demanding that the French remove themselves from these lands, as they were lands that the British declared they had already claimed. The French captain demurred. Although he replied that he was in charge of the Ohio region, he told the major that he really should bring this letter to the commander of Fort Le Boeuf another fifty miles away. The major was dismayed at having to ride such a long distance again the next day, but he accepted the captain's offer to eat with him and his officers. Though the two men with him stayed as well, the major had left the other Native Americans behind by design. He feared that the captain might somehow influence them.

As the dinner wore on, the Frenchmen drank wine freely, and tongues loosened. The French openly declared their intention of claiming the Ohio lands. Oh, they knew that the British would fight them for them, but they believed that the French would best them in the contest. The British, they confidently declared, were too slow to stop them. Besides, a Frenchman named La Salle had made it to the Ohio Forks region first. And now, Joncaire told them, the French were already chasing British families from their settlements, and they were determined to prevent any more from coming to the region under their control.

The major, who had remained perfectly sober, jumped at the opportunity to ply the inebriated Frenchmen for more information about their troops, supply lines, and forts. The French officers answered freely, seemingly unworried about the information they were letting loose.

The weather the next day prevented the party from riding out. Even if the weather had been favorable, by this time, Washington was now missing an important part of his party.

While the major and his men had been entertained by the French, the Seneca leader Half King and his men had visited their Delaware allies to hold council regarding the return of tribal treaty belts to the French.[2,3]

Onondaga, Cayuga, Seneca, and Tuscarora nations.

[3] Tanacharison, or Half King as he was called by the British whom he had befriended, was a staunch and intelligent Seneca leader with a broad knowledge of the white men and

Half King had a deep hatred for the French for a number of reasons. When he was a boy, the French brutally murdered his father and dishonored his corpse afterward.[4] More recently, he had become bitterly resentful of the insolent and insulting treatment given to him by French Captain Pierre-Paul Marin de la Malgue. But his reasons for siding with the British were not strictly personal. With two large empires pressing in on the Six Nations' lands, it seemed unavoidable that sides would need to be chosen. The British seemed like the best of the two bad options available.

Half King had gone to Marin with a similar message as the British—leave the Ohio watersheds. But it was not due to an unwillingness to share the land and its resources. He told the Frenchman that the natives would have happily traded and lived beside the French settlers in the area had they been as friendly to them as the British had been. Instead, the French had come and taken their land by force. Half King declared that the natives could not submit to this treatment. They officially called on the French to leave the area.

Marin told Half King that wampum or no, he would not listen to his words. He then referred to the natives as "flies or mosquitos," adding that he was afraid of neither. Marin continued, defiantly telling Half King that the French would indeed continue to build on the river. He practically dared the natives to try and oppose him. After flinging the wampum belt at Half King, he said the land belonged to the French and that no one had the right to say otherwise. Half King left the meeting with Marin incensed and offended.

---

their ways. The Six Nations' Grand Council appointed him as a leader and diplomat between the tribes, as well as a spokesman between the nations and the British. His leadership role earned him the moniker "Half King."

[3] Also called wampum or wampum belts, these articles made of strung-together white and purple clamshell beads held meaning and value. Wampum of different colors and styles held different meanings and were used for numerous purposes. In this instance, the return of the treaty belt meant that the agreement between the giver and the receiver was being terminated.

[4] He claimed that the French killed his father, boiled his body, and then ate it. The account is generally thought to be true.

Half King did not accompany the British in 1753 to reiterate his message to the other French commanders; rather, he looked for the support of the local tribes. He informed Delaware Chief Custaloga (also spelled as Kustaloga) that the "king" of the Delaware, Shingas, had ordered the tribe to return the treaty belt as well.[5] But Custaloga wanted to keep the peace and was reluctant to incite the French. He discovered a technicality through which he could refuse the order from his potentate. If Half King wanted to return the treaty belts to the French, he had to take the risk and do it without the Delaware tribe.

Once Joncaire got wind of the meeting that had occurred, he did exactly what Washington feared he would—he cordially invited Half King, White Thunder, and Jeskakake to his cabin for drinks, treating them as old friends and allies despite never having met them before. The men drank and drank, and not one word was uttered about the French leaving the valley.

Major Washington left in disgust. He knew exactly what game the French were trying to play, and he did not like it one bit. Joncaire was trying to win the native guides over to the French, and he was doing it right under his nose. The battle the French were fighting at the moment was one of diplomacy, and they excelled at it.

The next day, a sober Half King was determined to give his defiant "leave our land speech" to Joncaire. Washington tried to dissuade him, telling him he should wait to deliver the message to the fort commander. Really, though, he didn't care who heard the message; he just wanted to keep his native guides from further contact with the wily and persuasive Joncaire. However, he lost the argument, and Half King proceeded with the formalities.

After Half King's speech, Joncaire politely refused the wampum belt and told the native men to present it at the fort. But Joncaire was not about to end his bid to win over the natives. Washington's frontiersman guide, Christopher Gist, wrote that "Joncaire did everything he could" to get the natives to stay behind with the

---

[5] Traditionally, the Delaware (also known as the Lenape) did not have kings. Shingas's brother had been named the "king" by the British, and when he passed away, the title went to Shingas.

French. If he succeeded, it would be a huge blow to Washington, who relied on Half King not just to help him navigate the landscape but also in helping him navigate relations with the numerous tribes in the area.

That night, the major, his men, and four French escorts rode out toward the fort, joined by their four native companions whom they narrowly missed losing as allies. After four days of riding, the men arrived at Fort Le Boeuf.

Major Washington and his men were politely received and presented Governor Dinwiddie's letter to the fort commander, a tough Canadian named Jacques Legardeur de Saint-Pierre. It was to be the first formal confrontation between the British and French during this period. The message that Washington delivered announced to the French that it was a well-known and established fact that the lands around the Ohio River belonged to Great Britain. As such, the British Crown was surprised to find the French building forts and settlements there. Dinwiddie requested that the French leave in a peaceful manner.

While waiting for a reply, as the letter had to be translated into French, the major and his men took the time to inspect the fort, the barracks, and even the number of canoes the French had, taking notes so they could report their findings when they got back to Virginia. By the time they completed their inspection, the French had a reply and invited Washington to discuss it civilly over some wine. Despite all the courteousness, the answer was not appealing to the British. The Ohio River did not belong to the British but to the French, and the British did not have any right to use the waters for trading. In fact, any Brit caught doing so would be arrested. The French were prepared to defend their territory.

The French then tried to compel the major to bring his letter to the governor of Quebec, but Washington had grown tired of being bounced from one French commander to another. Besides, Legardeur had already given his answer, and Quebec was just another deflect and delay tactic. Washington wanted to allow Half King to have his say and then leave as quickly as possible.

But the French at Fort Le Beouf continued the same diplomatic battle that Joncaire had started. Though the French tried to put off hearing Half King, he was finally able to gain a private audience with the fort's captain. When the native leader tried to return the wampum belt to Legardeur, he refused it, declaring that he wanted to continue good relationships and trading with the natives.

If Half King found this refusal offensive, Legardeur was sure to make up for it by giving the Native American men every consideration. He knew how important Half King was as a path to gaining an alliance with the Six Nations, so he continued to employ crafty delay tactics in hopes of winning new allies and taking them away from the British. The French openly and unabashedly used the promise of liquor, guns, and other gifts in a brazen attempt to woo the natives away from the British, and it nearly worked. It gave George Washington some of the worst anxiety of his life, as he did not know whether he would lose his native allies that were so important to his current mission and the British cause.

The return trip, which took place in late December, was cold and snowy. The icy trails and difficult conditions strained their horses. Frostbite set in, rendering three of the men helpless. Yet the major was determined to get the French commander's answer back to Virginia without delay.

Not wanting to be held back by the ailing men and the wait for fresh horses, Washington took a backpack and had Gist follow him on foot. They trekked through the woods, even though it went against Gist's sage advice. A frontiersman like Gist had no trouble making the trek, but Washington was a gentleman and had difficulties. Their progress was slow.

The journey back was fraught with dangers and harrowing experiences. A native guide they picked up along the way tried to shoot them, narrowly missing both men. Half-frozen rivers with broken ice had to be perilously crossed using a hastily constructed raft that the men made using timber they cut down with a hatchet. Rough conditions caused Washington to fall out of his raft into the frigid waters, barely clinging on as Gist pulled him up. The men were unable to navigate the raft to shore, so Gist and Washington were forced to spend a freezing, ice-encased night on a small island. They then moved through the same woods where French Ottawa tribesmen had recently murdered and scalped an entire family.

Finally, on January 16th, 1754, one month after he left Fort Le Beouf, Major George Washington reached Williamsburg, Virginia. He was eager to hand in his reply and also report that the French were planning a seizure of the Ohio Valley, most likely in the spring. There was no time to waste.

Chapter 2 – The "Jumonville Affair"

Governor Dinwiddie frowned, dismayed as he read the letter. The French commander had written that he was not obliged to leave Ohio as the British had commanded. According to him, they had committed no acts of hostility toward the British, nor were they in violation of any treaty or trade agreement.

Dinwiddie was disappointed yet remained resolute. He saw the bigger picture and agreed with Washington that speedy action was paramount to their overall success. Preparations were made for the major to return to the Ohio Valley with a contingent of militiamen, including traders familiar with the Native Americans of the region.

That was easier said than done. Few voluntarily enlisted or were inclined to comply with the demands to muster. Angry, Dinwiddie began to invoke penalties on those who refused, hoping to motivate others to fall in line. Meanwhile, reports from native allies came in, telling of four hundred French reinforcements that were on their way to Ohio. Time and the ability to secure the Ohio Valley were rapidly slipping away.

Meanwhile, Dinwiddie ordered Captain William Trent back to Ohio to build a small stockade fort near the forks, which ensured the British continued to stake their claim to the area. Dinwiddie knew this was sure to provoke the French, but he would play this dangerous game nonetheless.

By March, Major Washington had three hundred unruly, undisciplined, and nearly ungovernable militiamen at his disposal. There was a promise that one thousand Native Americans would meet up with them. As much as these numbers might look sufficient, they did not tell the true picture. Some of the men had been released from prison just to join up. Many were without even the most basic supplies, including shoes or clothing, let alone guns. But they were all Washington had. He would have to make do.

Major Washington was also handed a commission that he had longed for—a promotion to lieutenant colonel and the assignment to finish building the British fort in Ohio that Captain Trent had started. With the minimum number of preparations now made, Lieutenant Colonel George Washington and his men set out for Ohio in mid-April 1754. After the treacherous Appalachian crossing, Captain William Trent raced to the party on horseback, delivering urgent news.

Upon opening the letter, Washington was delivered a shock— eight hundred French troops were about to descend on the unfinished British fort in Ohio. An attack was expected at any moment. Back in January, the native allies of the French had warned Governor Michel-Ange Duquesne about the British incursion, and they immediately began preparations to expel them from the lands. When the British came, the French were ready and waiting.

Since the small British column was still in West Virginia, there was no way they could make it in time to save their compatriots! Washington tried once again to hasten their journey, but slow wagons, the unavailability of horses, and lack of supplies made for an agonizingly sluggish pace. Just two days after Trent had delivered his news, another report was delivered on April 22nd. It confirmed the commander's worst fears—the unfinished fort had been taken by the French. Control of the fort meant control of the Ohio Forks. The British had lost before they had even begun.

Ensign Edward Ward, the messenger, was able to give an eyewitness account of what had happened. With Captain Williams away and Lieutenant Fraser indifferent to his duties, Ward became the senior officer of the forty-one soldiers guarding the unfinished fort. Upon hearing that the French were on their way, he enlisted the help of Half King and other natives, who advised a wooden stockade be built.

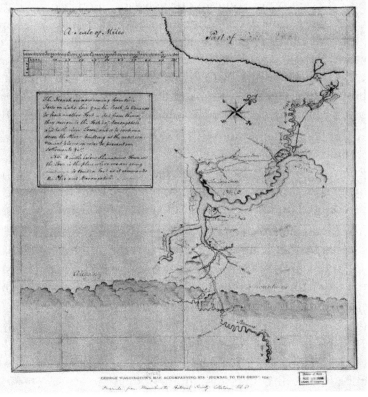

Map accompanying Washington's journal courtesy of Library of Congress.
https://commons.wikimedia.org/wiki/File:Gwash_map01.jpg

On April 17th, as the last gate was finished, the French arrived by canoe. They demanded that the British surrender immediately and leave with all of their belongings. Doing otherwise would have dire consequences for the outnumbered Brits.

With about one thousand French soldiers to his forty-one men, Ward had no choice but to leave. As they marched out, an angry Half King shouted to the French that the fort had been built on his authority and that he had laid the first post. He might be walking out at the moment, but for him, this wasn't over.

After Ward related his story, he handed the letter to Washington. In the letter, the French accused the British of disrupting the peace and harmony of the region when all the French wanted was to be able to use the area for trade.

The second letter Ward handed over was from Half King. He implored his old friend to come to their aid against the French, stating, "If you do not come to our assistance now, we are entirely undone, and I think we shall never meet together again. I speak with a heart full of grief." Tanacharison was greatly angered over the whole fort affair. He was the one who had made the decision to back the British, and he had convinced the other chiefs that it was the best option. But now, it looked like he had chosen poorly. For the sake of his honor, he needed to win against the French.

George Washington was grim. Even with native reinforcements, how could the 159 men he had left take on 1,000 French, especially given his military inexperience? There were a few other companies within marching distance, but they were weak and could not be counted on for much. The situation could hardly be worse.

Yet, Lieutenant Colonel Washington was compelled by Half King's plea for help, although he perhaps did not fully understand that the indigenous leader had his own agenda—revenge against the French. A victory would also help strengthen his position with his own people, as it would prove he had made wise decisions.

After strategizing, Washington decided to station his company at the British-fortified storehouse at Red Stone Creek and hold out for reinforcements. Hopefully, he would receive more commissioned officers because, up until then, he was sorely lacking those in his militia. He sent Ward and an escort of natives back with letters to Dinwiddie. He also sent messengers to Half King to meet with him to strategize.

The young commander had a lot on his plate. In writing to Dinwiddie, he expressed his concern, telling the governor, "Upon the whole, I find so many clogs in the expedition that I quite despair of success."

To add to his troubles, Trent met up with Washington's column with a group of militia volunteers he had raised. That would have been good news except that these hardscrabble traders were idle, greedy, and unable to be reasoned with. However, some of their protests for better pay were not without merit. But after a few days, Washington needed to separate them from his own men. They left in a huff, scattering and going about their own business. It was more of a relief than anything.

On May 24th, while waiting for reinforcements to take back the stolen fort, Washington set up camp at Great Meadows on a place he called a "charming field for an encounter." Chilling reports of French reconnoiters sniffing around their camp came in from Gist and other traders. Further reports said that the French mood was foul and ugly. They would surely find out about the meager numbers of British soldiers in the area. Immediate defensive action needed to be taken, and preparations were made to build a hasty fortification.

Three days later, with more reports of French activity, Lieutenant Colonel Washington sent out a scouting party of seventy-five men, which included Half King and his men. When they returned, they were eager to report that they had found a well-hidden French encampment deep in a forested gully. The camp contained a small company of no more than fifty men. Why would the French have a small hidden contingency so close by when they already had command of the fort? The possibilities filled the commander with concern, and he did not want to wait to be surprised by the answer.

With this new information, the British felt the necessity of striking first. They could easily sneak through the woods and surround the French. Washington hoped the element of surprise and having the high ground would make up for their lack of experience and numbers.

The night of May 26th was black and wet. Regardless, preparations needed to be made, and the lieutenant colonel sought Half King for a council. Fearing that an attack could occur at any time, the men agreed that they would not wait for the French to find them and make the first move—they would attack the encampment together.

At 7 a.m. the next morning, a company of forty British and a number of native allies stealthily crept through the woods as the French were stirring from their beds. One hundred yards from the French camp, they stopped. Washington sent Captain Adam Stephen and his men to the left. The native men would silently surround the far side of the camp, and Washington would take a contingent of men to the right. He knew going in that direction meant they would be exposed and in the open, and he was up for the challenge.

Modern-day Jumonville Glen.

Once everyone was in attack position, the tall, imposing figure of Lieutenant Colonel Washington stepped out into the glen and ordered the attack. The startled French soldiers jumped up and ran for their rifles.

Shots rang out on both sides, and men began to fall.[6] The French did their best to return fire, but the readiness and high position of the British had them at a disadvantage. Bullets whistled through the air. Washington heard the sound as they passed his ears, missing his head.

The French were quickly overcome. Those who tried to run into the woods were intercepted by Half King and his contingent. After less than fifteen minutes of battle, it was over, and the French had surrendered. As many as fourteen French lay dead or wounded in the glen, among them being their commander, Joseph Coulon de Jumonville. The British had suffered only one or two wounded.

As Jumonville lay on the field, he tried to call for a ceasefire as the battle waged on. But in the heat of the fray, his call went unheeded. Now, as the smoke was clearing, he implored Washington to read the letters he clutched in his hands. If what the letters said were true, Washington had just committed the gravest

---

[6] French reports stated that the British shot first, but a British soldier involved in the conflict claimed it was difficult to know who actually took the first shot. In all likelihood, the British shot first, and the French scrambled to return the volley.

error.

Before the lieutenant colonel could react to the letters, Half King walked up to the injured Jumonville. It was now his moment to enact his revenge for the humiliation at the half-built Ohio Forks outpost. As the Frenchman lay helpless and wounded, Half King allegedly said to him, "Tu n'es pas encore mort, mon père." ("Thou art not yet dead, my father.") He then took his tomahawk and crushed Jumonville's skull, killing him. He allegedly washed his hands in the dead man's brains.[7] He had sent a clear message to the French that he was not to be trifled with.

Though short, those fifteen minutes, later dubbed the "Jumonville affair," were crucial to colonial American history.[8] In those fifteen minutes, a young, twenty-two-year-old Lieutenant Colonel George Washington had started the French and Indian War. He would not yet understand the consequences that had been set in motion.

---

[7] Accounts vary on Jumonville's death. Some accounts state that he was killed in the first volley of bullets, while other accounts tell of his death at the hands of Half King and his tomahawk. The most compelling of these is John Shaw's sworn deposition based on soldier's eyewitness accounts.

[8] Earl Horatio Walpole described the military action as "a volley fired by a young Virginian in the backwoods of America that set the world on fire."

Chapter 3 – Vengeance Visits Fort Necessity

As the British rounded up and identified prisoners, Half King and his men were feeling less charitable toward the French.[9] They plundered the dead men, and those who lay wounded were killed and scalped. In his quest for vengeance against the French, Half King also demanded that the twenty-one unwounded prisoners be turned over for the same treatment. Washington would not concede to this; he could not surrender unarmed men to be butchered, especially after he heard who they claimed to be.

Jumonville's second-in-command, Drullion, earnestly backed up Jumonville's last words and the letters he carried. He told Washington that they were emissaries on a diplomatic mission and that they had been sent to give the British a message. The letters they were bringing to the British called for their removal from the Ohio Valley.

Further inspection of the letters only confirmed what the Frenchmen told them. The French claimed they wanted to keep the peace and were diplomatically demanding that the British leave their lands in the Ohio Valley under threat of forcible ejection.

---

[9] Only one man escaped, a French-Canadian soldier named Mouceau, who was in the woods relieving himself when the fighting broke out. He was able to report the Jumonville defeat to French commanders.

This mission was very similar to the one Washington himself had undertaken the year before.

Jumonville had also been under orders that if he found any British east of the Great Mountain, he was not to disturb them. But Washington and the British officers did not see this as the French trying to maintain peace. Instead, they believed these instructions painted the French contingent in the glen to be spies, sent to locate the British and scope out their numbers and positions. The British believed that the ambassadorial messages were simply a cover for the French in the event they were caught, a ruse designed to give credibility to their claims.

Furthermore, the British argued, it was quite suspicious that a supposed French ambassadorial detail would be hiding and "camping in a skulking place" deep in the glen. It was apparent that the French knew where the British were, so why would they not have already delivered the message to them? Washington wrote to Dinwiddie, giving this reasoning as a defense for his actions. He also took pains to make sure he accused the French of being the instigators.[10]

Though the Jumonville affair had been the first armed conflict of the French and Indian War, the French had previously made claims and threatened hostilities. In the minds of the British, the war had already started before the first shot was fired, and it was started by the French. Half King agreed with them on this. In his opinion, the French had always intended for hostilities to occur.[11]

However, all of the prisoners unanimously denied the claims of the British. They continued to persist in their claims of being an embassy. Unmoved, Washington sent the French prisoners to Dinwiddie in Williamsburg. He warned the governor not to be swayed by their "many smooth stories" and that he thought "they ought to be hanged as spies of the worst sort."

Dinwiddie did not buy Washington's defense of his actions, nor his claims that the French started the affair. He knew he would have to do some damage control. In his eyes, Washington had

---

[10] However, Washington's actions belied that claim.

[11] This book is not intended to lay the blame on either side. All sides would have their obvious biases, and their stories and opinions reflect that.

opened fire on a camp of sleeping Frenchmen while both sides had still officially been at peace, uneasy as it was. With political suaveness, Dinwiddie told his London superiors that Half King and his men started the conflict and that Washington and his men had just backed them up. Still, Dinwiddie had a bad feeling that Earl Horatio Walpole's words were ringing true—Washington had "set the world on fire."

But Washington had bigger worries than the French prisoners or arguments over who started the conflict. When the French at Fort Duquesne heard of the essentially unprovoked attack in the glen, retribution was sure to follow. Washington believed that they would be "attacked by considerable forces" sooner rather than later. Their current camp at Great Meadows afforded no protection from an onslaught. He hadn't intended to make his stand here. Instead, he hoped to take on the French at the fortified Red Stone Creek, but he would have no choice but to make the best of it.

From the end of May to the beginning of June, the 150 men of Great Meadows tirelessly worked to build a circular fort, cutting down trees and forming them into thick stakes of seven feet high palisades covered in barks and skins. They also dug deep trenches around the outside, although the marshy ground surrounding them was thought to give the British an added advantage. When it was finished, Washington proudly bragged that when the French came against them, the fort would hold strong even if it "must withstand 5 to 1." He aptly named it Fort Necessity.

Fort Necessity today.

While the British were building the fort, Half King went on his own diplomatic mission of sorts. He carried the scalps taken from several French heads as he made his way to make a bid to persuade the Seneca, Delaware, and Shawnee warriors to join him and the British in the fight against the French.

As soon as the fort was finished, Half King showed up with about eighty Native Americans. There was not one warrior in the group. These were elderly men, women, and children seeking protection from the French. More families trickled in over the following days, but Half King's promise of warriors continued to fall flat. Not only would the British have to fight this battle on their own; now, they also had vulnerable people to protect.

That was a difficult task considering that food was running scarce. Despite writing to Alexandria, additional food provisions never came. And now Washington had native families to feed on top of his men—and he could not give them less than he was feeding his own men. When the last sack of flour was used, the people had to endure four days of hunger before an Ohio trader came through. He sold them provisions at an exorbitant price.

Just a few days later, on June 9th, Washington saw the sight he had been waiting for—the rest of the Virginia regiment filing into the Great Meadows. The relief he felt was short-lived. These men had little battle experience and even less in the way of provisions. To top it off, the regiment's commander, Colonel Joshua Fry, was not among them. He had fallen from his horse and broke his neck, dying of his injuries. Washington would now be the senior field officer in command of the fort until the North Carolina regiment arrived. The problems they faced remained his to deal with.

Over the next few weeks, more army regulars from South Carolina made it to the fort, along with nine small swivel cannons. The sight of the small crudely built fort was enough to give the professional soldiers pause. The fort was only fifty-three feet in diameter. It contained some meager food supplies, a few tents for shelter, and numerous muddy puddles, courtesy of the weather. The soldiers did not feel confident in its protection. Instead of staying with the provincial militia inside the fort, they opted to make their own camp nearby. This was headed by their own commander, Captain James Mackay, who told Washington that he was not about to take orders from a colonial colonel. Despite the obvious snub, Washington was glad to have a force of four hundred fighting men at Fort Necessity. All the while, the French were gathering their own forces.

On June 18th, Washington had a highly disappointing meeting with Half King and the Six Nations' Council at Onondaga. Not only were they reluctant to join the fight against the French, but Half King himself was also beginning to waver on the decision. When the natives saw the British fort, it seemed like an unstable fence compared to the stronghold of Fort Duquesne. They questioned whether they wanted to ally themselves with soldiers who would barely be able to defend themselves in such a shoddy structure. The native chiefs did not like how the odds looked for the British and would not risk taking sides with an army that was sure to lose in battle. Realistically, they worried how defeat would affect their own people, fearing that a loss would bring further hostility and vengeance upon themselves should they align themselves with the British and lose.

In the end, Washington's diplomatic prowess proved embarrassingly ineffective with the native chiefs. The council, having lost trust in Washington's ability to win and fearing the superior strength of the French, decided that the Six Nations would remain neutral in the white man's fight. They took their people from the fort and left. Half King stood by Washington, and a few loyal natives joined him.

The loss of these expected native allies was a hard blow to Washington and the British. Not only was their fighting force reduced, but they were also left more vulnerable, as they now had fewer native scouts and guides. Disappointment turned to distrust. The British could not help but see the natives who refused to ally as "treacherous Devils." Some even believed they were spies for the French. Washington could not let his men see the deep concerns he had. They must press on, especially with the French numbers at Fort Duquesne growing larger and larger by the day.

Concerned with French movements, Washington ordered all of his men to clear the roads and fields in the wilderness to get back to the fort at Great Meadows. The same day he gave his order, June 28th, an avenging force of seven hundred French, Canadian, and native warriors left Fort Duquesne and headed their way.

However, the British were unaware that a smaller French force had left ahead of the main army. On July 3rd, they stood at the tree line, staring in full view of the stockade fort. The man leading the charge was none other than François Coulon de Villiers, Jumonville's older brother.

Washington's actions alone during the Jumonville affair would not have likely triggered an all-out war, insulting as the French may have found it. But the savage butchery of Jumonville and some of the others was more than the French could let slide.

When Villiers heard of his brother's death and the questionable actions that led up to it, he petitioned his commanding officer, Claude-Pierre Pécaudy de Contrecœur, to allow him to lead the retaliatory charge. He was given permission to take five hundred men and advance. Before making it to Great Meadows, he stopped at the glen where his brother had died. The bodies had been left unburied, and the summer heat created an unbearably putrid smell. Scalping and wild animals had rendered the corpses completely unrecognizable. Still, the men took the time to bury their fallen compatriots before marching on, their revenge now refreshed. They used the very road the Virginians themselves had just built.

From the tree line above, Villiers could make out the fort's stockade. He watched as the soldiers laboriously dug trenches in the viscous mud caused by the previous night's heavy rain, which had created marshy ponds around the stockade and turned the trenches into streams. This "charming field for an encounter" had been turned into a muddy, watery death trap.

As colonial sentinels looked out into the tree line, it was their turn to be surprised. Though their reconnaissance parties had brought back sensational and sometimes dubious reports of large numbers of French and native warriors, all naked, on the march to attack the British over the past week, Washington and his men were literally up to their knees in mud trying to make preparations in and around the fort. They had expected to meet the French face to face on the battlefield, but the ambush had come with unexpected swiftness.[12]

The sentinels grabbed their muskets and fired hastily before running back toward the fort. The French did not hesitate. The three well-disciplined columns behind Villiers advanced. They halted to fire and then continued downhill toward the trenches. The fort's soldiers positioned themselves in front of the watery trenches, ready for a full-frontal assault. Then, the French made a sudden change in direction.

Washington scrambled to position his entire force in the open field. It was a dangerous gamble, but it was the only one that could slow the French advance. But even this was just delaying the inevitable.

A chill went through the Virginia regiment as the natives gave "a great cry" and led the French charge down the hill. Mackay and his men held fast, waiting until the French were within firing range. The French were unintimidated by the British showing, and as they drew closer, shots were fired, and cannons cut down the advancing native warriors.

Washington turned to his men, only to be shocked at what he saw—none of them were there. They had fled, vaulting themselves into the watery trenches.[13] He ordered the men to fire, but their nervousness combined with battle ineptitude caused them to miss their targets. Instead, they shot too high, hitting the trees and raining down nothing more than leaves and branches upon the French.

The French, however, did not want to take any chances that those in the trenches would better their aim. The French and Native Americans dropped suddenly to the ground, concealing themselves behind any stones, stumps, trees, or bushes nearby.

To the British, it would have appeared as if their enemies had instantly vanished, except for the persistent firestorm of bullets coming toward them. But the French did not only fire upon the men. They targeted every horse, dog, and cow belonging to the

---

[12] Meeting armies face to face on the battlefield was typical in European-style battles

[13] One soldier later wrote that Washington's second-in-command, Lieutenant Colonel George Muse, "frightened his men back to the trenches," leaving Mackay and his men vulnerable in the open.

fort, ensuring that they took out the enemy's transportation, canine warning system, and meat sources. Dead animal carcasses soon littered the field.

To add to their already muddy woes, "the most tremendous rain that could be conceived" began to fall. It had been hard enough keeping their gunpowder and weapons dry amidst the mire and puddles, but now it was impossible. The waterlogged, mud-laden British soon became exhausted, and the firing of their soaked flintlock weapons gradually died out. They were perplexed at how the French could possibly be keeping their own powder and weapons dry, as they seemed to have no trouble continuing to fire upon them.

At 8 p.m., the French called for a ceasefire. Raising the white flag, they shouted an invitation, "Voulez- vous parler?" It was an offer to talk. Although Washington knew they were beaten, he adamantly refused. He would not allow the French to come within the fort. Washington feared it was a ruse designed to check out their situation, which would better enable them to complete the demise of the fort and those within.

Well, Villiers told Washington via messenger, if they did not want the French to come to the fort to talk, they were more than welcome to send someone to the French camp. He was willing, perhaps with gritted teeth, to negotiate with the man whom he blamed for his brother's death. But better that than to risk colonial reinforcements arriving and the possibility of dying by the British sword.

Only two soldiers of Washington's men spoke French: Dutchman Jacob van Braam and Ensign William Le Peyronie. They were sent to the French camp for talks. Villiers did not hide the fact that his assault stemmed from the need to avenge his brother's death. However, he told the men he was feeling generous; if they vacated the fort, it would satisfy his vengeance. Their countries were not officially at war, so he did not feel the need for further hostilities.

Peyronie and van Braam trudged back to the fort through the rain and mud, the ceasefire agreement in their hands becoming soggy and limp. The articles, with the ink runny from the rain, were translated to Washington. The British were to leave the fort, taking everything but their arsenal, and they were to do it quickly lest the French and their native allies got restless. They were also to leave behind two officers as hostages to be used in a prisoner exchange.

However, the articles also contained two interesting phrases that were not translated to Washington. Whether it was on purpose, poor translation, or the wet pages rendered unreadable by the rain, van Braam failed to say that the articles mentioned "vengor l'assassin" and "l'assasinat du Jumonville."[14] These phrases were a critical omission. The document implied that the British agreed that Jumonville was intentionally assassinated, not simply killed in battle. Signing it was as good as a confession to the crime.

The next day, July 4th, the French saw the British army out "with honors." The British banners waved in front of the departing columns, and the drums turned out a solemn beat with which to march away. The fleur-de-lis flag raised above the fort, waving above van Braam and Captain Robert Stobo, the two hostages who had been left behind.

The departing regiment had no wagons or pack animals to carry their belongings or rations, so they could only take what they could carry.[15] The French promised to guard the rest of their baggage until the British could send wagons to retrieve their things. Agreements on both sides were immediately broken.

As Major Adam Stephen, wet, stockingless, and muddy up to his thighs, was walking away, a servant shouted that the French were stealing his clothing. Already hot-tempered, the incensed major ran to the thief, ripped the trunk from the man's shoulders, and kicked him in the rear end. As he walked back to his line, two French soldiers stopped to chastise him, telling him if any Englishman struck one of their soldiers, they would not be responsible for the resulting retaliation. After delivering a swearing reply in which he "damned the capitulation" and pointed out the French had already been the first to break the terms, the amused

---

[14] Neither British nor French were van Braam's first language, so there was bound to be a margin of error in translating.

[15] The French agreed under the terms of the surrender to let the British take their arms and munitions with them. Unarmed, they would have been vulnerable to attack on their march out.

Frenchmen asked if such a "dirty, half-naked" fellow could possibly be an officer. In response, he opened his trunk, pulled out a "flaming suit of laced Regimentals,"[16] and put it on over his mud and gunpowder encrusted clothes before walking away from the astonished soldiers.

However, Major Stephen was not the only one to suffer the theft of his things as they marched away. As they moved away from the fort, the natives allied with the French besieged and harassed the departing army. Having already plundered the belongings they left at the fort, they stole and mocked the exhausted soldiers. Some soldiers thought they recognized familiar faces—those of the Delaware chiefs who had only a few weeks before considered an alliance with them.[17]

Each day, the ranks of the army dwindled as deserters fled by night. Half King and the natives slipped away under cover of darkness to return to their own families and villages. Half King returned to his home in disgrace, losing the clout he had hoped to gain.[18, 19] The defeat did not only reflect badly on him but also the Iroquois leadership whom he had promised a victory.

Washington had been seeking fame, and he quickly found it as news of Fort Necessity circulated. Only this was not the type of fame he had been looking for; he knew the defeat portrayed him in a poor light, especially after the Jumonville debacle. As with the Jumonville affair, his correspondence shows that if he thought he had made any mistakes, he wasn't admitting them. He blamed bad weather and the indifferent attitude of the soldiers for the fort's demise, never mentioning that the poorly chosen location and weak commanders under his control were the major contributing factors.

To the French, the British baggage left behind was too irresistible of a temptation. But they found more than just clothes,

---

[16] A formal uniform.

[17] The Delaware, along with many other tribes, fell under the umbrella of Iroquois rule. They, along with other western tribes, did not want to be under the Iroquois dominion and found it advantageous to ally with the French.

[18] His home was near modern-day Harrisburg, Pennsylvania.

[19] Half King died just a few weeks later.

surveying equipment, and other mundane objects. One item caught their eye in particular—Washington's personal journal. Of course, Villiers's curiosity got the better of him, and after reading it, he forwarded it to his commanders. It eventually made it into the hands of Governor Duquesne.

Washington's innermost thoughts did nothing to endear him to the French governor, who declared that "there is nothing more unworthy and lower, even blacker than the sentiments and way of thinking of this Washington." He then wistfully stated that he wished he could have had the "pleasure to read his outrageous journal in front of his very nose." He may have missed that opportunity, but he wanted to make sure every French person knew just what a villain Washington was. So, he had the journal sent to Paris, where it was published and made available for anyone to read.

Chapter 4 – "You Should Have First Asked Our Consent"

Once back in Virginia, Washington fully expected heavy criticism and blame for the loss of the fort. Although he received a mild rebuke from Dinwiddie, he was even more surprised when the House of Burgesses passed a vote thanking him and the other officers. Some of them personally approached him. If Washington basked in their thanks and condolences on his defeat, it didn't last long.

Dinwiddie wanted to send a regiment back to Ohio as soon as possible. But he was without the manpower, so he was stuck waiting for British reinforcements. In the meantime, sick of squabbling between colonials and regulars, he decided to reorganize the Virginia regiment into smaller units headed by captains. Dinwiddie offered Washington a captaincy with the regular army. Apparently forgetting the fiascos he was recently the cause of, Washington was offended by the offer of a lower rank than the one he currently held. He told Dinwiddie that there was no way he could be satisfied with a lower rank than he deserved or "thought he had the right to." He resigned from the army and went back to tending his farm.

Though the story of Washington's involvement at the beginning of the conflict was crucial to the events that followed, it was not the only story. Those first conflicts touched off an intricate web of other conflicts, allies, enemies, and trading partners that was spun throughout the colonial empire. Alliances, particularly with the indigenous tribes, were of the utmost importance. But negotiations, diplomacy, and maintaining good relationships proved tricky for some.

Various colonies took advantage of the decentralized system that imbued local governments with a lot of power.[20] They took it upon themselves to form their own relationships with the tribes of the Six Nations. The alliances in themselves were not a problem, but the fact that each colony was invested only in their own interests and made deals without concern for the well-being of any other colonies or those with whom they were allying themselves proved problematic. This became a real concern to British leadership overseeing the individual colonies. If alliances with the natives were not carefully managed, it would be harmful to the British cause.

The greatest and probably most disastrously chaotic example of this problem happened at a meeting in Albany, which had been called by the newly appointed governor Sir Danvers Osborn. The New England states, Virginia,[21] Maryland, and Pennsylvania[22] were called to meet with the Iroquois confederation.[23] Osborn, however, would never make it to the meeting. Tragically, two days after his arrival in New York City, he was dead, a victim of suicide by his own handkerchief. This left a heavy-handed Lieutenant Governor James DeLancey in charge, a man who let the power he had just gained go to his head.

---

[20] Some historians believe that local governments were allowed too much power. As a result, conflicts over trade and land were common.

[21] Dinwiddie refused to send a representative despite the invitation.

[22] Pennsylvania was reluctant to send a representative at first. Benjamin Franklin was eventually sent to join the meeting.

[23] Prior to this meeting, the Iroquois council had a meeting amongst themselves. They saw "the storm clouds of war" on the horizon and needed a strategy. But it seemed like a lose-lose situation. Though this was a "white man's war," fighting for one side or another would likely mean fighting against other native tribes who allied themselves with the opposite side. But if they remained neutral, they were likely to be just sitting idly by as their land was stolen by the warring powers.

After the delegates took their seats in Albany, five weeks of bickering commenced. The delegates knew that everyone was serving their own interests, so deep distrust had infected them before the talks even began.

New Yorkers, who were backed by DeLancey, considered the Iroquois "their" allies and were aggravated by any other colony trying to "interfere" with what they had going on. Using the authority of his gavel, DeLancey maintained strict control of the floor, claiming it was his right of superiority, considering he was the only governor present. Delegates objected to his handling of the talks, but he would not allow anything to be discussed that might cast New York in a bad light or conflict with its interests. This served to stifle discussions that might bring about solutions to problems like corruption.

On July 2nd, DeLancey began to discuss the French threat and the importance of native allies in helping to neutralize it. After weeks of colonists squabbling over who had the right to ally with native nations, it was finally time to hear from the Iroquois delegations. King Hendrick, a Mohawk leader, took the floor. What he said was meant as a knock on the heads of colonial representatives, calling them to their senses.

After noting the governor's opening comments, Hendrick took the stick in his hand and threw it behind his back. The dramatic move certainly caught the attention of the delegates, and they listened to his next words. Directing himself to DeLancey, Hendrick revealed the meaning of the stick. "You have thus thrown us behind your back and discarded us."

The Iroquois felt that the British had taken their good relationship and alliance for granted, and it did not go unnoticed. One of the biggest complaints was against the Albany colonists. Due to their proximity and other factors, they had a monopoly on the fur trade with the indigenous tribes. Knowing that, the colonists slyly offered to pay low prices, knowing there was no one else to offer more. As a result, the native tribes did not get much money to buy trade goods, so the trading became unfair and one-sided.

But as the British colonies made alliances based on their own interests with little regard for the people they made them with, the French took a different approach—and it worked very well.

Hendrick pointed this out, "The French are...ever using their utmost endeavors to seduce and bring our people over to them."

However, the biggest issue the Iroquois had with this situation was their lands. They were being fought over and taken without even consulting the people who had the rights to them, not to mention the long-term consequences it would have on the natives. Hendrick's sentiments echoed those of Tanacharison's, as he had believed that the land given to his people came from a divine source. But now the French and British were coming in on either side of the river to divide it up. Where would it leave his people?

The Mohawk king did not mince words when he said directly, "The governor of Virginia and the governor of Canada are both quarreling about lands that belong to us, and such a quarrel as this may end in our destruction." He further added a condemnation of their actions. "[The governors] have made paths through our country to trade and build houses without acquainting us with it. They should have first asked our consent."

With a scathing denunciation of their strategies, he concluded his speech, saying, "Look at the French, they are men, they are fortifying everywhere. But we are ashamed to say it, you are all like women, bare and open without any fortifications."

If King Hendrick had meant to shame the colonists into taking more honorable actions, it did not work. His forthright speech fell on deaf ears. The delegates kept their focus on their interests—taking more land. The motives may have varied. Some wanted land for profit,[24] others had political motivations, and others had more grandiose notions of a national council over local and native affairs. The delegates promised to consider the native council's complaints and demands, but they had little power or motivation to actually do anything about them.

However, the delegates were unwisely ignoring the fundamental issues that Hendrick had pointed out—not only the taking of land and resources without the consent of the natives who owned the land but also the lack of any reciprocation, which is the very foundation of an alliance.[25] The only reason more tribes hadn't

---

[24] Some delegates plied the natives with liquor until they agreed to sell their land.

[25] This was more than just the taking of the land; it was about broken promises made to

taken sides with the French was out of fear of British military power. It was also pointed out to them that if they wanted to battle the French for the lands, they were way behind their rivals. They were failing to take the most basic necessary actions to even hold the lands they were claiming.

The colonial delegates seemed to think these issues were of almost no consequence. It couldn't be further from the truth. George Washington himself insightfully pointed out the importance of maintaining good relationships and native alliances, noting, "Indians are the only match for Indians, and without them [on our side] we shall ever fight on unequal terms." The French knew this important truth as well, even if Washington's comrades did not see it. And it was that willful ignorance that would come back to haunt them.

---

the native people just a few years earlier. In 1752, Half King negotiated on behalf of the Iroquois nations. He was told that the Virginians wanted to *buy* the land from them so that they could resell it to the settlers. These would be "bought" by trading with cheap goods. A colonial spokesman further tried to reassure the tribes, promising, "Brethren, be assured that the King...by purchasing your lands, had never any intention of taking them from you, but that we might live together as one people, and keep them from the French, who would be bad neighbors." Ironically, it was now they who were being condemned by the indigenous people as "bad neighbors."

Chapter 5 – Wilderness War

As the colonies bickered amongst themselves, the clamor was but a mere buzz over in London. But despite the political wrangling going on amidst the British aristocracy, everyone agreed on one thing—the French needed to be expelled from "their" North American territories. This means more troops needed to be sent to Virginia. That is, *almost* everyone agreed with this. Secretary of State Thomas Pelham-Holles, Duke of Newcastle, believed that the French threat was being overly exaggerated. He believed that, overall, the French were peaceable, and diplomacy over force was the answer. King George II agreed with him. After six years of official peace with France, he was reluctant to set off another war.[26] He and Newcastle held a "let Americans fight Americans" attitude and refused to send more British soldiers.

But after several months of pressure and prodding, Newcastle finally caved. It was obvious that the colonial militia alone was not up to the challenge. Two regiments of Irish Redcoats under the command of Major General Edward Braddock were told to set sail across the Atlantic.

Though Braddock was well-connected, the major general had far too little experience on the front lines. His strengths lay in logistics and administration, but the London leadership felt he was

---

[26] Despite the armed conflicts occurring in North America, no official declaration of war had been made.

the most obvious choice to help halt the growing crisis in America.[27]

Braddock was about to experience wilderness warfare in a baptism of fire. He was given four specific assignments—get the French out of Ohio,[28] take the New York forts at Niagara and Crown Point from the French, and then destroy Fort Beauséjour in Nova Scotia.

It was to be a ridiculously daring and difficult three-pronged simultaneous attack. That tour covered a dauntingly long distance through the harsh and unforgiving mountain wilderness. Braddock would have his work cut out for him.

He left in late December 1754, and the winter trip across the ocean was risky. But as stormy and miserable as the six-week journey was, Braddock was determined to beat the French across the ocean. He had the advantage over the French preparations, as he was able to land on the more moderately temperate Virginia shores even though it was winter. The French, however, were locked out of continental Canada by ice-enclosed ports and would not be able to disembark until sometime in the spring. That gave Braddock several months to prepare.

Braddock would desperately need that time too. Though his regiments looked good on paper, the Irish units were relatively weak. However, Braddock was under the impression that the backwoods forces of the French, Canadian, and tribal fighters would be no match for his army regulars. Still, his forces would need the colonial numbers, especially with such ambitious assignments ahead of him.

Putting together a worthy army would prove harder than Braddock thought. He wondered what the colonists had been doing all this time. There were no weapon stockpiles, no major numbers of new recruits, and those who had been recruited were not properly trained and disciplined. Braddock also faced the logistical nightmare of getting men and supplies over the mountains into Ohio.

---

[27] Braddock had also held the post of governor of Gibraltar.

[28] This would be accomplished by capturing Fort Duquesne, near present-day Pittsburgh, Pennsylvania.

By spring, Braddock had two thousand British regular soldiers, nine hundred colonial militiamen, and fifty native warriors ready for battle. A detailed map of Fort Duquesne, which had been drawn by a British officer imprisoned as a war hostage, was intercepted in an attempt to smuggle it to Williamsburg. It proved to be a highly valuable capture. The British found out that Fort Duquesne now only had four hundred men garrisoned within its walls rather than the one thousand plus previously reported. Braddock was confident that he had the statistical advantage over the fort. The biggest problem he would face was getting there.

He and his men would have to march over one hundred miles, crossing the Allegheny Mountains on the way. It would be a challenge for a leader not accustomed to the wilderness and a large army carrying supplies. He would need an aide—someone familiar with those mountains and forests. The man he needed was George Washington.

Braddock didn't know it yet, but he also sorely needed Washington to bridge the gap between his royalist sensibilities and the rugged provincials living off the land. Braddock threw the full weight of his royally commissioned position around, and the more he did, the more his demands angered the locals, who were already looking to live a life free from the royalist yolk. They cared nothing about the empires that fought over the land and were not sympathetic to the cause.

Braddock soon realized he was facing an issue he was wholly unaccustomed to—nobody in the colonies, not even the governors, felt compelled to follow orders. They bickered, made promises they never intended to keep, and regularly indulged themselves in petty jealousies. It was a far cry from the strict army discipline and obedience to orders he expected.

Despite Braddock's political ineptitude and lack of military experience, the governors agreed to a preposterous plan that would bring nothing but utter disaster. It was decreed that Braddock's four missions would be conducted *simultaneously* despite the great distances between the forts they were tasked to seize.[29] But this way,

---

[29] Each task commander would face their own immense challenge. Braddock took on the key operation of Fort Duquesne, a crucial location on the Ohio Forks that basically

Braddock could metaphorically kill four birds with one stone, and the governors benefited from supply contracts, prestigious military commands, and receiving favor from British authority. The overreaching ambition of Braddock and the governors would be their doom.

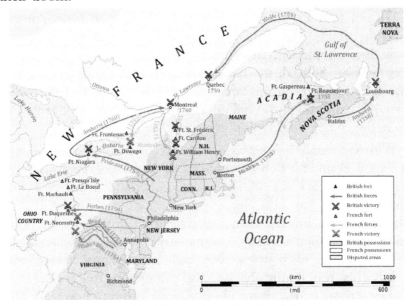

Map of British campaigns against French forts.
Hoodinski, CC BY-SA 3.0 <https://creativecommons.org/licenses/by-sa/3.0>, via Wikimedia Commons https://commons.wikimedia.org/wiki/File:French_and_indian_war_map.svg

Besides being too ambitious in his campaigns, Braddock made another fatal error in judgment. When the native chiefs offered men to help him conquer Fort Duquesne, he brashly refused.

---

guarded the entire Ohio Country. Next, the highly inexperienced Massachusetts governor William Shirley was assigned to take his two American militia regiments the three hundred miles from Albany to Fort Niagara, crossing difficult terrain that included slow, arduous ship portages and traversing a lake. Once there, he would come against a formidable French force sitting among the easy protection of Lake Ontario and the St. Lawrence River. Colonel William Johnson was assigned Fort Saint-Frédéric, an imposing, well-manned fortress at Crown Point that would require the help of the Iroquois to conquer. Nova Scotia Lieutenant Governor Charles Lawrence was assigned to take on Fort Beauséjour. Although the fort itself was weak from disrepair and had few soldiers holding it, the Acadians and Micmac natives who lurked there played by their own rules. They used the crumbling walls to their advantage and held it as a point from which they could conduct guerilla warfare.

Despite Washington's solid belief in the necessity of indigenous allies, Braddock's arrogance told him differently. He believed that European battle tactics were far superior to anything the indigenous warriors and scouts could offer, even telling Benjamin Franklin that "Duquesne can hardly detain me three or four days."

He not only declined the help but also heaped further insult upon the chiefs. He bluntly told them that the army would not allow their people to remain in the Ohio Valley once the British won the war. Soured, the chiefs told him that "if they might not have liberty to live on the land," they would refuse to fight for it. Then the native men who did not return to their villages traveled to where they might be better appreciated—Fort Duquesne.

With George Washington by his side as a volunteer aide and Benjamin Franklin's deft negotiations to secure wagons from local farmers, Braddock set off for Fort Cumberland, which was one hundred miles from Fort Duquesne. The men began their trek on a hopeful note, but the reality of traveling through dense, virgin woods and difficult, rocky, mountainous terrain soon crashed down on them. Even where they built rudimentary "roads," the pack horses were hardly able to travel the muddy, tree rooted, and boulder-strewn paths, never mind wagons carrying howitzers and other artillery and supplies.[30] Progress was painstakingly slow. Some days the caravan only made it seven miles over the course of eight hours. The trek took over two months.

When they reached the crudely built Fort Cumberland on Saturday, May 10th, 1755, it was not much to look at. The men set up camp. To their surprise, no locals came to sell them fresh food. Assuming the men were intercepting the locals and buying it on the sly, Braddock threatened death to any man caught doing so. He had not yet realized that they were very alone in the wilderness. There *were* no locals. The supplies they brought were all they had.

Still, the arrival of the troops to the fort created an atmosphere of a bustling, if not rowdy, town. Though Braddock tried to keep the troops occupied with drills and training, they often found better

---

[30] Once they began their inland march, there was nowhere to resupply for miles, so they had to bring what they could.

uses of their time, at least in their eyes.[31] Natives led by Tanacharison's successor, Scarouady, came into the camp and helped stir things up. They amused and impressed the soldiers with wild stories of their adventures and performed native war dances. However, it all became too much for Braddock when he found out that the native women were coming in and "entertaining" the troops for money and that soldiers were freely sharing liquor with their new indigenous friends.

Fort Cumberland, 1755.
https://commons.wikimedia.org/wiki/File:Fort_cumberland.jpg

Widespread drunkenness, bad behavior, and the lack of even the most basic military discipline among the men were huge problems for Braddock. He ordered harsh punishments for anyone found carousing with women, sharing liquor, or being otherwise disorderly—anywhere from garnishment of wages to 250 lashes to a death sentence. It was a look into how the imperial army was run, and many of the colonists did not like what they saw.

They were not the only ones. Disgusted by what they felt was Braddock's "bad heart," heavy-handed tactics, and general scorn for them, the majority of the fifty native men who enlisted to help the British left. Only eight stayed, including a now sullen Scarouady and his son. Again, the allies they sorely needed were driven away.

---

[31] Almost a third of his men were militiamen—nonprofessional soldiers recruited into the army. They had little to no training as opposed to the army regulars who were professional, trained soldiers.

Braddock turned his attention back to his mission. Although he had absolutely no concrete knowledge of what was happening at Fort Duquesne, his arrogant nature once again assumed that the enemy there was weak and nearly defenseless.[32] He believed the moment they saw his mighty army march up, they would abandon their post and run northward.

But not long after they left Fort Cumberland, native scouts began to report that French reinforcements were on their way to Fort Duquesne. Braddock cursed their slow movements and likely cursed Benjamin Franklin's erroneous prediction that the trip would be "light and easy."

After three days of agonizingly slow progress, Braddock decided to send the heaviest wagons back. The problem was, they contained the howitzers and a large chunk of their powder and munitions—supplies that were exactly essential in a battle.

Washington told Braddock that there was no way he was going to be able to capture the fort since they were bogged down by their snail-like pace. He suggested that they break up their forces and send a smaller contingent to ride ahead of the main column. Braddock liked the idea, but it was one that would prove to be disastrous.

On June 18th, Braddock set out with about half his army and as many munitions as they could quickly haul. However, he would leave the rest of the men to follow with too few wagons and horses, and they quickly fell behind. Even unburdened with half his army and supplies, Braddock's progress was still too slow. He now had two choices, and neither of them was great. He either could continue on at the same pace and risk French reinforcements beating him to Fort Duquesne or ditch more of his artillery and munitions but face the possibility of a siege he was unprepared to win. His caution won out, much to the exasperation of Washington.[33]

---

[32] This was mainly due to his lack of native scouts. He told his superiors in London that he doubted he could rely on them for accurate information anyway.

[33] Because they were traveling through the wilderness, men had to go ahead of the wagons to cut trees and clear paths to build crude roads that made the way passable, making for a slow and difficult passage.

On June 23rd, scouts came back to the camp to deliver good and bad news to Braddock. The bad news was that the reinforcements had reached Fort Duquesne. But the good news was that they were desperately low on food and supplies, making a long siege untenable for those inside.

However, unbeknownst to Braddock, the French were fully aware of his mission and had been almost from the beginning. French spies knew what he was going to do almost the moment he opened his commission letter. Accordingly, the French put their highly skilled Canadian Marines and local woodsmen militia into action to prepare and wait for Braddock to show up. They were also aware of Braddock's slow pace and aimed to take advantage of it. Stealthy French soldiers and their equally ghost-like native allies went out from the fort on a mission to terrorize the already unnerved British and colonial soldiers. Though Braddock's men increasingly saw evidence of the enemy in the woods around their encampment, the enemies themselves remained unseen.

Whether this rendered Braddock's men complacent to the danger or just reckless, three soldiers wandered from Braddock's camp one evening. Suddenly, the sound of musket fire crashed through the June air. Men ran from the camp in search of their compatriots, fearing what had caused them to fire. It did not take long for them to find out. The three bodies of the missing soldiers lay in the dirt, their scalps having been removed from their heads. Braddock was angered, and hunting parties went out. But fear of their ferocious and nearly invisible enemy got the better of them. Every creak of the branch and rustle of the leaves set their trigger fingers in motion, and the men fired about wildly and without discipline. But there was no one there to receive their shots.

Only three soldiers may have died, but the action was highly effective in throwing Braddock's men off-balance. The French were not done with them, but they had bought themselves some much-needed time.

In truth, Duquesne commander Claude-Pierre Pécaudy de Contrecœur was worried about how well the fort walls would be able to hold up to the British cannons. He knew his best chance at victory was meeting the British outside of the fort walls, and he set his men to clearing fields on which they could "greet" the British army. While some worked on clearing the area, Contrecœur had soldiers and natives form raiding parties to help break the British advance as well as their morale.

With the bulk of the Troupes de Marine scattered about French Canada in small detachments, it would take time to get them to Fort Duquesne. Fortunately, some surprising yet welcomed allies showed up at their gates. The Ohio natives were offended by Braddock, and they were now eager to make amends with the French, especially since it appeared they had the superior fighting skills. They begged the French to forgive them for choosing to take sides with the British. They realized their mistake and wanted to pledge loyalty to and fight for the French.

The French now had many native allies, but Contrecœur proved to be a problem. Besides the poor state of the fort, his age was catching up to him. On top of this, he did not have enough men to comfortably take on the much larger British force. He called north for reinforcements. At the end of June, Contrecœur had a moment of relief when he saw the canoes of French Captain Daniel Hyacinthe Liénard de Beaujeu coming to the riverbank. Relief quickly turned to alarmed disappointment when he saw that only two hundred men had come with Beaujeu, which was far fewer men than anticipated or needed. There were also no additional weapons.

After conferring on the state of the fort and the number of men there to defend it, both men agreed that the fort was a lost cause. There was no way they could hold it when the British showed up— they didn't have the manpower or the weapons. They felt that the best course would be to do what the British anticipated they would—retreat north to the safety of the much larger and more important Fort Niagara.

However, Beaujeu came up with an idea. Maybe, just maybe, a small contingent could stay and deal the British a quick blow by using the element of surprise. They would send out raiding parties to ambush and harass Braddock's men. There were no fantasies of winning against the British; this was just a plan to buy time so that the bulk of the garrison could escape north. But Beaujeu would need to get the help of their native allies.

Beaujeu had been friendly with the local tribes for many years, so he was well-acquainted enough with their ways to know that they would never want to make a last stand in a doomed French fort. But perhaps they would help with their delay tactics.

He met with a council of twelve nations from the colonies and Canada, which included the Abenaki, Shawnee, Delaware, and members of the Six Nations. When Beaujeu told them he wanted help against the British, they scoffed and told him that he had "no sense." Even with the natives, the French would be outnumbered, and they were unwilling to sacrifice themselves for a cause that was not even their own. Still, they told him they would sleep on it and give an official decision the next day.

On the day he was to head out, Beaujeu first stopped and asked the chaplain for his blessing. As he left the chapel, dressed in native war clothes and painted skin,[34] the native chiefs were waiting for him with their decision. They would not fight. While Beaujeu pleaded with them, a native scout ran into the camp. The British army was close; they had already crossed the Monongahela River. Beaujeu made one last pleading speech. Whether he felt emboldened or put on a façade for the natives, he told them, "You see my friends, the British are going to throw themselves into the lion's mouths. They are weak sheep who pretend to be ravenous wolves." He told them all they needed to do was wait in hiding until he and his men made their move, and then they could come out and back them up in battle. He confidently told them, "The victory is ours!" His speech worked. He was greeted with war whoops in response, and 650 native warriors were now ready to fight with him.

Unlike the British, who were loudly and methodically marching with drums and fifes signaling their every move, the French and Native American forces stealthily ran undetected through the forest toward the advancing army. The British engineers, who were at the front of the column, continued their work of cutting and clearing the way, making it possible to drive the wagons through.

So, wholly unaware of the French and native presence, the morale among the British and colonists was high. Braddock

---

[34] This was done as a symbol of friendship and solidarity.

believed that by the evening, they would be drinking champagne and celebrating their victory behind the walls of Fort Duquesne, which was now only seven miles away.

Their high spirits changed to fear at the speed of light. It seemed as if Beaujeu and his horde instantaneously appeared, crashing out of the brush and landing in front of them, whooping and firing scattered shots. As a British horseman called back that a native attack was upon them, Beaujeu and his men disappeared back into the dense woods as quickly as they had come out.

Although Braddock and his officers had expected the French to meet them in battle along the way to Fort Duquesne, this had caught them by surprise. The British quickly fell into ranks and dropped to one knee, beginning their volleys. One rank would shoot and then fall back for the next to take their shots, reloading as fast as they could. They shot blindly into the woods, the smoke created from the volleys further blinding them to the enemy's whereabouts. Panic began to take hold.

Yet, unbeknownst to the British forces, a shot from their third volley hit its mark. Beaujeu lay dead on the forest floor with the fatal musket ball still in his head. Captain Jean-Daniel Dumas was now in command of the French effort.

Still under cover of dense foliage, the Canadian and native warriors swiftly moved to flank the British grenadiers, who were distracted by the formation of French regulars who came out to meet them face to face on the road. From their invisible perches, they carefully aimed and sniped each of the grenadiers one by one. Whereas the British were firing blindly at the invisible snipers in the woods, French eyes carefully marked their easy targets since they wore red coats and clumped together. Within minutes, the majority of General Thomas Gage's officers lay dead or wounded. Though some brave soldiers stayed and fought fiercely after the death of their commanders, most broke rank and scattered.

Braddock tried to bring the remaining eight hundred men and their munitions forward. But the road was in no condition to support a quick advance of this kind. With the first flanks now running back toward them, the situation descended into chaos. The confusion allowed the French and Native Americans to get to higher ground, allowing them to have the advantage. They fired shot after shot into the reeling British ranks.

Washington had knowledge of the guerilla-style warfare the French and natives were now bringing down upon them, and he begged Braddock to let him take his Virginia regiment into the woods to do the same. Stubbornly, Braddock refused to allow any of his men to deviate from the traditional battle formations.

As Braddock was trying to bring things back under control and shouting orders at his men, his voice suddenly fell silent. The next moment, he slid from his horse's saddle and fell to the ground, struck by enemy fire. However, the aging Braddock survived and mounted another horse. He persevered in battle as, one by one, his horses were shot out from under him. Four of his horses fell that day.

Braddock's officers did not fare as well as he did. The French, who especially targeted the commanders, shot until all were dead or wounded. By mid-afternoon, Braddock saw that their situation was dire. Almost half of his men were down, either dead, dying, or wounded. He had to order a retreat. The men did not have to be told twice.

While retreating, Braddock suddenly felt the hot tear of his flesh as a shot ripped straight through his arm and into his side. He fell from his fifth horse, mortally wounded. The British abandoned everything and everyone as the French and natives chased them back across the river. They continued to slaughter or capture anyone they could reach. The small river ran red with blood.

The British retreated back to their wagon train. Seeing the state of their compatriots as they fled back, the wagon drivers began to panic. They cut the horses loose and rode away, leaving their wagons behind.

George Washington, who was unhurt but horrified, later said that what he saw that day was nearly "indescribable" in its nature and that the sounds of the dead and dying were enough to "pierce the heart" of even the most stoic warrior. But Washington was also disgusted by what he felt was cowardice on the part of the enlisted militiamen who were the first to turn and run. However, he desperately needed their help in getting the gravely injured Braddock to safety. Washington and another officer promised money to any who would assist them in moving their dying general.

They were finally able to put Braddock in a cart and get him back across the river.

In the days after, those who had not deserted made it back to Great Meadows. Braddock was also brought there, arriving on July 13th, the same day he died from his wounds. General Thomas Dunbar, whose men were in poor shape, then took the remainder of the army back to Fort Cumberland.[35]

Washington decried the execution of Braddock's operation as "folly." He knew that the French would likely try to meet them in the woods outside the fort, but Braddock's overconfidence and inflexibility kept the men from being prepared and fighting in a style that matched that of the enemy.

Meanwhile, back at Fort Duquesne, the French and native warriors were celebrating. They were not interested in pursuing the British across the river to finish them off, which was what the European soldiers would have done, but the native allies of the French returned to the battlefield to collect their spoils.[36] The warriors scalped and stripped every dead and wounded British soldier left on the ground while the French collected all the wagons, weapons, and munitions the British left behind.[37, 38] It was quite a surprise windfall, especially given that they were not expecting this sort of outcome.

---

[35] Fifty-four women had also gone on Braddock's march, working as cooks and laundresses for the soldiers. Only four returned with the defeated army. Though some died, likely by the hands of indigenous warriors, many were kidnapped and taken to Canada to be ransomed by the French.

[36] The native warriors had not joined the fight for power or supremacy; they were satisfied in their victory of driving the British from their land.

[37] The British and colonial forces lost nearly one thousand men, while the French and native contingent lost only twenty-one men.

[38] James Smith, a British soldier being held captive at Fort Duquesne, quietly awaited the British victory, fully expecting to see his own army come to claim the fort and rescue him. Instead, he saw the French and native warriors return on the road with about a dozen captives. He was horrified to see one man tied to a stake and burned, which was somewhat common in the native tradition of torturing captives. He was later adopted into a Native American family and lived with them for six years.

But the biggest prize came in a small box. Someone had found Braddock's dispatch box, and it contained the best surprise of all—information. The French now had all of Braddock's secret war plans in their hands, including instructions for the four big missions and a planned attack on Fort Oswego in western New York. The dispatches were immediately sent to Quebec. The British may have had the superior numbers, but the French now had the upper hand.

Chapter 6 – Canadian Campaigns Bring British Victory

As Braddock marched toward disaster, Lieutenant Colonel Robert Monckton was headed toward the first and only British victory of the year. His aim was the seizure of Fort Beauséjour, which was strategically located on the Isthmus of Chignecto.[39] Though it was small, it was important for French movements between Quebec and Nova Scotia,[40] and the British were keen on disrupting this key advantage.

Monckton and 2,400 men left their base at Fort Lawrence on June 4th, 1755. Monckton was aware of his superior numbers, believing that there were one thousand men at the fort. But he had heard rumors that the Acadians and Micmac natives who lurked around the fort played by their own rules. They used the fort as a strategic location from which they could conduct guerilla warfare, making the situation unpredictable for the British.

Fort Beauséjour's commander, Louis Du Pont Duchambon de Vergor, was well aware that the British were on their way. However, this was little comfort to him. He knew the crumbling

---

[39] Located in Nova Scotia.

[40] Part of a region known as Acadia at the time

fort walls were weakened by disrepair, and they were absurdly outnumbered—only 165 men held the fort. Even after coercing the local Acadians to help him come hold the fort, there were only four hundred French, Acadians, and native warriors.[41] Fear began to rise. Vergor knew that their only chance for survival lay in shoring up their defenses.

He set Louis-Thomas Jacau de Fiedmont to lead the men in strengthening defenses around the fort as well as burning bridges and destroying roads to slow the British advance. Meanwhile, Vergor wrote desperate letters to nearby Fort Gaspareaux, as well as Quebec and other Canadian forts and settlements, begging for reinforcements that would never come.

Fort Beauséjour

Verne Equinox, CC BY-SA 3.0 <http://creativecommons.org/licenses/by-sa/3.0/>, via Wikimedia Commons https://commons.wikimedia.org/wiki/File:Beausejour2006.jpg

As the British rebuilt the bridge Fiedmont had destroyed and crossed the Missaguash River, minor skirmishes with French patrols erupted. The first of these was very telling. On June 4th,

---

[41] The Acadians, who were French Catholics, were resistant to a takeover by the British Protestant forces, fearing religious intolerance. They were reluctant to help Vergor, afraid that if they fought on the French side and lost, they would face the possibility of execution by the British. So, they made Vergor "force" them to fight so that if they were captured by the British, they could claim that the French commander had given them no choice.

French forces faced off against the British in battle formation, but things quickly fell apart and ended in a retreat. The incident only served to strengthen British confidence while exposing the French forces' weaknesses and causing their morale to tumble. It was blatantly obvious that the Acadian militia was weak and inexperienced in battle. A deeper problem than training was also glaringly exposed—the Acadians' fear and lack of motivation to fight was going to be an issue on the day of battle.

Vergor's desperation was also out in the open. Seeing the weakness of his offensive earlier that day, further defensive action seemed to be his only choice. That same night, he took drastic action, burning homes, shops, and other buildings around the fort. As the Acadians saw their residences and livelihoods going up in flames, morale further plummeted, along with their motivation to fight or work on defenses.

Skirmishes continued over the next few days, but on June 8th, the native allies brought an unexpected "guest" to the fort. They had captured a British officer. Vergor and the French officers pressed him for information, but what they heard caused their hearts to drop. The British officer was all too glad to let them know that the British were on their way with a large force, and it was backed up by heavy artillery. That heavy artillery was sure to be the end of the fort.

As small skirmishes continued to be lost in the succeeding days, the situation continued to darken for the French. When British artillery began to shake the enfeebled walls of the fort, the full weight of how badly they were outmatched fell on Vergor. The Acadians saw it clearly as well, and many began to desert the fort. Vergor's only hope was that the letters he sent out would see results and that reinforcements would show up at any moment.

That last hope was dashed on June 14th. The worst news Vergor could hear reached the fort—the British were blocking the port at Louisburg, and French reinforcements could not make it. No help was coming. Vergor could not bring himself to tell his men, fearing it would break their already weakened spirits. Still, word got out, and once it did, the men of the fort became hopeless. Those who didn't desert right then and there pushed Vergor to surrender. But

Vergor was not ready to give up the fight, even if his men were.[42]

The British continued their artillery assault without letting up. The final straw came on June 16th when mortar fire hit the fort's mess hall, killing several French officers and their British prisoner. This was the end. The white flag of surrender was raised, and the terms of surrender were drawn up.[43] The same day, the British flag was raised over the fort.

Emboldened, Monckton next set his sights on nearby Fort Gaspareaux. He offered them the same terms he offered Vergor, and they were immediately accepted. However, when Monckton turned toward Fort Menagoueche in New Brunswick, French Marines commander Charles Boishébert refused the terms. He was not about to hand his fort over to the British. Instead, he burned it down and took his men up the river into the wilderness, where they could better position themselves for guerilla warfare.

Though the British claimed victory over a small number of French forces in Canada, the battle was a pivotal point in the history of North America and Europe. It not only changed the fate of the Acadians but also reshaped Atlantic Canada. It was also the opening British offensive victory in the Seven Years' War, an epic struggle for supremacy between the British and French empires.[44]

However, farther south, more dramatic but less successful events were unfolding for the British.

---

[42] Eighty men deserted at the news of the blockade.

[43] In the terms, Vergor insisted that protections for the Acadians be included. Though the British spared their lives, the Acadians were driven from their home. Many were taken south to Fort Edward, a British garrison in New York. Eventually, the Acadians were driven farther south, all the way down to French-held Louisiana. Today, the descendants of those Acadians are known as Cajuns (the French word Acadian was, over time, shortened to Cadian, which later morphed into Cajun).

[44] The Seven Years' War, a conflict that stemmed from European succession arguments, took place mainly in the European arena, though it is generally considered to be the first global conflict in history. However, as the war ran concurrently with the French and Indian War (1754-1763), tensions between the British and French empires spilled over into the North American colonies. In the end, it would have a dramatic effect on French occupancy and power in Europe and North America.

Chapter 7 – The "Bloody" Battles Set the Stage in New York

As the British were gaining victory in their goals in Canada, taking over the New York forts was not going as well. Governor William Shirley began his trek to Fort Oswego, which he would use as a base to launch an attack on Fort Niagara across Lake Ontario. Shirley was another inexperienced commander, and he was unaware of just how daunting a mountainous wilderness march would be, especially with winter weather looming. Thus, Shirley underestimated the difficulty of bringing his two regiments from Albany to Oswego.

Wrapped in a logistical nightmare, Shirley was forced to give up after a few weeks. He knew he would not be able to reach the fort before the cold weather set in, and continuing the trip through the harsh Adirondack winter would be equivalent to a slow, painful death. He was forced to abandon his plans and return to Albany. However, he didn't want this prong of Braddock's plan to sit in hibernation all winter. He knew that even if he had made it to Oswego, the fort was in such poor shape that it could not be defended against a French assault. So, he sent seven hundred unfortunate men to the fort to make repairs over the winter in the hopes that the plan could be revisited once the ice melted.

Farther south, as Braddock was fighting for the Ohio Forks in the summer of 1755, Irish General William Johnson was on his mission to take over the Lake Champlain/Lake George region.[45] Like Braddock, he was wealthy and well-connected, but since he was a merchant, he had little experience on the battlefield. However, unlike Braddock, Johnson had some very important qualifications to bring to the battlefield—he had an intimate knowledge of native culture and politics. With those qualifications came an important friend: Mohawk Chief Hendrick. Johnson was diametrically opposed to Braddock's contemptuous outlook on the native people. He had embraced their culture, and it would make a world of difference for the British.[46]

Even though he had about 1,500 colonial militiamen for his campaign, no native allies had signed up to accompany him. This presented a real problem, as it would leave him at a great disadvantage, especially since the French would have native allies fighting with them. But given the recent record of the British army, along with the shadow of the Albany tensions still looming over them, how could he make such an offer sound appealing?

Besides the Iroquois Confederacy's general policy of remaining neutral in the fighting, the Mohawks were a divided nation.[47] This not only posed a problem for them—many New York Mohawks were reluctant to fight their Canadian brethren allied with the French—but it was a problem for the British and French who each mistrusted their Mohawk allies, thinking they wouldn't help their cousins. But Johnson knew he had to put his suspicions aside.

Johnson, who became the newly named British liaison to the Iroquois, had a meeting with 1,100 men, women, and children of the Six Nations council in the field around his home. He tried to persuade them that the British were there for the benefit of the indigenous tribes—to protect them and their land. And he told them that it was in their best interest to help him do that. In an impassioned speech, he told them that his "war kettle is on the

---

[45] At the time, it was known by its French name: Lac du Saint Sacrement. It was renamed Lake George by Johnson in honor of the British king.

[46] The Mohawk nicknamed Johnson "Chief Big Business."

[47] The Mohawk tribe is part of the more encompassing Iroquois Confederacy.

fire" and that his weapons were ready for war. He asked them to "take up the hatchet" and join him. However, they were reluctant. They had heard about Braddock's disaster.

In the end, only two hundred agreed to follow King Hendrick and Johnson into battle. When Johnson brought the native warriors with him to the newly built Fort Edward,[48] his militiamen gawked and noted with awe the "juels [sic] in their noses" and "their faces painted with all colors." For many, it was the first time seeing the wild appearance of the warriors up close.

Three days later, Johnson and his men made the twenty-mile trek to the southern shore of Lac du Saint Sacrement. Staring out over her clear waters, Johnson, wanting to "honor his Majesty" King George II, declared the lake had a new name—Lake George.[49]

Having heard sensational reports that there were eight thousand French waiting for him at Crown Point, Johnson was understandably nervous.[50] He set to work building a fort near the water's edge, not only as a place to launch his offensive up the lake but also in a bid to defend themselves from what he thought was an overwhelming French force.

At the very north end of the lake, the commander of Fort Saint-Frédéric, Jean-Armand, Baron de Dieskau, had "eyes" on the south end of the lake.[51] As "unreliable" as his Iroquois scouts were (in his words), he did pick up some interesting information—there was a lot of British activity to the south.[52] Suspicious of Johnson's activities, he had two choices—he could wait and see what Johnson

---

[48] Fort Edward was built on a narrow section of the Hudson River near a portage called the "Great Carrying Place." It was originally called Fort Lyman. Tiny Rogers Island, which is part of the fort enclosure, is considered the "spiritual home" of the US Army Rangers. It was where Robert Rogers wrote his "Ranging Rules" in 1757, which became a guide for irregular military tactics that have been used by armies around the world ever since.

[49] The beauty of Lake George is renowned. Thomas Jefferson called it the "queen of the American lakes."

[50] In reality, there were only about three thousand men at the fort, about the same as Johnson's forces.

[51] Frédéric is the French name for Crown Point.

[52] Lake George is thirty-two miles long from north to south. Given the distance and topography of the lake, it is impossible to visually see from one end to the other.

was up to, or he could nip any British activity in the bud before the campaign season ended for the winter. Dieskau knew he could not stand idly by as he watched the British prepare to encroach on French territory. Instead of obeying Governor Pierre de Rigaud de Vaudreuil's orders to stay and hold the fort, he decided that another surprise attack was in order.

On September 7th, Johnson received news that the French were on their way, along with seven hundred Native Americans who were said to be "panting for the attack." But their noiseless movements through the woods made it difficult to know where they were. And then additional news reached him—the French were not marching toward his position on Lake George. They were aiming to attack Fort Edward.

Although Johnson said that he "did not dread a surprise," he was disconcerted by the state of his militia at the fort. Hundreds had been ravaged by dysentery, and others suffered under "disorderly management." They were not in prime shape to take on a surprise attack from a large French contingent.

Johnson conferred with King Hendrick. He wanted to split his forces, taking one thousand of his militia and two hundred native warriors through the winding, narrow, hilly path to go protect Fort Edward. The rest would be left behind to continue building the fort. Hendrick immediately pointed out the problem of splitting up the forces. He believed it was a tactical mistake, especially on a road with little visibility. Johnson ignored his advice.

At eight the next morning, the eerie silence of the lake descended over the British, with the haunting call of the loons the only sound that broke through. Under Colonel Ephraim Williams Jr. and King Hendrick, the British column moved toward Fort Edward, with the Mohawk chief in the lead.

Dieskau's Mohawk scouts knew every move the British were making and warned him they were on the way to Fort Edward as well. He quickly organized an ambush, knowing the British were unaware of their exact movements. The Kahnawake Mohawk watched silently as the British column passed, waiting to surprise them from the rear.[53] The French regulars were hidden beyond a

---

[53] The Kahnawake Mohawks were a Canadian branch of the Mohawk tribe allied with the French.

small rise, and they waited ahead to block any advance while the Canadians flank took the road, ready to rain a hail of musket fire from either side. The British didn't know it, but they had walked right into a trap.

In an unexpected move that stunned his commanders, a French Mohawk warrior was seized by his conscience. He broke orders and called out to King Hendrick. In what Dieskau called "a moment of treachery," the Mohawks had a conversation as hidden French officers looked on in bewilderment and anger. The French-allied Mohawk warrior not only ruined the ambush by revealing himself, but he also tried to convince Hendrick to take his warriors and run, letting the white men fight their own war. The Kahnawake did not want to kill their own people.

Before King Hendrick could respond, a shot reverberated through the forest. The Mohawk leader slowly fell from his horse. He hit the ground, dead. The opening shot of the battle had been taken; the war was on. At first, the French had the clear advantage of surprise and position. The British Mohawk were also unnerved by the swift death of their leader, which was followed not long after by the death of Colonel Williams.

Johnson, who was still at the lake, could hear the gunfire from three or four miles away. Fearing the worst, he quickly took three hundred men to go to Williams's aid. As the sound of musket fire grew louder, Johnson and his men were met by Williams's retreating militia. Quickly gathering brush, branches, wagons, and anything they could find, they hastily created a barricade on the road. Johnson had brought a cannon with him to back up his defense. Those two quick decisions were what would save him and his militia.

Two hours later, the French regulars came marching in formation toward their barricade, many of their militia bristling with reluctance to face such an entrenched position. Their open position had them at a clear disadvantage, and their fears were not unfounded. Dieskau, however, hardly batted his eye as he led what was practically a suicidal assault.

Though the colonial militia would never be able to match the French army in formation, they performed adequately from behind their protective barrier. As musket fire was exchanged, a large, smoke-filled boom shook the air. Dieskau was taken by surprise by the British cannon. His regulars and their Mohawk allies scattered as they retreated, the heavy artillery firing shot after shot into the thick forest. Scenes of abject horror unfolded as bloody, dismembered limbs were flung about the brush and as disemboweled bodies lay limp.

Once the French salvo was halted by the cannon fire, Johnson's Mohawk warriors leaped over the barricade, whooping with tomahawks in hand. Fierce, close combat went on for several hours, exhausting both sides. The French, who were overwhelmed by Johnson's assault, fell back first, leaving their commander on the field propped up against a tree, riddled with four musket ball wounds. He was now in the hands of the British as their captive. Johnson himself did not fare much better than Dieskau—he was down due to a wound to his groin. The French retreat ended the engagement that came to be known as the Battle of the Bloody Morning Scout. But the fighting was not yet over—the worst was yet to come for the French.

As the wearied French, Canadian, and Mohawk fighters fled, their exhaustion caught up with them. They stopped to catch their breath and rejuvenate themselves at a tiny, forested body of water called Rocky Brook, believing they were safely out of distance from the enemy. They let their guard down, which was a fatal error.

New York Captain William McGinnis snuck through the woods with his two militia regiments to take the resting French contingent by surprise. It worked. The fatigued French fighters were overwhelmed and routed. By the time the skirmish was over, between two hundred and three hundred French lay dead. McGinnis and his men rolled their shot-riddled bodies into Rocky Brook, their seeping blood rendering the quiet pond a grotesque red color. It was hereafter known as Bloody Pond, and the battle ended the group of skirmishes collectively known as the Battle of Lake George. But the picturesque lake had not seen the last of the fighting and bloodshed.

Bloody Pond

Chris Light, CC BY-SA 4.0 <https://creativecommons.org/licenses/by-sa/4.0>, via Wikimedia Commons

https://commons.wikimedia.org/wiki/File:Bloody_Pond_used_by_both_sides_P6250137.jpg

Chapter 8 – The Rules of Battle Change

As 1756 dawned, the rules of war were changing. As Governor Pierre de Rigaud de Vaudreuil wrote to Paris, "wars in this country are very different from the wars of Europe." For the French, it wasn't such a bad thing; in large part, they were the ones changing the rules. Their strategic departure from traditional European battlefield formations to the use of guerilla warfare with the help of native warriors had proven very effective for them. Also, unlike European warfare, they were specifically targeting civilians in a bid to create terror and drive out the British.

The native allies had similar goals and methods. They had been fine with trading with the white men who came across the ocean. They even lived alongside them as friends and neighbors for many years. But as the Europeans encroached on and fought each other for their territory, they could no longer continue the peace. They wanted to discourage more settlers from coming, so they started their own campaigns of terror against the people living on their land.

This was typified in the story of Mary Jemison. She settled in Pennsylvania with her parents and siblings, and she and her Irish family experienced this terror firsthand. A few years after they had settled in America, when Mary was fifteen years old, a group of Shawnee and four Frenchmen came to their home and, unprovoked, attacked the family. The family, who was held captive in their home, spent a terrifying night awaiting their fate. The next day, the very thing Mary spent the night fearing became a reality in front of her eyes. Her parents were brutally massacred and scalped, and her brothers were sent off with the French. The Shawnee men kidnapped Mary and forced her to trek seventy miles over several days. During the night, as the Shawnee sat around the fire preparing the scalps of her family, they told Mary that had the white men never come, this would not have happened. They believed their encroachment had forced them to such extreme and hostile measures.[54] For them, the loss of land and the deaths of their people due to this war were very personal.

The British, however, were used to strict military discipline and rigid battle structures. They did not show the flexibility of the French or the passion of the native nations when it came to battle. It reflected in their losses the year before. Only one of Braddock's targets had been met, and their year ended with one victory, one major loss, and Shirley and Johnson hunkered down, waiting for the action to resume. But they were beginning to realize, late as it was, that they needed to make some changes if they wanted to win.

Plagued by the colonists' insubordination and desertion, as well as a power struggle between Shirley and Johnson, the British had a number of internal struggles to deal with.[55] But even more detrimental to their victory was the fact that they were slow to realize just how much they needed native allies. As for the French, they may have embraced the guerilla-style warfare that most of their native allies employed, but those fresh from the continent were not ready for the native rules of warfare. These truths were highlighted

---

[54] Mary was brought unharmed to a Seneca village and given to two Seneca women who had lost their brother in war. The natives had a custom of taking prisoners to compensate for family members that had been lost in battle. Sometimes the prisoners would be tortured and killed in the most savage way the grieving family could imagine in a bid to satisfy their grief. But in most instances, as in the case of Mary, the prisoner was adopted into the family to replace the deceased relative. Mary said the Seneca women adopted her and treated her very kindly, basically as a sister born from the same mother. She lived a long life with their people as a tribe member and died among them at the age of ninety-one.

[55] Shirley was named Braddock's successor after his death.

at the Battle of Fort Oswego, which commenced again in the spring of 1756.

Johnson had sent Captain John Bradstreet and a sizable force to the fort over the winter to shore up its defenses. However, by the spring, the men garrisoned there were in poor shape. The men foolishly brought only a month's worth of supplies with them, and they quickly found themselves in dire straits. No supplies could come over the frozen waters during the winter, and the French ambushed supply lines coming from Albany. In March, the French and their native allies also captured used snowshoes and skates to attack the weakly defended Fort Bull, taking more British food and supplies for themselves.[56]

Having faced months of starvation, the subsequent scurvy, and Native American raids throughout the winter, the fort's commander, Lieutenant Colonel George Mercer, still believed that they could hold the fort. The French, knowing Oswego would be a tougher battle, had concentrated on the weaker forts, but as winter thawed, they turned their attention back to the Great Lakes outpost. It would not fare much better than the unfortunate Fort Bull.

In order to kick up their offensive, the French sent forty-four-year-old war veteran Louis-Joseph Marquis de Montcalm over to New England in May 1756.[57] The French were in even higher spirits now, as they had more native allies join them over the winter. This move was triggered when a number of chiefs were killed by the British. Even the steadfastly neutral Iroquois broke their policy, and sixty warriors joined the French. Montcalm, however, began to be disturbed by reports of brutal Native American savagery, even though these attacks were committed against his British enemies.

---

[56] The French and natives took the sixty British inside Fort Bull by surprise. Within an hour, the French had killed almost everyone. Those who escaped were caught in the woods and massacred by the French-allied Mohawk and Abenaki warriors. The French then took all the food and supplies they could carry before setting the fort on fire.

[57] Montcalm arrived on May 11th. Less than a week later, on May 17th, Britain formally declared war on France, officially beginning the Seven Years' War.

The British were aware of Montcalm's arrival at Fort Carillon, which was north of Lake George.[58] They began frantic preparations at their fort at the southern end of Lake George in anticipation of a French attack. However, Montcalm had his sights set on Fort Oswego. In early summer, Montcalm prepared the noose and began to tighten it around Fort Oswego. Montcalm snuck up to Montreal in order to sail down the St. Lawrence River with the French regulars and Troupes de Marine. He knew the British were expecting him to attack from the south, so the wily general decided to change the game and defy expectations.

Once he was at Fort Frontenac, Montcalm joined forces with two other commanders. Their combined forces created the largest European army the North American wilderness had seen to date. With war whoops from their native allies, they went to take up their position near Fort Oswego and the two other British forts nearby.[59]

Montcalm's native allies told him that they would not fight in the European style but would keep to the woods in line with the style of fighting they knew best. Montcalm agreed and busied himself getting cannons set up on the hill overlooking the fort and digging siege trenches.

The British had been aware of the French advance for a couple of days, and they were frantically trying to fortify the crumbling Fort Ontario. They put a cannon on the roof of a building they thought would be barricaded, but it had to be abandoned when the cannon fire recoil caused the roof under it to collapse. If there was bad foreboding for the fort, this was it.

On August 11th, French commander François-Pierre Rigaud took a group of native warriors and snuck close to the walls of Fort Ontario to snipe the defenders standing atop its crumbling stone. The next day, Fort Ontario felt the full power of the French artillery. A furious barrage of heavy guns and cannon fire from the surrounding cliffs rocked the fort and the men hiding inside. The French had a nearly direct line of fire into the fort from above.

---

[58] This was a large and important fort guarding the waterway between the northern end of Lake George and the southern end of Lake Champlain.

[59] They were also planning to take the nearby outposts of Fort George and Ontario.

Mercer knew there was no way that he and his men could survive this attack.

Taking advantage of a gap in the French siege lines surrounding them, Mercer ordered a daring evacuation of the fort. They would have to leave the fort and cross the river in a bid to make it to Fort Oswego—in broad daylight.

As much as abandoning the fort may have been necessary, they were handing the French a gift in the form of a fortified position that they could use to shoot directly at Fort Oswego. After taking over the abandoned fort, the French trained their heavy guns across the river. As the French began to bombard Oswego's walls with their artillery, Rigaud and his men left Fort Ontario, jumped into the river, and swam toward Forts Oswego and George. They would surround the area to make sure no one could go in or out. The British were trapped.

The British were surrounded and under constant bombardment from the other side of the river. They knew their situation was hopeless. The walls of the fort crumbled more and more after each hit. Little did they know that General Daniel Webb and his men were struggling to reach them, but it would not be in time. After three days of heavy bombardment, there was no choice but to surrender.[60]

Montcalm further insulted the British by forcing them to leave without the traditional war honors.[61] He rejoiced over the impressive wealth he had captured. Besides 1,700 prisoners, he had gained hundreds of bateaux (a kind of boat) as well as a stockpile of artillery and munitions. His native allies, on the other hand, seethed with anger. They waited eagerly for the chance to strip the British prisoners of their personal effects, but Montcalm would not allow it.

---

[60] There were many women and children inside the fort as well.

[61] A ceremony where the enemy is allowed to march from their fort and lay down their arms as a way to show them honor and appreciation for their valor in fighting. However, Montcalm, even though he was very staunch in sticking to the etiquette of surrender, refused the British this honor. He believed that Lieutenant Colonel John Littlehales, who took over command when Mercer was killed by French mortar shells, should have put up more of a fight and so did not earn any war honors.

Angry, they took matters into their own hands. Some rushed into the hospital, mercilessly killing and stripping the wounded prisoners as they lay in their beds. Others tried to reach the prisoners under French guard. As some British tried to flee the fort, Abenaki chased them down and killed them with blows from their tomahawks.[62, 63] No one was spared. Every British soul they could lay their hands on, even women, children, and babies, were killed or captured.

The native warriors were bent on taking plunder and captives back to their villages in a show of honor and proof of their victory. However, what they see as honor, Montcalm saw as barbaric. This was nothing like the civilized European codes of war that he was used to.

As much as the British were his enemy, he could not bear the thought of what the native warriors might do to the one hundred men they captured if they did not get the ransoms they were seeking. He offered his own money to ransom them to ensure they didn't meet a horrific end. Although he downplayed the savagery in his report back to Paris, Montcalm vowed he would never again allow this to happen. But that vow would prove to be meaningless.

Montcalm trying to stop the massacre of the British.
https://commons.wikimedia.org/wiki/File:Montcalm_trying_to_stop_the_massacre.jpg

---

[62] Some French soldiers, drunk on the barrels of rum found in the fort, followed suit and also killed the fleeing British.

[63] Not even Littlehales escaped this brutality. A group of Abenaki warriors grabbed hold of him and beat him near death, saying he was a "coward and had behaved ill" because of his "quick" surrender.

Chapter 9 – The Tragic End of Fort William Henry

By 1757, the war clouds had again gathered over Lake George. Though Montcalm and the French were busy for the remainder of 1756, they had not forgotten about the fort that Johnson and the British built on the southern end of Lake George. If Montcalm could take the now fully built Fort William Henry from the British, the French would control all thirty-two miles of Lake George. It was the next link in the French bid to control the entire series of waterways that linked the Atlantic Ocean near New York City to the northern Atlantic outside of Hudson Bay in east-central Canada.[64]

---

[64] Known today as the Trans Adirondack Water Route, the chain goes from the Hudson River to Lake George, then to Lake Champlain via the La Chute River. It then goes from Lake Champlain to the Richelieu River and then to the St. Lawrence River. From the St. Lawrence River, it goes to the Gulf of St. Lawrence, which eventually spills out into the Northern Atlantic. This was the most strategically important chain to both the British and the French, as it would allow them to easily move men, weapons, supplies, and goods through the New York wilderness. Much of the fighting was done between the forts that guarded these waterways, including Fort Edward on the Hudson River, which was several miles southeast of Lake George.

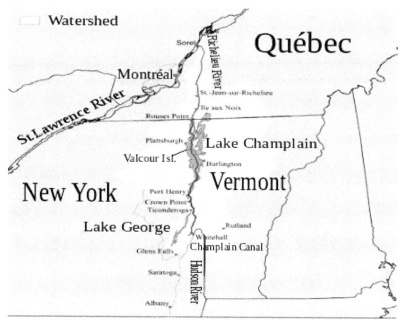

Important waterways fought over by the French and British.
Champlainmap.png: Kmusser / derivative work: Pierre cb, CC BY-SA 2.5
<https://creativecommons.org/licenses/by-sa/2.5>, via Wikimedia Commons
https://commons.wikimedia.org/wiki/File:Champlainmap.svg

While Montcalm was gathering troops at Fort Carillon in preparation for an all-out assault down the lake, General Webb sat virtually idle in Fort William Henry. It was not due to a lack of information—he constantly got reports about French activity, and it was fairly obvious that the French were going to launch an attack. Webb just chose not to do anything about it. He and John Campbell, Earl of Loudoun, who was now the commander of the British forces in North America, didn't believe Montcalm would be foolish enough to launch an attack over the iced lake during winter. Montcalm himself thought it was a waste of time and energy.

However, even though it went against Montcalm's advice, Governor Vaudreuil was determined to launch a surprise winter attack on Fort William Henry. Rigaud was given command of the mission, and he took three columns of soldiers and skirted the frozen west shore of the lake. Men went ahead of the columns and poked the ice with picks to check its thickness and how safe it was to walk across.

Rigaud intended to surprise the fort, but he did not seem to realize the sounds of their footsteps crunching across the snowy frozen lake and the strikes of their ice picks carried down the lake. Their approach was no surprise to those in the fort.

The British called everyone into the fort, and the French, unable to do much else, burned their outbuildings and three hundred bateaux sitting on the shore. Determined to complete his mission, Rigaud and his men attempted to take the fort. But they were missing an important component to victory—heavy artillery. Without it, their feeble attempts fell flat. When a late March blizzard dumped three feet of snow on Rigaud and his men, their four-day siege ended, and they retreated back to Fort Carillon. With a weak, not-so-surprise attack like this, it was no wonder Webb felt secure sitting behind the fort's walls. But the lake would eventually thaw.

Despite the failed winter assault, Fort William Henry remained too tempting to the French. They would mount another attack with a bit of an advantage—the British had been dragging their feet about repairing the outbuildings burned over the winter. This allowed the French to concentrate their full might on the fort walls.

By mid-July, the British were getting nervous about what the French were doing at Fort Carillon. In order to find out, Colonel John Parker and 350 men paddled north up the lake. Unfortunately for them, the French were already one step ahead. Almost as soon as the British boats had hit the water, the French knew about it. All they had to do was wait.

The next morning, the three boats that Parker had sent ahead were set upon by Ensign de Corbiere and 450 men, mostly native warriors. After taking men captive and bringing them ashore, the French were able to extract information from the British. They found out that Parker and the rest of their contingent were planning to land at Sabbath Day Point, a little more than halfway between the two forts.

When Parker and his fleet rounded the point the next day, they saw their own boats by the shore, leading Parker to believe they had reached the rendezvous point safely. But when they got closer to shore, they were stunned by a hail of musket fire from where the French and natives were lying in wait. Before the British could retreat, they were quickly surrounded by fifty canoes. As they tried to flee, the French opened fire, the sound of gunshots reverberating between the mountains on either side of the lake. The French-allied natives jumped into the waters and, with surprising agility and ferocity, chased down the rest. Cries of the wounded and those being overturned could be heard across the serene waters as the warriors capsized or dragged their vessels under. Those who fell in the water were "speared like fish" or drowned. Only one hundred of Parker's men survived, with many being taken captive and brought to Fort Carillon.

To their horror, the captives were not treated according to the European code of war etiquette—they were in the hands of the natives, who played by different rules. The unfortunate prisoners had ropes tied around their necks and were forced to walk to the camp outside of the fort. As the day wore on and as the natives freely drank the British rum they had confiscated, their ferocity increased, leading to the shocking instance of one prisoner being boiled and eaten. Any information the British gained had come at a devastating price.

There was now no doubt in the minds of the British that another attack on Fort William Henry was imminent. British regulars and colonial militiamen gathered at the fort in a bid to try to defend it. They hastily built additional timber and brush barricades around the fort walls for an extra layer of protection. The men waited, not knowing when the French might arrive.

General Webb then stunned the officers of the fort when he left them, hurrying back to Fort Edward. He gave command of the fort to Lieutenant Colonel George Monro. His final words to Monro must have chilled the officer to his core. He told Monro "to make the best [surrender] terms left in your power." His belief in the fort's imminent defeat, though perhaps realistic, must have been highly unsettling.

By the time Webb left, Monro had 2,300 men to fight for the fort—technically. These numbers are frightfully deceiving. Only one thousand of the men gathered were in fighting condition; the rest were plagued with injuries or illness. On the other end of the lake, Montcalm's force of 9,200 was in prime shape and ready for battle.[65]

The first indications that the French forces were on their way came during the night of August 2nd. Bonfires could be seen on the shore farther up the lake, burning brightly against the pitch-black silhouette of the mountains.

When day dawned on August 3rd, the British were awakened by the booming of French cannons. Though they were not in range of the fort, the French were announcing that they had arrived and were heavily armed. A fuller picture of what was coming emerged for the fort's inhabitants. They could see bateaux tied together to create large pontoons carrying French cannons and heavy artillery coming down the lake.

It was easy to see the French had landed along the shore only a half-mile from the fort, outside of the range of fire. Shortly after, the clanging sound of French shovels could be heard, the noise carrying across the water. They wasted no time building trenches, digging their way toward the fort. Within a short time, the British were under siege.

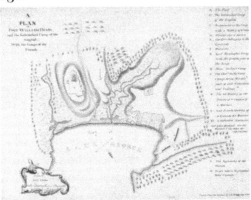

Fort William Henry and surrounding landscape Library of Congress
https://commons.wikimedia.org/wiki/File:Plan_du_si%C3%A8ge_de_fort_William_Henr y_en_1757.jpg

---

[65] Sixteen hundred of these were native warriors, gathered from 33 different tribes. In preparation for taking Fort William Henry, Montcalm had gone on one of the biggest French campaigns to gather Native American allies. He promised them that they could ransom British prisoners and that the British fort was "swimming in brandy" for the taking. Montcalm's contingent also consisted of Canadian Troupes de Marine, the toughest fighters in the army.

Montcalm and his men furiously rushed to set up their defenses along the lakeshore. The star-shaped outpost was strategically located on a twenty-foot hill with the lake in front and swampy marshland around two other sides, forming a sort of wetland moat. But as well constructed as its thirty-foot thick walls were, complacency remained a constant enemy.

This was where Monro made his first mistake in being distracted and reacting to only what he could see. As they busily fortified the fort from the lakeside, Monro was unaware that three thousand French soldiers and natives had snuck up behind the fort and were deeply garrisoned in the woods at their back. They set to work cutting off the road to Fort Edward. The British didn't know it yet, but they were already surrounded.

Once Monro found out that they were surrounded, he knew his situation was desperate, maybe even more desperate than he had anticipated. Webb's final words may have rung in his ears, but he was not ready to do himself and the fort the dishonor of surrendering without firing a shot. He believed that if he asked Webb for reinforcements—the men at Fort Edward were sitting only sixteen miles away—the general could not turn down the request. Messengers were sent out, and Monro waited confidently for help to arrive. He just needed to hold the fort for a few more days until help arrived.

Before their classic European-style battle even began, the French tried to break the British down with psychological warfare. French soldiers and native warriors shot at the walls of the fort day and night, hidden in the dense trees around the fort. As the French dug trenches closer to the walls, snipers followed the path, getting close enough to shoot soldiers on top of the wall. Though the British on the wall were able to defend and hold the snipers back, their unfortunate oxen outside of the walls were easy targets. One hundred dead animal carcasses soon littered the grounds around the fort walls, and the French and their allies continued to relentlessly fire on the fort for five days.

Montcalm was confident that he had the victory. As a man bound by war etiquette, he would prefer to take the doomed fort without further bloodshed. Walking under the red flag of truce and accompanied by drummers and fifteen grenadiers, Montcalm's aide-de-camp Louis de Bougainville marched to the fort to meet with Monro.[66] The French would offer a peaceful surrender.

Bougainville was greeted civilly at the gates of the fort, but he was blindfolded before being taken to Monro. Once in the commander's presence, his blindfold was removed. He formally and politely informed Monro that the French were calling upon them to abandon the fort on what they considered to be their territory.

The French would give Monro just one hour to decide the fate of the fort. Offering added incentive to answer on time and answer correctly, Bougainville warned, "Once our batteries are in place and the cannons are fired, perhaps there would not be time, nor would it be in our power to restrain the cruelties of a mob of Indians." The menacing message was clear—surrender, or we will not restrain our native allies, and we will not be responsible for the savagery that they inflict.

Bougainville drove home the point by reminding the commander of the bloody massacre the British had suffered at the hands of native warriors after the fall of Fort Oswego. Surely Monro would not want the same fate to befall him and the men, women, and children inside his fort.

As if reinforcing Bougainville's words, an Abenaki warrior came near the fort walls and shouted a menacing message to the British in French, "Ah, you won't surrender. Well fire first...then take care to defend yourself because if I capture you, you will get no quarter." Failure to surrender would mean there would be no mercy in defeat.

Under the rules of European warfare, Monro was fully expected to surrender since his defeat was certain. However, he did not want to give up with reinforcements expected at any moment. The fort was too important to give up, and he would continue to defend it until General Webb sent reinforcements. He did not need the full hour to make his decision.

Monro bluffed, telling Bougainville that he could not surrender because his orders were to hold the fort. Putting on a brave front,

---

[66] The French flag was white, so they used red to denote messengers coming in a peaceful fashion.

he then told the Frenchman that the barbarity of the natives does not scare him. He told them, win or lose, they would fight down to the last man. But despite his show of bravado, Monro was extremely nervous. He sent more messages to Webb, letting him know the situation was becoming increasingly dire and begging him to send help quickly.

After receiving the refusal to surrender, Montcalm continued his dig toward the fort, setting up his cannons for heavy bombardment. Monro's men frantically fired cannons and guns at the advancing French. Even if they couldn't stop them, they needed to at least slow them down until help or news from Webb arrived from Fort Edward. They just needed to hang on a little longer. Little did they know that General Webb had already sent a messenger with his reply; he would just never reach them.

The situation became grimmer for the fort over the next few days. Although fire was exchanged back and forth, and while the British, for the most part, were able to keep the French at bay, they could not sustain this siege for long, especially once the French cannons were positioned and ready.

On August 6th, cannon fire cut through the air on both sides, the deafening sounds echoing between the lake's mountains in a constant cacophony. Howitzers shook the ground, and muskets sent a hail of metal toward the fort. Although the sand beneath the fort's logs helped to dampen the blows, French artillery soon started to devastate its walls. Mortar shells were lobbed over the walls, and the casualties began to mount.

Casualties were not just coming from outside the walls either. Four British cannons and a mortar gun exploded behind the walls, killing the men around it. The British were in as much danger from their own cannons as they were from those of the French.

Desperately, Montcalm ordered that the roofs of the barracks and other buildings be quickly ripped off to prevent fires from starting or spreading around the fort when hit by mortar shells. When French fire stopped for the night, Montcalm and his men could be heard, though not seen, digging their way to the walls in the dark. It was just another masterful piece of psychological warfare on the part of the French.

On August 7th, mortar fire tore a hole through the British flag flying over the fort. The carpenter who was sent to fix it was killed immediately by incoming fire. Sensing this as a symbolism of their doom, morale inside the fort tumbled. The symbolism of it was not lost on the French either. Knowing the fort was lost, Montcalm halted the barrage and again sent an offer of surrender under the red flag of truce.

Bougainville again approached the gates and told the sentries that he had a letter for Monro. When Monro opened the letter, he expected to read the terms of surrender. Instead, his heart sank in horror. The letter, stained red with blood, was from General Webb. Several days before, a Mohawk scout named Kanectagon was lying in wait next to the road to Fort Edward, waiting for someone whom he could capture and ransom. His patience was rewarded when the messenger with a letter from General Webb passed by. A Frenchman who was traveling with Kanectagon searched the British soldier and found the letter in a secretly sewn pocket in the dead man's coat.

When Montcalm was given the letter, he was overjoyed. It was the best news he could have hoped for. And not only that, he could use it to his advantage. Wanting to destroy any hopes Monro had left, he sent the letter with Bougainville, along with the letter of surrender.

A tornado of thoughts must have swirled through Monro's mind as he read Webb's words. The general succinctly wrote that he did not think it "prudent" to send more soldiers to the besieged fort and that Monro should try to get the best terms of surrender possible.[67] There would be no rescue from Fort Edward, and the news was reaching Monro devastatingly late.

Monro next read the letter of surrender, which was what he was expecting. The French hoped the blow of Webb's letter would be devastating enough to get Monro to surrender. Monro looked up at Bougainville and told him that the French had been a most

---

[67] Webb knew that the fort was almost sure to fall to the French. When that happened, Fort Edward would be the only outpost held by the British in this important region. If he took soldiers from Fort Edward, he would leave it too poorly defended if the French tried to take it after Fort William Henry fell.

pleasant enemy. Yet his next words shocked the Frenchman. Monro told him that he could not yet surrender. The walls of the fort had not yet been breached, and if he surrendered now, it would be a terrible dishonor.[68]

Though the British had spent five sleepless days and nights defending their fort and waiting for reinforcements that would never come, they would continue to fight until the walls of their fort crumbled. As the French recommenced their salvo, morale inside the fort was shattered. Although the walls were still standing, the situation was utterly hopeless. The militia fighters were not only exhausted but also traumatized. They were running out of food and munitions, and their artillery was succumbing to metal fatigue, creating a higher chance that they could explode each time another shot was fired. With no help coming, surrender was the only option left.

Montcalm's terms of surrender were carefully crafted so as to avoid the fiasco of Fort Oswego, where the natives took scalps and captives. Montcalm promised the British they could leave the fort unbothered by the French native allies, although they could only take their personal items. Everything else would become French property, which would be sent to supply their Canadian forts. But the native warriors wanted their share of the spoils, so the French made a deal with them that if they left the departing British alone, they could have whatever was leftover at the fort.

On August 9th, at 7 o'clock in the morning, the white flag of surrender was raised over the fort. The British would negotiate the terms of surrender. As per their custom, the French terms were rather generous to the British. Among other things, they would be allowed to leave the fort with honors and with a guarantee that the French would not allow their native allies to harm or harass them on their way out. It was a complete contrast to the fiasco of Fort Oswego.

However, the native chiefs allied with the French did feel that the terms were generous toward them. They had been left out of

---

[68] Monro was following the European military code of honor, which stated that until the fort walls were actually breached, it would be a dishonor to surrender, inferring that there was cowardice on the part of its commander.

the surrender negotiations altogether. Montcalm gathered them and informed them that under the terms of surrender, they were not permitted to take captives, pillage, or strip the defeated enemy as they left the fort. Although the chiefs listened politely to Montcalm, it belied the anger that boiled up inside of them. They cared nothing for the European code of honor—their honor was dependent on returning home with captives and spoils. It was the only reason they had agreed to fight. They felt betrayed by the French, who were now going back on the promises they had made when recruiting the warriors. They had sacrificed their fighters to the war and now were getting nothing in return. It was humiliating.

The tribal warriors were further insulted when Monroe threw a banquet for Montcalm and his officers, graciously toasting them as worthy opponents. The native fighters had not been asked to join this peaceful gathering, essentially treating them as if they had been of little consequence in the battle. It also raised fears that should the white men on both sides become friendly, they might decide to come together against their people. The Native Americans could see no upside to having allied themselves with the French in this war.

When the fort was officially handed over to the French at noon, trouble began brewing immediately. The British soldiers laid down their weapons and marched out of the fort walls to an encampment not far away, but many of their people still remained inside the fort.

Soon after they left the fort, screams from behind them pierced the air. Native warriors, intent on taking spoils and captives, had forced their way past the French guards and made their way into the fort. The French soldiers tried in vain to stop them. The warriors pillaged, drank until they were drunk and angry, and terrorized the British prisoners. One ran out of the area where the wounded were held, grasping "a human head, from which trickled streams of blood."

Montcalm desperately tried to get the situation under control, but due to the many languages spoken by the various tribesmen and a sad lack of interpreters, communication was nearly impossible. He was going to have to find a way to get the British out of the fort, and quickly.

He devised a plan to spirit the British away from the fort during the night. The French hoped that under cover of darkness, the fort's inhabitants could safely leave while the native warriors slept. That plan did not go over well.

As they were leaving, the warriors woke up. Upon realizing what was happening, they swarmed the French encampment and angrily threatened their officers. The British were brought back to the fort. They would have to leave in daylight so as not to further anger the French allies.

When the sun dawned over the mountains on the eastern side of the lake on August 10th, the British began their march out of the fort under their mortar-torn flag. Escorted by French grenadiers, the well-organized British regulars marched out first, followed by a disorderly line of the colonial militia. Camp followers brought up the rear.[69] All were unarmed.

The tension was thick. The French could feel it, and it worried them. As the grenadiers escorted the column away from the fort, the natives had already begun to make their move. They broke back into the camp, killing and scalping the wounded left behind.

The disillusioned native warriors care nothing for the terms of surrender given by the French. The French promises to the British meant as little as their promises to them. And trying to sneak the British out from under their noses had further antagonized them. They went ahead of the British and laid in wait on the side of the road leading out from the fort. They were determined to take the spoils that were their due.

With terrifying war whoops, they launched themselves from their hiding places and set upon the regulars in front. They took what they wanted, including Monro's horse. The French, who were nervous about what might happen and wanting to avoid more bloodshed, advised the British to just give the warriors what they wanted and to not put up a fight. Monro urgently passed the message down the column as the warriors took everything they had, including their hats.

---

[69] These were women who stayed with the soldiers to help with chores, such as sewing, cooking, and laundry.

Understandably, the column began to panic. They expected the terms of surrender to be adhered to and that they would peacefully march to Fort Edward. This turn of events was shocking and frightening. The situation had surprisingly and quickly spiraled out of control. But as frightening as it was for the regulars in the front, they had actually been relatively lucky. The situation became far more terrifying for those following behind.

Not content with taking what few belongings they had, the warriors quickly surrounded the militiamen and the women and children following behind. The ever-dreaded "hell whoop" rang out, signaling a massacre. With ferocity and without restraint, the warriors took hatchets and tomahawks and leaped at the men, killing and taking scalps as trophies of war. Hundreds were taken off as captives, many with the intent of being ransomed back in Canada. One hundred and eighty-five people who had left the fort lay dead along the road.[70, 71]

The attack lasted just a few minutes, but it was intensely terrifying. When Montcalm heard what was happening, he personally rushed to the scene. By the time he got there, it was over. Monro was courageously rescuing captives, some of whom had lost all their clothes and were brought back stark naked.[72]

When General Webb found out about the surrender, he sent five hundred men to meet those on their way to Fort Edward. Expecting to see an orderly column calmly marching down the "King's Road," the soldiers were shocked to see thirty of their people crashing out of the woods and running down the hill toward them, many without shirts or even pants.

Montcalm had lost his native allies and had a lot of explaining to do as to how this massacre occurred despite his orders. He would

---

[70] Numbers of those killed vary. Original sources said 1,500 were killed, but the report was likely sensationalized to spark outrage among New Englanders. After much research, scholars believe the dead was actually 185, though some sources say as low as 75 or 85.

[71] Though the book is highly fictionalized, this event is the foundation for James Fenimore Cooper's *The Last of the Mohicans*.

[72] After taking anything of value from the fort, the French burned it to the ground. Today, Fort William Henry has been rebuilt as a museum on the hill adjacent to its original location.

not pursue a seizure of Fort Edward. He had worse things to worry about. Word spread about how the French treated their native allies, making it highly unlikely that new warriors could be recruited. Those already allied with the French broke or threatened to break their alliance in the wake of the battle.

The easily won French victory, which had relied so heavily on native warriors, was now leading the French to their greatest crisis. Without their native allies, they would find that winning North America would be out of their grasp. The many battles they had won over the past few years would all be for naught.

Chapter 10 – The Battle on Snowshoes and the Legend of Rogers Rock

The year 1758 started off with a lesser-known battle that would become local folklore centuries later. In late February, still the dead of winter, the British decided to cancel their planned attacks on Fort Carillon (Ticonderoga) and Crown Point. Instead of sitting idly by, they would send out a reconnaissance mission headed by Captain Robert Rogers, the smart, fearless, and cunning founder of the Army Rangers. Rogers was to take four hundred of his Army Rangers to scout out the situation just north of the forts.

In the days before he left Fort Edward, he found out that the fort's commander, Lieutenant Colonel William Haviland, had made his mission public to everyone in the fort. Rogers was angered that a security breach could compromise his mission. He was further angered to find out a few days later that a servant at the fort was captured in a French and Native American ambush. He felt sure the man had talked and revealed his mission. Although he felt that his mission was compromised and the French knew he was coming, he prepared to set out anyway.[73]

---

[73] Rogers did not appear in any French reports or sources until after his mission, making it very unlikely that the French knew about his mission.

Rogers faced another setback on the day he was supposed to leave. Instead of 400 men, Haviland was allowing him to take just 184, including officers. Rogers argued that since he was sure the French knew he was coming, he would need *more* men, not less. Haviland didn't budge on the issue, and Rogers found his decision incomprehensible in the face of the situation. Still, he had no choice but to bitterly obey his orders.

The second day of Rogers's journey, March 11th, saw him and his men march past the depressing sight of the burned-out Fort William Henry. The men could not take the time to dwell on the past defeat and its aftermath. They donned ice cleats and started their long haul over the frozen waters, making it about a third of the way up the lake by the end of the day.

The first sign of danger appeared the next day, and it ran across the lake on four legs. The Rangers spotted a dog coming from one of the small islands in the lake—a sure sign that native warriors were nearby.[74] Scouts on ice skates were sent to check out the situation.

Though they could see no one, Rogers did not want to take any chances, as the native warriors were masters of hiding and ambushing. He and his men hurried into the densely wooded shoreline and exchanged their ice cleats for snowshoes—they would move where they had more cover. Just to be sure, they would wait until night to continue their trek.

Over the next couple of days, they marched in snowshoes during the night, resting in the frigid cold and the deep snow of the woods during the day without the warmth of a fire so they would not give their position away. When they did move, the unnatural gait required to walk on the snowshoes slowed them down. The cold and the journey quickly took their toll on the men, causing considerable fatigue as they pushed through the snow.

On March 13th, Rogers stopped his men within a few miles of a French advanced post and, after conferring with his officers, made a plan. But what he didn't plan for was what was actually happening at Fort Carillon the day before.

French Marines, along with two hundred Iroquois and Nipissing warriors, had arrived at the fort to help defend it. That night, the

---

[74] It was commonly known that Native American raiding parties took dogs with them.

warriors held council and had their medicine man speak. Unaware that Rogers and his men were in the area, he delivered a shocking prophecy—a British war party was already near. By the time the news reached the Marine commander Sieur de La Durantaye, native scouts had come back with a report that seemed to confirm the medicine man's words. They had come across the tracks of two hundred men with snowshoes, and scouts at the top of Bald Mountain could see soldiers moving into the area—it was the foretold British war party. Fort Carillon sent out three parties of French militiamen and native warriors to meet them.

Rogers expected the French to come across the ice, so he brought his men inland, trudging between Bald Mountain and Trout Brook through four feet of snow. Before long, advanced guards sent back news—the French had been spotted. They did not know it was only one of the parties that had been sent out, and so they spread themselves along the river to meet the ninety-seven Frenchmen and natives coming their way.

Once the French contingent passed in front of their left wing, Rogers took the first shot. Caught by surprise, the first volley killed forty of the French-allied natives. The rest retreated. The first confrontation had been a success for Rogers—he had played the French and native game of ambush and won. However, Rogers had no idea that the other two French units were waiting to ambush *them.*

Not wanting to allow those fleeing to regroup, Ensign Gregory MacDonald and Captain Charles Bulkeley took their respective divisions and set off in hot pursuit. Little did they realize they were chasing them back to their larger French contingent and straight into mortal danger.

The triumphant Rangers, who were exhilarated from their recent victory, ran straight into Ensign Jean-Baptiste de Langy and his men, their guns at the ready. The French opened fire at close range, catching the Rangers by surprise. The Rangers could hardly react before Bulkeley and all his officers were on the ground, dead or wounded. MacDonald and another officer, though mortally wounded, rallied their men who were still standing and led them back to Rogers and the main column.

Rogers and his men were unaware that their compatriots were in dire straits. They were combing the area of their victorious ambush, scalping and stripping the dead. The scattered Rangers were caught off guard and were out of battle-ready formation when the French swarmed in on their right flank. Rogers was able to think quickly on his feet, and he immediately ordered his men toward the higher ground of Bald Mountain. There, they would either shake the French or die making their last stand.

The French, hot in pursuit, were not about to give up that easily. The hated Rogers and his Rangers had been a serious thorn in their side.[75] They could not let this chance to rid themselves of such troublesome enemies while they were within their reach slip away.

Rogers and his men fought fiercely as they were pushed higher and higher up the mountainside. Greatly outnumbered, Rogers and his men resorted to woodland fighting tactics, something they were quite experienced with. They were able to hold the French advance back for some time, but they could not hold out forever. British Lieutenant William Phillips and his men fought to guard the rear, but their small unit was slowly surrounded.

Some of Phillips's unit was able to break away and escape, but Phillips, who had been promised protection by the French if they surrendered, had little choice but to capitulate. However, when the native warriors found the scalps of their dead tribesmen on the surviving soldiers, they became enraged. There were no French promises that could hold them back from taking revenge. After tying Phillips and his men to trees, the natives took out their fury on them. Only three of them would survive.[76] As brutal as it was, their surrender bought Rogers some time and allowed him and the rest of his men to get away for the moment.

Rogers's last-ditch effort to get to the high ground was not without sacrifice. Fifty men were lost as they scrambled up the

---

[75] Rogers specialized and was an expert at harassing the French, even boldly and brazenly jumping into the trenches around Fort Carillon and taking prisoners from right under the noses of the rest of the garrison.

[76] Phillips and the two other survivors were eventually taken north by the native warriors and paraded around their villages in a show of victory. Phillips endured a number of harrowing experiences before escaping and making it back to the British army. The fate of the other survivors remains unknown.

mountain, but Rogers, with less than 120 men, many of whom were wounded, continued their difficult ascent up the snow-covered slope. Most of them would not make it.

As darkness neared, Rogers hoped to hold out until he could make a nighttime escape with the twenty men he had left with him. The French, on the other hand, were desperate not to lose them to the night. They caught up to Rogers; they came so close that hand-to-hand combat nearly started. Defeat and likely death were close at hand for the British.

It was now time for Rogers to follow his own advice that he set out in his "Ranging Rules." One rule states that "If the enemy is so superior that you are in danger of being surrounded by them, let the whole body disperse, and everyone take a different route to the place of rendezvous appointed." If possible, one should hold firm and wait until night to escape. Now was the time.

The Rangers each scattered into the gloom of the mountain, hoping to hide until nightfall and then make for the rendezvous point. With the natives in close pursuit, not everyone was able to escape; some were taken as prisoners. Rogers, however, made what became a legendary escape.

Throwing off his coat, Rogers fled through the woods along the flat mountaintop. The French, believing him dead, gave up trying to find his body. However, the Iroquois warriors persisted. Rogers made it to the eastern side of the mountain but stopped dead in his tracks. Looking down, he saw a precipitous slope leading seven hundred feet down to the frozen lake. He was trapped. But he was also crafty.

Taking off his snowshoes, he turned them around and tied them on backward, walking away from the edge and back into the woods. He hoped to make it look like his escape ended at the cliff's edge. When the Iroquois pursued his tracks later, they found two sets of snowshoe prints ending at the edge and assumed that Rogers went over the side.[77]

---

[77] This cliff face is now famously known as Rogers Rock.

Rogers Rock.
Internet Archive Book Images, No restrictions, via Wikimedia Commons
https://commons.wikimedia.org/wiki/File:A_battle_fought_on_snow_shoes_-
Rogers%27_Rock,_Lake_George,_March_13,_1758_(1917)_(14596080357).jpg

A little while later, the native warriors saw a sight that greatly frightened them. There was Rogers, whom they had assumed died going over the cliff, running across the frozen lake. They reasoned that no regular man could have survived the drop to the lake and believed that Rogers could have only survived with the help of spirits. Believing that he had supernatural support behind him, the Iroquois refused to pursue him any further.[78]

Rogers managed to rendezvous with the other survivors at the point near the lake where they left their packs and sleds. Messengers on ice skates were sent to Fort Edward to let them know what had happened and to get help in bringing the wounded back. After spending two nights on the frigid, wind-whipped Sloop Island in the middle of the frozen lake, Rogers and his defeated men dragged themselves into Fort Edward on March 15th.

---

[78] Local folklore tells a fantastic legend of Rogers sliding down the rock face to the lake and escaping, his slide being what cleared the slope of its vegetation. This is no doubt taken from the Iroquois belief about what happened, but surviving such an escape down the icy slope would have been virtually impossible. Rogers did not give an account of his escape in his narrative, but the story of his escape has been pieced together by various reports and probabilities.

For his courage and leadership, Rogers was shortly thereafter promoted to major. The French would soon find out how wrong they were about his death when he reconstructed his shattered Army Rangers and took them to Crown Point to continue harassing the garrison.

Chapter 11 – A British Victory and a Humiliating Disaster

Up until June of 1758, the British had suffered one demoralizing and humiliating defeat after another, with a few exceptions. Part of the problem lay with the trouble brewing from within.

The commander of the British army in North America, John Campbell, Earl of Loudoun, had faced nothing but years of problems from colonial assemblies, with Massachusetts being a particularly sharp thorn in his side.

The colonists continued to argue for the same rights as British citizens living over in the homeland—they considered themselves subjects of the Crown as well. They just happened to live on the other side of the ocean. Why should they be treated differently than any other citizen of Britain? In protest, they began refusing to pay taxes imposed by England. They reasoned that if they were not afforded the same rights and protections as citizens, then they were not obligated to pay taxes.

Loudoun was not used to being defied, and he was flummoxed over why the colonists were so rebellious. He could not understand their valid fears. The colonists realized they were obligated to wage war for empires that did not consider them citizens. This risked bankrupting their fragile economy, and in addition, their tenuous grasp on the rights they did have might be taken away at any time. Issues over money and morals heavily divided the colonists from the British. But instead of acknowledging their concerns, Loudoun only viewed colonial Americans as troublesome rebels.

London saw the issues and problems mounting, prompting the government to fire Loudoun as the commander. The man to take his place, Lord William Pitt, was much more astute when it came to dealing with the colonists. He knew that no matter how demanding or headstrong they were, he absolutely needed them in order to win this war. And to win the war, he must first win over the colonists.

He started by having money sent over for the army—a smart move considering that the military salaries were a point of contention for the colonists. Feeling that some of their concerns had been addressed and heard, the colonists were elated and more willing to cooperate. Whereas it had previously been incredibly difficult to get militiamen to enlist, they were now signing up by the thousands. Pitt's strategy worked, and it was the first step toward turning things around.

Despite their issues, the British never took their eyes off their goal—control of the New York route and, ultimately, Canada. But in order to do that, they would have to do what seemed nearly impossible—defeat a sizable French force at the formidable Fort Carillon.

To round out their plan for Canadian domination, they planned to take Fort Louisbourg and Fort Frontenac in Canada, as well as make a second attempt on Fort Duquesne. A major offensive aimed at crushing the French was about to begin.

The first offensive movement began in June when Major General Jeffery Amherst seriously outmanned the French by bringing eleven thousand soldiers up against the three thousand men garrisoned at Fort Louisbourg. After landing at Cape Breton, Nova Scotia, the British easily took Lighthouse Point.

Fort Louisbourg.
Pierre-Charles Canot, CC0, via Wikimedia Commons
https://commons.wikimedia.org/wiki/File:Pierre-Charles_Canot_-
Views of Montreal and Louisburg, A View of Louisburg in North America taken
near the Light House - B2001.2.1498 - Yale Center for British Art.jpg

From the point, the British army launched a punishing 49-day assault, bombarding the besieged fortress with cannons from land while 157 British ships silently sailed into the harbor and decimated the entire French fleet. It was a crippling dual assault, and with their fort ablaze, the French had no choice but to surrender.

When the French finally surrendered the fort on July 26th, 1758, the British showed that they had not forgotten the tragedy of Fort William Henry. The French were accorded no honors of war, and all those who had fought against them were taken prisoner. To complete their seizure of the region, all eight thousand inhabitants of Cape Breton Island were deported back to France. The British had their first real victory in years, and they were one step closer to their goal of taking over Canada. However, things were not going as well farther south at Fort Carillon, where the bloodiest battle of the war raged.

Under Brigadier Lord George Howe and Major General James Abercrombie, the British were preparing to take on Fort Carillon in early July. They had high hopes for Howe's leadership; according to his fellow officers, he was considered "the best soldier in the British army." But would he be enough to take on Montcalm and his seemingly impenetrable fortress?

The British were taking no chances. They gathered one of their largest forces—fifteen thousand men and eighteen siege cannons—believing that their much larger force was assured of victory. But they were about to find out that larger numbers did not necessarily equate to an easy victory, nor did it assure any victory at all.

On July 5ᵗʰ, with a fleet of one thousand small boats, the British set off, heading up the lake as the sun crept over the eastern mountain range. Their many boats covered the width of the lake, dotting the waters from the eastern shore of the lake clear to the western shore. Bagpipes and bugle music danced across the waters and echoed among the hills. The colorful coats and banners of the British, Scottish Highlanders, and colonial militia created a brilliant pageant the likes of which the lake had never seen before nor would see again.

Before Montcalm could even see their fleet, he knew the British were coming and that they were coming strong. Lookouts on top of Roger's Rock saw the incredible flotilla silently rowing their way, and they ran to report to Montcalm. He knew that the guerilla warfare that had worked so well before would not work with an army that size. For what may have been the first time, fear set in.

Before they set off, Abercrombie ordered his men to lighten their weight by shedding some of their clothing. They cut their long coats to jackets and trimmed their hat brims. It not only relieved them from the July heat and gave them less to snag on the brush but also allowed them to move through the water less encumbered. It was effective, and the fleet made it up the lake in surprisingly good time, leaving the fort little time for reinforcements to reach it.

Abercrombie landed about an hour's march from the fort and waited a day before continuing, debating over the best route to take. The delay, seemingly innocuous, was, in reality, incredibly costly.

Montcalm used that day wisely; neither the British nor the French know it, but that day would make all the difference. He knew he was outnumbered five to one and that the small fort would be devastated if the British set up their artillery on the high grounds surrounding it. He had to act quickly. Knowing there was only one road onto the peninsula where the fort stood, he decided that was where they would mount their defense.

He brought his men to the hilltop about a mile from the fort, where they created a maze, using logs and sharpened branches to slow and tangle the enemy.[79] Montcalm was not certain they could win against such overwhelming numbers, but he would try to at least hold out until reinforcements—one thousand regulars and one thousand native warriors—arrived. Those hopes were soon dashed when the British reached him before his reinforcements. It would also be the first time the French fought without their native allies, furthering their disadvantage.

Montcalm also sent out regiments to guard the area where the British landed and the portage roads he was sure they would take. Colonel François-Charles de Bourlamaque was guarding a key bridge over the La Chute River. He burned it and took his men north to meet Montcalm and the main contingent.

The next day, the British began their march toward the fort. Hacking their way through the dense wild undergrowth, Lord Howe took a forward party of Army Rangers headed by Rogers and went ahead of the main detachment in order to check on the French position near the sawmill. Two more disastrous mistakes had just been made.

Howe and Rogers were met by a French detachment that was moving through the dense woods looking for them. Not long after the first shot was fired, a bullet found its way toward General Howe. It struck the left side of his chest, piercing his lungs and heart. He fell backward off his horse, dead before he even met the ground.

The Army Rangers, though aware of Howe's demise, held firm and quickly worked to surround the French. Trapped, the French were like fish in a barrel, the British fire decimating their numbers. Less than one hundred men escaped back into the woods.

Despite their victory, the rest of the British army had a difficult time following the example set by the Rangers. After they found out about Howe's death, they were gripped with anxiety and thrown into confusion. As darkness fell over them, the situation

---

[79] Aptly named Rattlesnake Hill at the time, it is now known as Mount Defiance.

worsened. Upon hearing screams coming from the woods, the nervous soldiers fired almost blindly, hitting many of their own with friendly fire. It took hours for Abercrombie and the officers to get their men back under control.

The confusion following the conflict gave the French additional time, time that Montcalm used to his utmost advantage. His men finished the outerworks log maze and took their positions, with each party stationed fifty steps apart along the road to the fort.

On July 8th, Abercrombie prepared to launch the assault. With confidence in Johnson and his four hundred Mohawk warriors, he decided that an offensive was better than a siege. In his haste, the meeting where he gave the officers instructions was hurried, and they left unclear about what exactly they were doing. Only Abercrombie's last words of the meeting rang in their ears. "We must attack in any way, and not waste time in talking or consulting how." That haste and lack of clear planning was another critical error in a string of many.

Abercrombie ordered the cannons on the lake to fire on the fort, but since they were out of range, the bombardment was nothing but a waste of time and munitions. Abercrombie may have been trying to make a show of force or distract or disconcert the enemy as he waited for more cannons to arrive by boat. But little did he know, half of his siege cannons lay at the bottom of the deep lake. Any other artillery they had would never reach them in time.

The rest of the army marched up the hill where the French were taking their stand behind their outerworks maze, with multiple skirmishes breaking out along the way. The British struggled up the hill with their heavy packs, stumbling on branches and stones and breaking the rhythm of their march.

When they got to the top of the hill, Colonel William Haviland led the charge. When the firing began, he mistakenly thought the main assault had begun. Telling his forward militiamen to "fall down," he marched his regulars ahead. It was yet another tragic error for the British. They marched straight into the fire of Montcalm's best marksmen, who were stationed behind the barricades, their guns positioned through narrow slits in the logs.

Haviland's men "fell like pigeons."[80]

The rest of the British frontal assault tried to reach the solid log breastwork, but first, they had to navigate the tangled maze of sharpened stakes and branches before it. The sharp stakes snagged their coats and tangled them in the brush, slowing their advance to a crawl. The maze-like barrier forced their well-formed lines to be dispersed. That division made them much easier targets. The French snipers fired from their protected positions, keeping the British from coming near their protective barricade. They were "cut down like grass," the ground "strewn with dead and dying. A man could not stand without being hit. Balls came by the handful."[81]

The French were firing furiously, sending a metallic blizzard of bullets toward the British line. For every three shots the British took, the French were able to answer with five and with more deadly accuracy. The screams of men went up through the woods as they fell, while others cowered behind stumps and boulders. The British commanders were quickly losing control of the army and the situation.

Now the fearsome, almost legendary division of the Scottish Highlanders, known as the Black Watch, launched themselves toward the barricade, their intimidating black tartan a blur.[82] They made it within twenty paces of the barrier, closer than any other regiment, and began a three-hour firefight with the entrenched Frenchman. They were only able to see "their hats and the ends of their muskets." They persisted, though, looking to find any weaknesses in the wall before them. The unceasing and fierce determination of the Black Watch managed to press the French, especially with a move that lived up to their reputation.

---

[80] The Mohawks had been left behind on the hill as auxiliaries and scouts while the British regulars marched forward. They watched as the British were mowed down by French guns before they turned and left without joining the fight.

[81] These were the eyewitness words of a Connecticut soldier who fought in the battle.

[82] The Black Watch was a royal regiment named for the black tartan they wore. They were known for their fierce, fearless fighting, which was compared very closely to that of the native warriors. Even the native warriors themselves viewed the Black Watch that way.

Some Black Watch members suddenly ran from the firing line, dodging the flurry of French bullets. They leaped onto the log barricade with terrifying ferocity, appearing like "roaring lions breaking from their chains." Despite their wild courage, those who made it over the wall were cut down by the French, taking the most catastrophic loss of any regiment.

By nightfall, two thousand British laid on the hill, dead or wounded, while those regulars who survived retreated behind the militia-held lines. In contrast, the French lost only 380 men. The British again found out that superior numbers did not necessarily equal victory, and they retreated. They tried to make a run for the lake, but they were slowed, as the thick mud consumed their shoes and took them right from their feet. The soldiers didn't care; in their frenzy to leave, they didn't even stop to pick up their shoes. Some ran barefoot or with only one shoe on back down the hill.

It was a day of glorious victory for Montcalm and his garrison at the fort. They were sure to see honor for their amazing victory.[83] But Montcalm was not so naïve to think he had seen the last of the British at the fort. The next time, he might not be so fortunate. He pleaded with headquarters for more men and equipment, telling them that "miracles cannot always be expected." However, he would never receive these two essential components.[84] The French Crown wrote back to Montcalm that since France was occupied with the war on the continent, it did not have the resources to send him more men. They told him, "When the house is on fire, one cannot occupy oneself with the stable." Unnerved by the large British showing and unable or unwilling to send help to North America, Paris officials told Montcalm and the French command in Canada to "think only of making peace."

---

[83] Despite the surprising win, Governor Vaudreuil condemned Montcalm for not chasing after the retreating British and finishing them off. Montcalm, however, would not have his victory disparaged and shot back at the governor, "When I went to war, I did the best I could...when one is not pleased with one's lieutenants, one had better take the field in person."

[84] The French Crown did send Montcalm eight hundred recruits who had no experience and needed to be trained, but what he asked for and needed were experienced regiments. The French king was more concerned with the costly war they were waging in Europe, one that was draining France's finances to the breaking point.

Abercrombie's reputation, on the other hand, was shattered. He felt the scorn of his men as they dejectedly rowed back toward Fort William Henry.[85] The British had all their hopes resting on his ability to win and, in this case, win quickly and decisively. All that was dashed within eight hours on a muddy hill. But despite the humiliating loss, the British still pressed on toward victory.

[85] The New England militia began to insultingly refer to Abercrombie as "Mrs. Nabbycrombie." Even the Iroquois warriors joined in with their own disparaging remarks, tauntingly referring to him as "an old squaw [woman]" that should "wear a petticoat."

Chapter 12 – The British Turn the Tide

The British were understandably angered and humiliated by the events at Fort Carillon. But instead of losing hope, it whipped them into a greater frenzy, making them determined to take Canada "at any cost." The French may have been thinking about peace, but the British were not.

They turned their eyes once again toward Fort Frontenac. Though they hadn't been able to take the fort in a previous attempt, General John Bradstreet suggested that since Abercrombie still had a large number of men under his command, they could be used for a successful strike against the Canadian fort.

It was a bold move—they would have to march the army 250 miles through mountainous wilderness inhabited by the Iroquois. But after their recent loss, they were looking for an easy win. Bradstreet called Frontenac "ripe for the plucking," and they bet on the French not expecting them to attack again so quickly. They hoped this would allow them to take the French by surprise. Their gamble would pay off.

In early August, Abercrombie and Bradstreet gathered 3,600 men, nearly all provincial militiamen, and set off on their difficult journey. The French might not have known that the British were on their way, but they did know that the fort was in dire straits. Almost all of the men garrisoned there had been pulled out to go to Fort Carillon. Only 110 men and 9 small boats remained to defend it. They just hoped that their cannons could prevent the British from making it across the lake should they come.

The trek was arduous for the British militia. Not only was their overland march made difficult by overgrown and uncleared roads, but it was also punctuated by low water in the rivers and creeks that ground their boats in silt. They had to stop and build dams to raise the water levels in order to move their boats. By the time they reached the mouth of the Oswego River on August 21ˢᵗ, 1758, six hundred men had deserted Bradstreet. But they continued to press onward.

The next day, the British boarded several hundred bateaux and set sail across the lake, heading straight for Frontenac. Had the French seen them coming, Bradstreet's fleet might have sustained some damage and given Frontenac a chance. But as fate would have it, the French boats never saw the British coming.

They landed and set up their artillery in secret, the French never suspecting what was coming their way. The next morning, the French were shaken from their beds by artillery fire. The British laid down a sustained barrage, bombarding the walls and trapping the French. The French knew within the first few minutes that they were doomed. They put up the obligatory token resistance in accord with European war etiquette, knowing it was the only way they could surrender with honor.

Within hours, the flag of surrender was raised. The British accorded the soldiers the honors of war and allowed the fort's elderly commander, Pierre-Jacques Payen de Noyen, to return to Montreal. Though the fort was small, it was a major victory for the British in a number of ways. Fort Frontenac was the key to the St. Lawrence River, which would allow them access to Canada. It was a strategic conquest—the way to Quebec was now wide open.

In addition, the British not only claimed the food, weapons (including sixty cannons), and supplies within the fort—a major windfall for them—but they also took the supplies meant for other French forts in the north, depriving them of critical essentials.[86]

---

[86] Eight hundred thousand livres' worth of provisions was captured, equal to more than $1.07 million today, making it quite a windfall for the British.

This short battle was an enormous and crippling loss for the French—a loss from which they could not recover.

Now that the British had control of the St. Lawrence on the northern end, they wanted to round out their seizure of the important waterway by capturing the southern end as well. The British now had decent control over the Northeast, but they knew that in order to win the west, they had to take the Ohio Forks area, the region that disastrously slipped through their grasp early on in the war. Taking the Ohio Valley meant another attempt at taking the indomitable Fort Duquesne.

Even though it had been three years, the British were wary about the mission, and they were determined not to repeat Braddock's calamitous mistake. They put Scotsman General John Forbes in charge of the mission, and they began to create a plan. Instead of taking Braddock's route through Virginia, Forbes planned to cut a new, more direct path through the dense forests of Pennsylvania. He would have six thousand men at his disposal. As they chopped their way toward Ohio, they would build outpost supply stations for themselves every forty to fifty miles. They did not want to get stuck without necessities in the middle of an unfamiliar wilderness again.

Aside from his logistical plans, the forward-thinking Forbes realized he needed to do something that Braddock or any other British commander had done before. He knew that what Washington had been saying, that they needed native allies, was true. And he needed a diplomatic envoy to actively woo the Delaware, Shawnee, and other Pennsylvania tribes. Without them, victory was all but hopeless.

Forbes enlisted the help of Delaware-speaking Christian missionary Christian Frederick Post, who had his work cut out for him. Post was determined to win the natives away from the French, and he held a multi-day council with several tribal chiefs, the most prominent among these being Teedyuscung, the self-styled "king of the Delaware." Post told the natives that the British wanted peace with the tribes and promised they weren't there to take their land but to drive the French out. But given the history of the British breaking promises, stealing land, and defrauding the native tribes, they were understandably doubtful about their claims.[87]

Post would have to overcome decades of rightful and justified animosity toward the British, who the natives believed had taken land that was their birthright and inheritance. He asked the chiefs to lay down their hatchet and form a treaty, promising that things would be different this time. He agreed that the British would not settle west of the Allegheny Mountains and would ensure the tribes had thousands of acres of land for themselves. After nineteen days, the chiefs finally agreed to the alliance—they knew they needed the British in order to keep their lands. However, they wanted the British to know that they were a power to be reckoned with and that they could make peace as well as break it if the promises were not upheld. Post agreed to bring their warning back to British command, though he knew all too well it was likely to fall on deaf ears. The British only cared that they now had the allies they sorely needed.

While the British were making treaties with the Native Americans, the French were losing their allies. Governor Vaudreuil knew that their native allies didn't truly fight for France; they fought for themselves and the land that was theirs. However, he also knew that he needed to retain their loyalty. It was the only hope for winning.

However, his retention of native allies came across three serious obstacles. First, Montcalm had been resistant to accepting help from the tribes. He was a staunch believer in fighting by the European battle etiquette and detested the "savage" battle tactics, which he found distastefully brutal. The second major issue was that the French no longer had what they needed to keep their native allies. With the supplies stored at Fort Frontenac now in the hands of the delighted British, the French had no gifts of guns or other goods to woo them. Without incentives, the natives would hardly look their way. The third problem lay within the native community itself. The war had taken a heavy toll on them. Smallpox brought by the Europeans, as well as hunger and warfare,

---

[87] One of the most outrageous examples of this was the 1686 Walking Land Purchase, an agreement made by William Penn and the Delaware. The vague terms originally laid out led to an egregious abuse of the agreement by the British in 1737.

had decimated their populations. In some places, entire villages had been wiped out. They were tired of war and had little more to give to this white man's conflict.

Issues with native allies weren't the only big obstacles that made Montcalm nervous. Like Fort Frontenac, Fort Duquesne was now weakly defended because the men garrisoned there were sent to fight on the Canadian front. Since the fort was in such an isolated location, it would be difficult to get enough men, munitions, and supplies to the fort to bring it back to its former strength.

But it was not just Duquesne that the French couldn't supply; the Frontenac debacle had deprived them of supplies for all their other forts. This problem was further exacerbated by corruption among the French, with sorely needed money being gambled or frittered away by the authorities. As a consequence, the French army was facing serious hunger. Montcalm was enraged. How could his men be expected to fight and fight courageously at that while weak and demoralized from hunger? Montcalm knew they were in trouble.

While Montcalm was anxiously trying to keep his army supplied and retain their native allies, Forbes and his men were chopping their way through the dense virgin forests of Pennsylvania—much to the chagrin of George Washington.[88] Washington was eager to return to finish what he had started in the Ohio Valley, so he joined Forbes. When Forbes showed him the route he wanted to cut, Washington insisted that Braddock's previous road was the better way to go. The two locked horns. When Forbes got his hands on a letter George Washington had written to another officer bemoaning Forbes's decision, he was angered, believing Washington to be a fool. The feeling was certainly mutual. Washington eventually lost this argument with Forbes, as well as his good relationship with the general.

When Forbes and his men were within fifty miles of Duquesne, they put the finishing touches on their last outpost, Loyal Hannon. It would be the key staging area to launch their assault. Scouts stealthily snuck out to high vantage points to try to find out just how strong the French force was.

---

[88] The route they cut still exists today; it is now the modern-day Pennsylvania Turnpike.

The French, who were almost always in the know about the whereabouts of the British, resorted to their old tricks. They sent out raiding parties to ambush and harass the British as they worked and hunted in the woods. Men often returned to camp bloodied and battered from surprise attacks, and inevitably, this began to unnerve the rest of the men.

However, the British were tired of the guerilla tactics used by the French and native warriors, so they decided to strike back. Major James Grant, a Highlander, proposed a bold plan to give the French a taste of their own medicine under the guise of a reconnaissance mission near the fort. However, he planned to take five hundred men with him—far too many for reconnaissance. It was fairly obvious that Grant had something up his sleeve.

Grant obviously had too few men for an all-out assault, but he knew that the French fort was weakly defended. With this knowledge, as well as his thirst for fame and glory, he wanted to make a secret bid to take Duquesne himself. Could he and his men possibly pull off such an ambitious plan?

Lieutenant Colonel Henry Bouquet encouraged Grant's audacious plan, giving him an additional 250 men. On September 14th, Grant set off and easily marched to within a mile of the fort. Grant's men then split into three units, and they confidently began their final march, bagpipes blasting the air and announcing their position. However, it didn't matter how much noise they made; the French already knew where they were, thanks to their native scouts. And the French were right there waiting for them. Fort commander François-Marie de Lignery, a battle-hardened marine, was no fool. He quickly went out with some troops and warriors and set a trap. And when the British advanced, the trap was sprung. Lignery's men swooped down on the surprised British and routed them. Three hundred of Grant's men were killed, and Grant himself was taken prisoner and quickly shipped to Montreal. Forbes, whose health was severely deteriorating due to dysentery, reeled under the heavy blow of the defeat and called Grant's actions rash.

The quick victory, however, did not change the dire situation Lignery and the fort were facing. With no way to get supplies, they were running out of food. Emboldened by his victory and motivated by desperation, Lignery shortly thereafter decided to launch an assault on Loyal Hannon, hoping to raid its storehouses.

They made three attempts at the outpost during the day but were beaten back every time. Lignery made one last attempt at night and managed to pick off some sentries but failed to breach the station. He and his men were forced to return to the fort, hungry and provisionless as ever. Despite their lack of success, the thought of facing starvation as winter approached was a strong incentive for Lignery to continue his attempts. For ten days, the French desperately tried to reach the British stockpiles, failing each time.

After the French attempted once again to steal horses and livestock, the British had had enough. Forbes sent Mercer to strike back in a woodland battle as the French again approached. However, once they engaged the French in battle, Mercer's provincials had difficulty attaining a victory. Forbes quickly sent Washington and his Virginia regiment to help Mercer.

Washington and his men approached the battle near dusk, the darkened light combined with powder smoke and fog making it difficult to see. Shadowy figures passed through the gray air, and the sparks of musket fire created brief flashes of brightness. Washington and his men fired toward the indistinct figures and flashes.

One of Mercer's officers, Captain Thomas Bullitt, saw the new volley of fire coming toward them, and he quickly realized what was happening. He ran straight toward the muskets of the Virginia regiment, screaming for them to halt their fire. The Virginians were firing straight into Mercer's regiment! Washington heard Bullitt, and he also stepped between the lines in an effort to halt their fire, even using his sword to push firing muskets up toward the sky.

When the firing stopped and the smoke began to clear, the gravity of the situation became obvious. Washington's horror mounted as they saw fourteen of their own dead on the ground, with another twenty-six wounded, all by friendly fire. Bullitt was incensed by Washington's carelessness. He blamed Washington for the incident and would never forgive him for it. Washington, however, somewhat spooked by his near-death experience, believed that divine providence had spared him for something greater.

As terrible as the blunder of the skirmish was, there was a bright spot. When the French ran from the fray, they left three of their men behind. The British took them as prisoners and pressed them for information about the fort. The information they dug up was pure gold. According to the prisoners, Fort Duquesne was weakly defended. It was so weakly defended, in fact, that the commanders were thinking of abandoning it. Forbes was overjoyed at the news. Now was the time to strike.

Within two weeks, Forbes was ready to mount his final assault. The British were so close to their goal, but Washington inexplicably started to press Forbes to abandon the plan and return to Braddock's already-cut road. The idea was ridiculous, and with provincial enlistments due to be up in a few days, Forbes was determined to press on.

French anxiety had grown, and they had finally come to terms with the fact that their situation was utterly hopeless. On November 18th, 2,500 of Forbes's men were marching toward the fort. There was no way Lignery's forces could repel them. Even their native allies had packed up and left the fort. It would be a complete rout.

Lignery ordered the evacuation of two hundred men to other outposts while the rest set charges around the fort. Now was not the time to worry about putting up symbolic resistance and being accorded the honors of war. After what had happened at Fort Frontenac, they wanted to leave nothing for the British but a pile of smoldering rubble.

When the British came within view of the fort, there was no army waiting to greet them—only an abandoned fort burning along the river. Forbes won the Ohio Forks without a shot, but he wouldn't have the security of the fort to spend the winter.[89] Leaving some men behind to rebuild it, he took the rest of his men back to Philadelphia.[90, 91]

---

[89] Before Forbes left, he renamed the area Pittsborough, now known as Pittsburgh.

[90] Forbes would never live to see the rebuilding of the fort or enjoy the British victory of the area. He died from poor health just a few weeks later.

[91] Afterward, Washington took some men and returned to the battlefield of Braddock's disastrous defeat. The remains of their dead fellow soldiers were never claimed or buried;

By the end of 1758, the British, despite many mistakes, had turned things around. But in truth, they had not done it alone. Without the Iroquois, who had given up their fifty-year policy of neutrality, as well as the other tribes who abandoned the French and came to their side, things might have turned out very differently for the British. However, just because things were looking up for the British didn't mean they had won the war just yet.

---

they had been left to nature and the elements those past three years. Washington had them buried with the military honors they were accorded. He then returned to Mount Vernon, once again retiring from military life and starting his new life by marrying Martha Custis.

Chapter 13 – The Fall of Quebec and the "End" of the True Canada

It was late July 1759, and Colonel James Wolfe paced the ground on the Île d'Orléans on the St. Lawrence River. After having received "secret instructions" from the king regarding a three-pronged attack centered in and near Canada, his journey north was difficult. He battled near-constant seasickness and braved an unusually severe winter, and he now found himself facing the core of the French forces.

He was anxious to take some real action against Quebec. The British had been successful in their other two campaigns. If Wolfe could pull it off, this would be the final and decisive battle in accomplishing their goal.

Only a few days earlier, William Johnson had taken one thousand British soldiers and a large contingent of native warriors against Fort Niagara. The French, who had only five hundred men at the fort and had lost the majority of their native allies, were at a disadvantage from the get-go. As French reinforcements made their way to rescue the fort, nineteen-year-old British army officer Joseph Brant was eager for the attack.[92] He and his men pulled a

---

[92] Brant (also known as Thayendanegea), a Mohawk officer in the British army, later

page out of the French playbook and ambushed the French as they marched out of the dense forest. The French took heavy casualties, the worst of these being the mortal wounding of the fort's commander. With their help neutralized, the fort was doomed, and they had no choice but to surrender.

Around the same time, the British returned to the site of one of their greatest humiliations—Fort Carillon. Knowing the British were coming with another large force of eleven thousand men, including that thorn in their side Captain Rogers and his Rangers, the French didn't believe that their good fortune would hold out a second time. They evacuated the fort, leaving only four hundred men behind to "take care" of the fort.

As the British dug siege trenches toward the fort, the French were turning their cannons toward their own walls, laying mines, and making a trail of gunpowder that led straight to their munitions storehouse. If the British wanted to take the fort, the French were going to give them an explosive surprise. The departing French quickly took torches and set the long fuses on fire before running.

The British caught a few French who were fleeing, and they informed the British that the fort was about to blow. British commanders wanted to save the fort at all costs and offered a king's ransom to anyone who would douse the fuses. But the British soldiers knew that those one hundred guineas would do them no good if they were blown to pieces.

That night, as darkness set in, the ground suddenly shook with a tremendous boom, and the sky suddenly lit up with a large explosion, the French flag still flying above the burning fort. Though the outer stone walls of the fort held up, the interior burned for two days. It was a tremendous victory for the British. Along with nearby Fort Crown Point,[93] the British controlled the Lake George/Lake Champlain region, allowing General Jeffery

---

became a tribal chief. (He was reportedly the great-grandson of King Hendrick.) He also acted as a liaison in efforts to bridge the gap between the white man's world and the Six Nations. He was also reportedly involved in two massacres, earning him the nickname "Monster Brant."

[93] This was built on the site of the conquered Fort Saint-Frédéric.

Amherst a clear path toward Wolfe and his men and Canada.[94]

Wolfe must have been encouraged by the British victories to his south. He only had 8,500 men, which was less than the 12,000 he had requested, but they were well-trained. They had faced skirmishes with Montcalm's sixteen thousand soldiers, but Wolfe was not concerned about the superior numbers of French soldiers. He wrote to his mother, telling her that Montcalm was "at the head of a great number of bad soldiers, and I am at the head of a small number of good ones."

But no matter how good his soldiers were, they had not made any headway against the impenetrable city. It sat safely in the high cliffs on the other side of the river, nearly impervious to a frontal water-born assault. Wolfe desperately looked for any "opportunity to strike a blow" on his enemy.

Montcalm, on the other hand, remained "entrenched up to the chin" within the city, refusing to be drawn out into a battle he would surely lose. That's not to say Wolfe didn't try his hardest to shake them out of their secure city fortress. But Montcalm wasn't falling for any of Wolfe's tactics. He knew that as long as the British could not get them outside the city and draw them into open battle, they had a chance. They would try to outwait the enemy, hoping to hold on until winter could drive them away.

Though Montcalm decided to concentrate his manpower on holding Quebec, he was no fool—he saw the writing on the wall for North America and the French. Eerily, he had predicted earlier in the year that "Canada will fall during the upcoming campaign season." And now the fulfillment of that prediction was staring at him from across the river.

Wolfe knew that even though Montcalm could wait it out within the city, time was ticking for him. Winter, which started early in Canada, was just over the horizon. If Wolfe was going to help bring North America under the control of the British that year, he was going to have to make some dramatic moves. Day after day, his cannons and mortars bombarded its walls, and day after day, they

---

[94] The British rebuilt the fort and renamed it Fort Ticonderoga (from the Iroquois word meaning "between two waters") and held it until 1775 when it was taken by colonial Americans under Ethan Allen and Benedict Arnold.

crumbled a bit more as the French scrambled to keep them intact. But despite the growing pile of rubble around the city, it was still not enough to win.

Boarding the HMS *Russell* on July 31ª, 1759, Wolfe, along with men on two other war vessels, surreptitiously made their way up the river under cover of darkness. They crossed the river to the area near Montmorency Falls, hoping to get a better view of French activities. Wolfe also had another plan in mind—attack the temporary French fortifications protecting the northern side of the city. He hoped to flush the French from their entrenched positions. Once they were out in the open, the British would have a clear line of fire into their ranks. What Wolfe hadn't realized until he landed was that from high on the hill, the French guns on the walls of Quebec could reach him and his men before they even made it to their redoubt.[95] That would make Wolfe's plan far riskier. He and his men would be caught in the open between two unreachable French defensive lines. Wolfe decided to go ahead with his plan anyway.

As he waited for the main body of his landing forces to arrive, Wolfe could see dire problems already brewing. The ships carrying his troops became grounded on the river's shoals, preventing them from reaching Wolfe. By the time they were able to get themselves loose and find another landing spot, the storm clouds had already begun to gather.

As Wolfe and his men finally advanced toward the redoubt, the French troops watched them from the hill. It must have been quite amusing to the soldiers who had fought outside Fort Carillon to see the British making yet another foolish attempt. They laid down withering fire, a rain of bullets from the French hill pummeling the British ranks.

The French assault slowed their advance, but it did not stop them. And it might not have stopped them if it had not been for the intervention of Mother Nature. Just a short while after the firing began, rain from the sky poured down on the British, wetting their gunpowder. With their weapons unable to fire, they were as good as unarmed. Wolfe had taken heavy losses in a short amount of

---

[95] Temporary fortification or defensive structure.

time, and he was forced to retreat across the mudflats in a confused, angry, and exhausted escape. Angry that he had persisted in such an ill-advised assault, he wrote, "Many excellent officers were hurt in this foolish business."

Although the French were victorious, Montcalm could not celebrate. He knew that the British would not give up when they were so close to their goal. He wrote to the French Crown, begging the king to send him reinforcements; otherwise, he could not hold the region for France. The reply he received was disappointing, to say the least. The king told him that he would not send more troops but instead sent his compliments, flattering Montcalm by saying he relied on the commander's zeal and knowledge to save Canada.

Montcalm was right about Wolfe; he did not even consider giving up. Instead, he continued to find ways to try to draw the French out into battle. Propelled by anger over his loss, the inability to conquer Quebec, and the insults the French had afforded the British, Wolfe and his men began burning everything they could reach on the other side of the river. The settlements and smaller towns outside the city bore the brunt of this rage, as 1,400 homes were turned to ash.

Wolfe also maneuvered some of his warships upriver. If he could not get to Quebec, maybe an attack on Montreal would anger the French into engaging in an open battle. British siege guns bombarded the city, setting it ablaze. Terrifying infernos raged, creating horrors this war had not seen before, especially for the many non-combatant refugees who had sought safety in the city. Montcalm, though shaken, refused to budge.

By September, Wolfe was in a desperate state in more ways than one. One-third of his army was incapacitated by illness, and Wolfe himself was gravely ill with fever and chronic maladies. He believed he wouldn't survive much longer, and it would be a disgrace to die without gaining Quebec. Despite his illness, he was highly motivated to form an audacious plan to attack the city.

On September 12th, Wolfe's plan went into action. Part of the British fleet sailed down the river and began to attack the city of Beauport. They hoped that the French would believe it was just another small conflict but large enough to distract them from what the British were really planning.

As the bombardment commenced, 4,500 men rowed across the river to the base of the cliffs named Anse-au-Foulon. They were going to scale the cliffs in the dark. The first troops up greeted the sentries in French. Believing that the men were French reserves, the sentries let down their guard. The British soldiers easily captured the bewildered guards and opened the way for the rest of the regiments to safely climb the cliffs. Within five hours, the British had scaled the cliffs and positioned themselves on the Plains of Abraham. When sunlight began to dawn, Montcalm was shocked. He saw the red coats of the British dotted across the field on the more exposed western side of the city. Wolfe's plan worked—to Montcalm, it was as if they had appeared out of nowhere.

Despite Montcalm's firm stance of not meeting the British out in the open, he saw something unusual that would inevitably cause him to change his mind. He was well aware that the British regulars were superior to his French militiamen, but he noticed that Wolfe had spread his men into two ranks instead of three—something Montcalm had never seen before. This formation caused the British to be spread out across the battlefield in a thin line. To Montcalm, this seemed to him to be a breach-able weakness.

Montcalm believed that he would only need one column to defeat the British, and he and his men marched out to the field. The two empires would meet in the classic European battle formation that Montcalm so loved. But as the not-so-disciplined French militiamen marched out of the city to meet them, things quickly began to fall apart.

Unable to keep their lines, the French began firing at the British. The Redcoats held fast, and not one of them fell to the ground—the French had begun firing before their guns were even in range, wasting valuable time and ammunition. The British did not even flinch, and they continued to stare down the blue coats of the advancing French forces. If this first volley was any indication of the state of French training, the British could remain confident in their fight.

The French continued their advance, but before they could position themselves, the British were ready for them. With two musket balls loaded at a time, the Redcoats decimated the French line. The field was quickly littered in blue.[96] In less than ten minutes, the surviving French fled back to the city, leaving 1,500 dead on the plains. It was clear that Montcalm was right all along—they were no match for the British in an open battle.

However, it no longer mattered how right Montcalm was. He had made a fatal error, and it would be his last. He was shot in the abdomen, the red blood stains spreading through his white undercoat as he was rushed to a physician's house. It was too late; he could not be saved. His end, however, was less dramatic or heroic than Wolfe's.

Wolfe took musket fire to his wrist and chest during the battle, and his men found him lying on the field. They quickly rushed to find a physician to save him, but he refused the help. He knew his body was too weakened by sickness and that he could not survive the mortal wounds. He bravely told his men that his end had come. However, he told them that he could die knowing that he had been a hero and that his name would be known all over the British Empire.

The French returned to the city utterly demoralized. Their fierce leader was dead, the city was in near ruins, and desertion from the army was rampant. With food and supplies running low, it seemed impossible that they could wait out a siege inside the city until the bitter winter winds brought them release. They knew another assault by the British would only lead to more unimaginable carnage. Four days after this decisive battle, the French had no choice but to surrender.

Such a climactic battle ending in the dramatic deaths of both brilliant commanders seemed like it would bring a decisive end to this war of two empires. Yet, it would rage on for another year. Peace had fled all of Europe since war raged there as well, and peace also remained the last thing on the mind of General Amherst. Despite their incredible conquest of Quebec, Amherst would not rest until the British had taken all of Canada.

---

[96] Later, British historian Sir John Fortescue called the action "the most perfect volley ever fired on a battlefield."

By the summer of 1760, Amherst was hellbent on taking the last French holdout—Montreal. The way there, though, was fraught with danger. He and his men would have to navigate the dangerous rapids rushing down the St. Lawrence River, and if they made it, they would still have to survive the gauntlet of French-allied Canadian Mohawk territory. In early August, he set off from Fort Oswego with an army of 10,000 men and 750 native warriors.

Amherst knew the Mohawks were his greatest weakness and the greatest strength of the French. In order to win, he needed to get rid of this threat, which he referred to as the "enemy's Indian scoundrels."[97] Amherst despised his own Iroquois allies, calling them the "savage enemy," but he knew he needed them to win. He also knew he would need diplomatic tactics to neutralize the Mohawk problem.

As Amherst and his forces made their way up the St. Lawrence River, they took the time to stop at various Mohawk villages. The British worked to convince the Mohawk chiefs that they just wanted peace with them and did not want to fight if it could be helped. Amherst's plan worked. The Mohawk agreed to stay out of the fight. Once again, the French lost one of their most valuable assets: native allies.

With the native "problem" peacefully taken care of, Amherst could now turn to organize his massive offensive against Montreal. Three British armies converged to finish this fight in Canada, creating an impressive and terrifying force that would come up against the city all at once.

On September 8th, 1760, the French in Montreal saw a crushing force of Redcoats at their doorstep. Not wanting a repeat of the previous year, they surrendered without a shot being fired. Though the surrender was bloodless, the French suffered the insult of not

---

[97] In a quest for vengeance against the Abenaki the November before, Amherst sent out Rogers and a unit of his Rangers on an ill-fated revenge mission. Although Rogers "successfully" attacked one of their villages, he and his men were chased by the French and Abenaki into a nightmarish retreat. Sick, weak, and starving, the Rangers eventually resorted to roasting their own shoes and powder horns for food. Some even turned to cannibalism, eating their own fallen compatriots. Many Rangers were lost on the return from the mission. Amherst's vengeance cost his men dearly and earned him virtually nothing.

being allowed to take their regimental flags. The British wanted to twist the knife and take their flags as trophies. The French burned them, preferring to turn their flags to ashes rather than see them in the hands of the gloating British army.

A week after Montreal surrendered, Robert Rogers, now a major, captured Fort Detroit for the British. With that, the French and Indian War was essentially over. However, the problems for the British were just beginning.

Conclusion

The British may have won North America, but the question was could they rule it?

The American colonists, who had willingly sacrificed men and money to the war, were disenchanted with British Parliament on the other side of the ocean. They believed that their efforts during the war should give them certain rights, specifically the right to be free from taxation by the Crown and to levy their own taxes through their own representatives.

Britain's wars were costly. By the end of the Seven Years' War, its national debt had doubled. It tried to recoup some of its money through what the colonists viewed as oppressive taxation. Since their bitterness had been brewing against their mother country for some time, the tax issue began to push them over the edge. It would spiral into a problem that the British would not be able to contain.

With the Seven Years' War still raging for another three years, Britain needed to send its soldiers from North America to the French-controlled West Indies, as well as Europe, West Africa, and Asia, to fight their war on new ground. In Austria, they would fight for control of northern Europe; in Africa, they would fight over control of the slave trade; and in India, they would fight for a stake in Asia. They fought because a historical empire was on the line, the likes of which had not been seen since Rome ruled the Western world.

In French Canada, British influence took a firm hold over the next century. It made the loss for French Canadians more than just losing their land and forts; they viewed it as a tragic loss of their culture as well. This caused some over the centuries to consider the day Quebec fell as the day "true" Canadian history ended. A few decades later, in "revenge" for Montcalm's death, the French would reemerge as important players in the new American history that began to unfold.

In North America, Amherst's contempt for the native people continued to grow, and it became more than just insulting words. He shunned any overtures of friendship and insulted the natives by refusing to stick with the long-standing customs that their people had shared. He would no longer give them weapons, ammunition, liquor, or any other gifts in an effort to retain peace.

William Johnson, who was serving as a liaison to the First Nations, was alarmed by Amherst's callousness toward their former allies. He knew that if relationships broke down, war would be inevitable—and it would be a war the British could ill-afford to wage. It was not just France that had suffered from the war; Britain had also faced severe financial losses, and there would be far worse long-term consequences to come.

As Amherst began to change the relationship with the native people, from one of powerful allies to that of subjects, the tribes began to balk at the attempts to subjugate them, as well as the further encroachment on their land. Almost as soon as they had made the treaty agreeing to not build west of the Allegheny Mountains, the British broke their promise. The tribes could see where things were headed, and they were very wary of the British, especially after having lost their French allies.

Johnson warned Amherst that continuing on this course would lead to war, but Amherst ignored his concerns. Convinced that the Native Americans were dangerous savages, Amherst knew the British must show their superior power and keep them in subjugation. By 1763, the situation had deteriorated.

In February 1763, the British signed the treaties of Paris and Hubertusburg, ending the Seven Years' War. However, peace in North America continued to elude them. That same year, Ottawa Chief Pontiac gathered a council of tribes to talk about the growing

British threat. He told them he had a divine vision where the Creator spoke to him and told him that the land was created for the native people and no one else. Pontiac then called his people to take action to preserve their rights. He further motivated them by saying that his divine vision instructed him to go to war with the British and drive them from their lands. The tribal chiefs agreed to ally to start a war against the British. Tribes that had previously fought each other for many years now agreed to come together for this common cause.

For the British, a new war began while a colonial revolution loomed on the horizon.

Part 3: The Klondike Gold Rush

A Captivating Guide to the Major Migration of Gold Miners to Yukon and Its Impact on the History of Canada and the United States of America

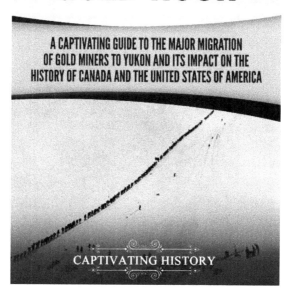

Introduction

In the late 1890s, a phenomenon occurred in the Canadian Yukon that still captures the imagination: the Klondike Gold Rush (sometimes spelled "Klondyke," though both are a mispronunciation of the First Nations word "Thron-duik"). At a time when the American frontier was beginning to close, an intense and long-lasting economic depression hit the United States and Canada. So, the prospect of quick, immense riches sparked one of the most intense and rapid movements of people in North American history. (As a note, we're going to be using the terms "Klondike" and "Yukon" interchangeably throughout this book— the Klondike is a river in the Yukon Territory of far western Canada where most of the gold during the Klondike Stampede was found.)

Though the Klondike Stampede, as it is often called, especially in Canada, lasted just under two years at its height, it captured the imagination of generations of young men and quite a surprising number of women in the last years of the 19th century. Even after the frenzy had subsided, the stories and images of this amazing period in history lived on, most famously in the stories of Jack London, the young American who went north to seek both fortune and fame in gold but also with his pen.

For a time, during Hollywood's Golden Age, movies about Canada's Northwest Mounted Police (more popularly known as the Mounties) brought in millions. Some of these movies costarred a comedic sidekick, usually a miner or tramp, and oftentimes a rowdy American who helped the Mounties due to his seemingly American trait of "bending the rules," which the Mounties were certainly *not* going to do (at least not at the beginning of the film!). In a number of movies, the bad guy was a bully who wanted to horn in on other people's gold claims.

Of course, the Stampede was caused by "gold fever." People in both the US and Canada literally lost their heads (and everything else they owned) for a chance at instant and untold riches. As you can imagine, most people that went to the Klondike came back empty-handed, some of them physically wrecked for life by what they experienced in the Great White North. A small few did become incredibly wealthy—at least for a time. Many of those who did find large quantities of gold spent it in the hotels, gambling halls, and brothels that were erected in nearby towns. Some used their gold to "stake out" a life for themselves and their families, most of the time far from where they had what most would have called "the greatest adventure of their lives."

Chapter 1 – Yukon Ho!

In the 1980s, the comic strip was Calvin and Hobbes" and even they got caught up in "Klondike Fever"—at least until their peanut butter and jelly ran out! It may seem a bit silly to add a bit about a comic strip from the 1980s, but Bill Watterson's amazing comic strip not only captured the limitless imagination of a young boy but also included a fictional Stampede so Calvin could leave behind the rules and regulations of his parents and society. Of course, Calvin and Hobbes went home after a couple of hours in the "Yukon" and got hugs and hot chocolate after their adventure. The miners and others in search of fortune spent months of misery dragging, carrying, pushing, rafting, and sledding their way through hundreds of miles of the roughest terrain in North America. Untold numbers of horses and dogs paid the price, along with quite a few men. No hot chocolate was waiting in the Klondike.

So, how did the Klondike Stampede begin? In 1896, an American prospector named George Carmack, who had found sizable coal deposits in the Yukon prior to the gold rush, was traveling south through the Klondike River area of the Yukon along with his wife and her relatives. Carmack had been on his own since the death of his mother at age eight and his father at eleven. In his late teens, he joined the United States Marine Corps and served at sea aboard a US Navy ship on the West Coast and off Alaska's coast. In 1882, he deserted after the Marines denied him permission to visit his sick sister. He wandered through California, and in 1885, he was in Alaska making his living by trapping, fishing, and occasionally trading furs and fish. In 1887, he and Shaaw Tláa (most commonly known by her English name Kate Carmack), a woman of the Tagish First Nation. The Tagish and their larger group of cousins, the Tlingit, were the most numerous but not the only First Nations living in the Klondike area.

George, Kate, her brother, and her nephew were fishing near the mouth of the Klondike River. At some point, a local prospector suggested that while the Carmacks and family were in the area, they might as well pan for gold since reports had come in recently of small finds in the general area. (Gold and silver were not unknown in the area, but no one knew about the colossal amounts of gold in the ground near the Klondike River.) That idea appealed to the adventurous George Carmack and his brother-in-law, famously known as Skookum Jim, although his Tagish name was Keish. His English name was James or Jim Mason. "Skookum" is a local Chinook First Nations word meaning strong, brave, great, or powerful, depending on the context. Skookum Jim met all those requirements.

For many years, people outside the Klondike area credited George Carmack with the initial find that began the Stampede, but in reality, it was most likely Skookum Jim who found the first gold in Rabbit Creek, a southern tributary of the Klondike River (today, it is known as Bonanza Creek). It seems to have been agreed by the group that it would be best if the white George Carmack established and legalized the claim with the Canadian government, as it was believed that a white man's claim would be recognized and protected by the government as legitimate rather than that of a First Nations man.

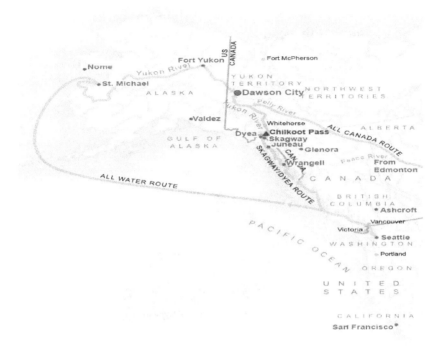

Yukon Ho! The two most popular trails were via Skagway and Dyea, Alaska.
https://en.wikipedia.org/wiki/File:Klondike_Routes_Map2.png

Though most historians believe that Skookum Jim was the one to originally find gold, it came to pass that in filing the claims, Carmack registered four with the authorities downriver while the others continued to work. Later in his life, Carmack divorced his common-law wife Kate (Shaaw Tláa) and essentially sent her packing home to the Yukon from California, where they had moved after the rush was over. They had a daughter, Graphie Grace, who later stayed with Carmack in California, leaving Kate alone to make a living making crafts and equipment for miners that remained in the region.

That being the case, it could be said that Carmack was a man who would take more than he was entitled to. Of the four claims he filed, two were for him: one as a normal share and the other for discovering the gold. (This was allowed by Canadian law. No other man was allowed to file two claims at the time unless he had the original claim.) There did not seem to have been any strife between the four at the time. George was even derided by other white miners and trappers in the area for being too friendly with the natives; he was called "Squaw Man" behind his back. So, perhaps Carmack did find the gold first, though most doubt it. At any rate, George got his two claims, Skookum Jim got one, and Jim's and Kate's nephew, Káa Goox, received the last.

Keish or Skookum Jim.
https://en.wikipedia.org/wiki/File:Skookum_Jim_Mason.png

George Carmack
https://en.wikipedia.org/wiki/File:George_W_Carmack,_one_of_the_discoverers_of_gold_in_the_Klondike_(CURTIS_1187).jpeg

Kate or Shaaw Tláa.
https://en.wikipedia.org/wiki/File:Shaaw_Tl%C3%A1a.jpg

Káa Goox, also known as Tagish or Dawson Charlie. Dawson City was the biggest boom town to rise up during the Klondike Gold Rush.
https://en.wikipedia.org/wiki/File:Dawson_Charlie_aka_K%CC%B2%C3%A1a_Goox%C
C%B1_-_01.jpg

There are two seminal works on the Klondike Stampede, both written by Canadians: Pierre Berton's secondhand account written a few years after the gold rush, *The Life and Death of the Last*

Great Gold Rush, and adventure writer/journalist Tappan Adney's *The Klondike Stampede,* a truly gripping firsthand account of the second wave of miners "going Klondike," which was a popular phrase describing someone heading out to find their fortune in the frozen north. These two books are the primary sources of information used for this short introductory book, and I highly recommend them for further reading. In Berton's book, he gives a great account of the moments leading to the discovery.

Before George Carmack dipped his pan in the water for the first time, he recited a verse from *Hamlet*: "To be or not to be." Tagish Charlie replied, calling the verse the Tagish/Chinook First Nations pidgin (broken, simple English mixed with native expressions) word for magic.

"'Wa for you talket dat cultus wa wa?' Tagish Charley asked him. 'I no see um gold.' 'That's all right, Charley,' Carmack told him. 'I makum Boston man's medicine.' He raised the pan with its residue of black sand. 'Spit in it, boys, for good luck.' ... At that instant, they were standing, all unknowing, on the richest ground in the world ... The south fork of the creek was as yet unnamed, but there could be only one name for it: Eldorado ... Who found the nugget that started it all? Again, the record is blurred. Years afterward Carmack insisted it was he who happened upon the protruding rim of bedrock from which he pulled a thumb-sized chunk of gold. But Skookum Jim and Tagish Charlie always claimed that Carmack was stretched out asleep under a birch tree when Jim, having shot a moose, was cleaning a dishpan in the creek and made the find. At any rate, the gold was there, lying thick between the flaky slabs of rock like cheese in a sandwich."

No matter who found the nugget, it was George who staked the initial claim, and he carved it on a nearby tree: "'TO WHOM IT MAY CONCERN I do, this day, locate and claim, by right of discovery, five hundred feet, running upstream from this notice, Located this 17th day of August, 1896. G. W. Carmack'"

The unwritten rule of gold prospecting was that no one kept a find to themselves. Carmack knew that prospectors were going to flood the area when they were told of the find, especially since it was a rich one. Strangely enough, though, Carmack and his party had been told of good prospects at Rabbit Creek by another old prospector named Robert Henderson. Henderson did not like First Nations people. While talking to George Carmack, he insulted Skookum Jim, Kate, and Tagish Charlie a number of times. Although what he said were not "fightin' words," the conversation left a bad taste in everyone's mouth. Later, Carmack would "pay" Henderson back, as he did not tell him of the find. Carmack met two desperate miners from Nova Scotia and told them of his claim and how to find the area. Remember, a man could not simply walk down the creek claiming the whole thing. There were two claims for the finder and one claim for others. Later, men would pool their claims and shares of the gold, but that was after tens of thousands of men and hundreds of women had come north.

The Klondike Stampede started when George Carmack went into town to get his claim registered. He was not a drinking man, but this situation made him a bit thirsty and anxious. He went into a saloon in the town of Forty Mile, about fifty miles upriver from Dawson City, and bought two glasses of whiskey for himself. Then he turned around and told the crowded room of the find. He was met with silence. George Carmack had a reputation for being a teller of tall tales. But then, he took out his four-ounce vial of gold (the first find panned out of the stream) and laid it on the bar. The men thought it was a scheme by one of the big upriver traders to get them to move north. "Is that some Miller Creek gold that Ladue [one of the traders] gave you?" one of the men asked.

Despite the skepticism, more and more people drifted into the saloon when they heard of Carmack's tale. One experienced Yukon miner took a careful look at the gold. Some men were so good at what they did that they could tell the general area in which the gold was found by the color, sheen, and shape. Gold could come in flakes, nuggets, and even strings that looked like small tree branches dipped in the precious metal. This miner pronounced that the gold came from somewhere he had never been and that it certainly wasn't Ladue or any other trader.

It was then that the whispering started. Slowly, men drifted off. Some went to the local surveyor and asked if it was possible. His answer? "The gold must've come from somewhere." On the night of August 16th, 1896, the Klondike Gold Rush began. All during the night, experienced miners and others drifted out of town to the river's edge and began to head toward Rabbit Creek. It wasn't a "stampede" yet, but that was coming.

What's left of Forty-Mile today; the town cleared out almost immediately, though it was used as a supply point for what was to come.

Chapter 2 – The Stampede

Eleven months after Carmack had announced his party's find, a number of very happy miners made their way back to San Francisco and Seattle. On July 15th, 1897, the steamer *Excelsior* docked in San Francisco (a town very familiar with gold rushes), and the steamer *Portland* docked in Washington State. Reporters put the value of the many sacks of gold coming from the ships at over a million dollars. At today's current gold prices, that would make it closer to one *billion* dollars, and at today's dollar value, given inflation, it would be thirty million. Estimates of the total amount of gold brought out of the Klondike by 1900 (though the "rush" effectively ended in 1898) range from fifty to one hundred million dollars. However, that was back in 1900. In 2022, that amount would be roughly worth an astounding two *billion* dollars.

That kind of money would make almost any person catch "gold fever," and in 1897, Americans and Canadians were desperate for good economic news, though quite a large number of British, Irish, Australians, and others made their way to the Great White North to seek a better life or at least adventure.

In 1897, the industrializing world was in a deep depression. The depression of the 1890s was the worst in memory, and only the Great Depression, which took place during the 1930s, was worse. The depression began with the failure of the Philadelphia and Reading Railroad in 1893, which caused businesses to suffer in the northeastern United States. This had a domino effect and was shortly followed by a stock market crash in May 1893. Foreign investors left the US and took their gold-based currency with them, which nearly wiped out the banking system. By the end of the next year, 12 to 15 percent of the US workforce was unemployed, many others were underemployed, and there was no real social safety net to speak of other than family, churches, and perhaps the donations of the incredibly wealthy "robber barons" of the time. Men, women, and children went hungry. Crime rose, health worsened, and despair set in.

Making things worse was an 1890 report from the Census Department. It said the frontier, the place where Americans had gone for more than two hundred years in search of a better and freer life (at the expense of the Native Americans living there, without a doubt), was gone. There was still land, but it was not going to be free. With the admission of Arizona and New Mexico as states in 1912, the continental United States was, for all intents and purposes, completely defined and mapped out.

The depression of the 1890s hit Canada hard as well, though its "frontier" was still open in many ways. However, the lands that were "leftovers" were in the far northwest: Alaska and the Yukon. In normal times, those remote and forbidding lands attracted adventurers, fugitives, and those desperate enough to risk the dangers of living near the Arctic Circle. For many, the dream of living in Alaska, which had been purchased from Russia in 1867 and which only became a state in 1950, was just that, a dream, maybe imagined in a moment of desperation in a saloon or in a crowded tenement full of screaming children and other families. The notion was often not taken seriously.

For many in 1897, though, the desperation had gotten bad enough for people to give the journey a try, especially if the newspapers and rumors were true. By those exaggerated accounts, gold was simply waiting on the ground to be picked up. The rush was on.

The headline that started the Klondike Gold Rush in the US.

https://en.wikipedia.org/wiki/File:Seattle_Post_Intelligencer_newspaper_front_page_for_J uly_17_1897_announcing_the_arrival_of_the_steamer_PORTLAND_in_Seattle_from_t he_Klondike_gold_fields.png

People from all over Canada and the US made the decision to "go Klondike," and with every new headline, adventure story, or tale of "big spenders" in the Yukon, additional hundreds, then thousands, of people followed.

There was a huge problem with this—well, actually, there were hundreds of problems, but the biggest one was *inexperience*. Since papers mixed the true with the false, many prospective prospectors thought they could simply load up a pack (or worse, a suitcase) and head off to the Yukon.

That was not the case, and the Canadian government was quick to let everyone know that anyone coming into Canada with less than a year's supply of food, clothes, and other necessities would be turned back at the border. That meant the people heading there needed to spend money—and not just a small sum. It also meant that goods could only be gotten in Alaska if they had been purchased and shipped beforehand, but with each passing day of the Stampede, goods got more expensive. "What the market will bear" was the economic theory of the day, and those who came to Alaska unprepared had to team up with others or seek a generous creditor. There were some, but they were few and far between. Many prospectors took jobs in the new boom towns of Skagway and Dyea, Alaska, and in Dawson City, Canada, hoping to earn enough to get equipment to get to the Klondike, a journey that was hundreds of miles through unbelievably beautiful and deadly wilderness.

The Canadian government did not want the death of countless prospectors on their hands, nor did they want their territory filled with "bummers" (an old US Civil War term for scroungers who lived off the land). It also did not want to bail out miners who were in distress because of their own unpreparedness, which happened countless times anyway.

In Tappan Adney's *The Klondike Stampede*, he lays out the typical load of one year's supply (per man) that was taken into the Yukon wilderness. Some of the items that were taken include flour, bacon, split peas, beans, evaporated apples and peaches, butter, salt, rolled oats, and rice, just to name a few. They also brought along pack straps, nails, saws, frying pans, and other essential items. A few of the items were shared among men in a party (going it alone was nigh impossible), so only one was taken.

As far as clothing went, Adney, who was better prepared than most, took the following: "Rubber hip-boots and an oil-skin coat are necessary. For the long, cold winter, misapprehension exists.

Those best qualified to express an opinion say that there is nothing better than a deer-skin coat with hood—an Eskimo garment, called a parka. Then, one should have a fur robe; one good robe is better than any number of blankets, and should be 7x8 feet. In the order of preference, arctic hare is first. Next is white rabbit, the skins being cut into strips, then plaited and sewed together. One needs nothing else in the coldest weather, although one can thrust one's fingers through it. Both rabbit and hare robes are scarce and last only a year. Lynx, fox, wolf, marmot, make good robes; bear is almost too heavy for traveling. I was fortunate indeed to pick up even a marmot-skin robe, eight feet long and five wide, lined with a blanket, Indian-made, from somewhere up the coast."

Put together, the supplies were about one thousand pounds—per man!

So, how did they do it? They did it in stages. In 2003, a reality show called *Klondike: Quest for Gold* aired in Canada. The show revolved around three Canadians and one American. They were all "average" people who wanted to test themselves, trace the footsteps of an ancestor, or find gold. There were also three Tlingit First Nations men who acted as porters for part of the route (one was a great-grandson of Skookum Jim). Like their kinsmen had in the 1890s, they carried three thousand pounds of supplies. In the end, this proved not enough; by the time they arrived in the Klondike, they were virtually out of food.

The first leg of the journey was roughly 450 miles. Though the trail was, for the most part, clearly marked, it was and still is absolutely backbreaking. It was also hell on their feet, shoulders, and backs, especially since the participants were outfitted with gear, food, and clothing from 1898. They wore hard leather and wool, which are both uncomfortable and, especially in the case of wool, heavy.

Wrap your head around this: for every ten miles of progress they (and the miners of the 1890s, at least those who pressed on) made, they actually walked two hundred miles. Why? Because each time, they had to retrace their steps to their last camp, load up, and go to the next staging point. They did this over and over again due to all the equipment they had to carry. Thus, 450 miles became 9,000 miles! It is no wonder that out of the approximately

100,000 men who set out for the Yukon, only about 25,000 to 30,000 made it. All the rest turned back at some point, dejected, worn out, diseased, and maybe even crippled for life. Some would quit and make a surer living in one of the towns that had sprung up along the route. Some of those who did this, especially the women who attempted the journey, ended up richer than the vast majority of men who sought gold in the streams of the Yukon, most of whom came back empty-handed. Many never came back at all; all along the trail, one can still see the occasional grave marker of an unfortunate Stampeder who didn't make it.

Two quotes, one from an unknown prospector who threw down his pack and headed back (probably one of many who uttered the same words) and one from Tappan Adney, describe the perils of the various trails leading to the Klondike. The prospector said, "Money ain't worth THIS!" Adney includes a short conversation in which someone asks, "Do you think I can make it?" An experienced prospector responds, "That depends on *what you are.*" Some called the Yukon the "Great Alone," and an inexperienced man or party could find themselves not only lost and in great peril but also on the verge of insanity, especially those from the great cities of the United States and eastern Canada.

That was all to come. First, they had to get to Alaska and decide what route to take into Canada. For most, to get there meant great expense. Not every man who dreamed of "going Klondike" could simply pack up and leave. Most had careers or jobs and families who relied on them. If they were unemployed or poor, they might not be able to even afford a ticket on a tramp steamer from Seattle or San Francisco, not to mention all of the equipment and its storage aboard the ship or have supplies waiting for them near the border. Lucky dreamers might have a relative or friends that might lend them the money in return for a percentage of the gold that most were *sure* they were going to find.

Seattle and San Francisco were the main departure points for ships leaving for Alaska, though many left from Portland, Vancouver, and Tacoma. Many of the men and women had never been at sea, and even in spring and summer, the North Pacific is not calm. Many spent the ten-day journey wretchedly sea-sick.

By far the most popular and easiest ways to head to the Klondike were through Skagway and Dyea, Alaska. The "Rich Man's Route," which was obviously longer and somehow "easier," according to contemporary texts, was limited to those who had both money and time. Amazingly enough, there were scores of men who did not need gold or were not actively looking for it; they were simply going to the Yukon for the adventure.

The existing literature, including the fiction of the great American writer Jack London, overwhelmingly reports and tells tales of the routes from the two Alaskan towns mentioned above. However, a great many Canadians journeyed to Calgary by rail, then either walked, rode, or took the few railways that went close to the Klondike, which was not particularly close. The railway running through the region today was not started until the Stampede was well over with.

The two main routes were the Chilkoot Trail and White Pass Trail. Of the two, the Chilkoot is the more famous, or rather infamous. The White Pass Trail had the reputation of being the "easier" trail, but the over three thousand horses, mules, and dogs that died on the "Dead Horse Trail" would likely have disagreed. Some horses literally launched themselves off the cliffs rather than go on suffering malnutrition, whipping, pain from worn or poorly shod hooves, spavin (the swelling of the horses' hocks, the joint just above the hoof), and much else.

Many prospectors brought horses with them if they could afford them. Many of those who brought their own animals assured their horses were in good health before starting out, but weeks or months on the trail destroyed most of the animals. Those that survived the trip were sometimes sold to miners returning to Alaska or Dawson City, Canada, with the trip back home killing them. Though many prospectors treated their horses well, many men who came to the Yukon had either no experience with horses or simply did not care about them. There were many occasions when horses suffered because a pack was poorly made and loaded by an inexperienced newcomer who was more concerned about making it to the goldfields than caring about the condition of their horses or mules.

There were instances of men taking horses from those who treated them poorly, often leaving some money behind so as not to be labeled a "horse thief," but these men were few and far between. Energy spent wrangling horses from those who mistreated them took away energy needed for the trail. The writings of Tappan Adney and Pierre Berton are full of compassion for the poor animals that died or were essentially tortured along the way.

Along White Pass or "Dead Horse" Trail, 1898. Even today, bleached horse bones are visible along the trail.
https://en.wikipedia.org/wiki/File:Whitepass-dead-horses.jpg

Before the prospective millionaires even made it to the trail heads leading to the Yukon, they had to make the journey by sea. Aboard the steamships, a loose "government" often formed. Tappan Adney gave an account of the three-men committee on his ship and an account of their responsibilities. These were the actual minutes of the first meeting of the committee on the boat:

"Upon arriving at Skagway a representative of the committee will go ashore and select a suitable place on the beach for landing and distributing the goods. This will be enclosed by ropes, and the enclosure will be policed by a committee of fifteen, armed with rifles, and doing police duty in shifts of eight hours each. No goods can be removed from the enclosure except upon a written order of the committee. On board ship, Messrs. S. A. Hall and J. Robinson will check the goods as unloaded and sent ashore, and on shore the goods received will be checked by Messrs. D. Orsonnens and

N. B. Forrest. Fifty volunteers will receive goods as landed, and, in conjunction with the subcommittee, distribute and arrange the same. Messrs. William Fuller and Duncan MacDonald will police the boat until freight and baggage are discharged." (As a note, the N. B Forrest on the committee was not the famous Confederate general; he had died in 1877.)

Adney went on to describe further actions taken by those on the ship, including an informal police force, which consisted of the biggest and toughest men on the ship. He also wrote of the men's constant wondering and worrying about what lay before them.

Once the ship arrived at Skagway, the passengers, their horses, and equipment had to be unloaded, which perhaps gave some of the miners-to-be a bit of an awakening. Horses were lowered over the side by a winch and strap mechanism and set loose in the water. They automatically swam to shore, where they had to be wrangled by their owners. Tappan Adney and the few other experienced outdoorsmen got a firsthand view of the ineptitude of most of their compatriots/competitors. Many flailed about, losing their horses and heads for a time. Some stood about wondering what to do next, which was to recover their one thousand pounds of equipment from narrow docks. It was a long wait for many.

Tappan Adney on the White Pass Trail, 1897.
https://en.wikipedia.org/wiki/File:Edwin_Tappan_Adney.jpg

Adney's ship carried 160 men and 100 horses, and he arrived in late summer of 1897. The next year, dozens upon dozens of more ships would arrive. Skagway grew in a fast but chaotic way to accommodate ships, men, and horses.

Though most men knew the distance to the Yukon goldfields was immense from maps and conversations aboard the ships, they were prepared for neither the ruggedness of the trails nor the weather. Though Tappan Adney arrived at Skagway in August, it began to snow in early October, and the temperature fell to -6°F during the first week of the month on one occasion. For most of October, it was warmer, although it was still below freezing.

The only way for someone to make it to the goldfields was to team up with another person. Parties of four or six were the general rule. The trek up the trails was slow, and larger groups of men found themselves in relatively close proximity. Luckily, the camaraderie of the long journey and a common goal helped most get by or at least get started, though as time, distance, and hardship wore the men down, the camaraderie petered out the closer one came to his/her goal. However, given the era and the rough justice meted out along the trail, the kindness and sharing of knowledge among the miners are truly remarkable.

Right from the start, Adney, other experienced men, and men with cooler heads and open minds could see that many of the men onshore were either going to have a very rough time of it or would not make it at all. The Yukon was not a playground. Many men simply loaded up their kit the best they could and set off, which was a big mistake.

Loading the horses and the occasional mule with a pack and harness was a task in and of itself. At least one man at Skagway and another on the trail had brought two huge oxen with them. A good healthy horse could carry anywhere between 200 to 250 pounds. In a pinch and for a short time, it could carry three hundred, but that would simply wear the horse out if done regularly, even under ideal conditions. An ox could take three hundred to four hundred pounds either on its back or dragging a sled, but the conditions on the trail were better suited to animals and men nimbler on their feet.

Even two hundred pounds could eventually overcome a horse that was not cared for properly, especially if the harness and load on its back were not balanced and tied properly. For Adney and other experienced men, the sight of many city slickers and others inexperienced with horses and the outdoors in general was a laughable and pitiable sight. They watched as novice men attempted to tie the most effective knot for fastening a load to a horse, the diamond hitch, which was a complicated affair. Those who took their time to learn the knot and many other things from those in Skagway and elsewhere generally fared well, at least for a time, although luck certainly played a role. There were likely many know-it-alls who either listened once or tried the knot and other effort- and time-saving tips one time and figured they would be "good enough" or that they would learn "on the way." Those men and their poor horses had a very rough time of it, and most of them gave up. However, many died or were injured, some for life, due to their arrogance.

It should be remembered that all of this effort had to be repeated every single day for literally hundreds of miles (thousands taking the return stages into account). The schedule went something like this. One would wake up, get a fire going (or keep it going from the night before), make coffee and breakfast, and then clean pans and plates. After this, you would break down and get your pack ready. Feed and water the horses, and inspect them for sores (many did not do this or did not know to do it). Next, you would stage the camp, which means you would put the items in the order they needed to be moved to the next staging point. It depended on the distance, but two or three trips were usually made. Camps were often stayed in for two nights under perfect weather and health conditions.

All of that took about three minutes to write out, but in reality, the steps would likely take *hours*. They would do all of that in the morning, and in the evening, the horses had to be unloaded and cared for. The men had to eat and set up camp. The journey was absolutely backbreaking, monotonous, and miserable, especially considering the swarms of mosquitoes that occasionally descended on the men in warm weather. There were also black and grizzly bears to contend with, though a smart bear kept its distance from the crowds of men invading its territory.

Some men had experience hunting, but that took time, effort, and energy. Most of the time, hunting simply was not worth it unless they stayed at a base camp for more than a couple of days, which sometimes happened when the weather was bad. However, bad weather in Alaska and the Yukon usually meant that it was safer to remain as warm as possible in the tent or stay near the fire. Fishing was done, especially after the men climbed the passes over the mountains, where alpine lakes and very swiftly flowing rivers would carry the mining parties hundreds of miles. Most of the time, however, fishing was too time- and energy-consuming. After all, the key was *speed*.

The most famous of all of the thousands of pictures taken of the Klondike Gold Rush is the one showing people climbing the Chilkoot Pass, which, even in June, could be mostly covered in snow. Those who did not plan well and arrived in the spring or late summer could count on snow, though, in a way, the snow could be a blessing. The thickness of it covered the incredibly tough boulder-strewn "trail."

Robert Service, who is considered the "Poet of the Yukon," penned the following about the trail to the pass:

"We landed in wind-swept Skagway.

We joined the weltering mass,

Clamoring over their outfits,

waiting to climb the pass.

We tightened our girths and our pack-straps;

we linked on the Human Chain,

Struggling up to the summit,

where every step was a pain."

--"The Trail of 'Ninety-Eight" by Robert Service

Before they could make the climb over the pass, the miners had to wait, sometimes for days, for either the weather to clear or for the parties in front of them to go over the top. At times, this meant waiting on the steep mountainside in snow many feet deep. This often led to frostbite because of the lack of mobility and, of course, broken ankles and legs, which could be life-threatening but would definitely end one's search for the motherlode in the Klondike.

The Chilkoot Pass was daunting at nearly four thousand feet, but if the Stampeders made it over the top, their journey became *somewhat* easier. They had to carry their "outfits" (their equipment, in the parlance of the time) a relatively small distance to Long Lake, then to Lake Lindemann, and then to Lake Bennett before they would reach the Yukon River. From there, they would be able to sail or paddle the rest of the way to Dawson City and the goldfields. To many of the men and women who went over either Chilkoot or White Pass (they were approximately parallel to each other but miles away), it felt as if they were "almost there." However, they had only gotten a third of the way to their goal. They still had approximately 375 miles to go. That is if they passed through Canadian customs with their paperwork to be in the country and paid their duties on goods being brought into the country from Alaska. By all accounts, most of the Canadian officials were fair and occasionally gave the Stampeders the benefit of the doubt by not checking their outfits too thoroughly.

Tappan Adney described what he saw when he visited the Chilkoot Trail. "The men take up the packs, and this is what happens: They walk to the base of the cliff, with a stout alpenstock in hand. They start to climb a narrow foot-trail that goes up, up, up. The rock and earth are gray. The packers and packs have disappeared. There is nothing but the gray wall of rock and earth. But stop! Look more closely. The eye catches movement. The mountain is alive. There is a continuous moving train; they are perceptible only by their movement, just as ants are. The moving train is zigzagging across the towering face of the precipice, up, up, into the sky, even at the very top. See! They are going against the sky! They are human beings, but never did men look so small."

It should be remembered that the miners making their way to the Klondike were, for the most part, not alone on their trek. Many, if not most, of the parties hired First Nations packers to assist them. As the Stampede grew, more and more of the Tagish, Tlingit, Chinook, and other packers grew richer and richer. The experienced outdoorsmen could carry nearly two hundred pounds on their backs by using special slings and rigs of their own making. Packers also knew the dangers of the trail and the ever-changing weather. At the beginning of Tappan Adney's journey, he negotiated a price of fourteen cents a pound for the native packers he hired, which was a good price. However, it was very common for the First Nations people to renegotiate their fees along the way, which was good for them but bad for the miners. Mostly, the packers would give their current employer a chance to pay the new price, but if he or his party hesitated, the First Nations men would leave to find another mining party that would offer a better price. Sometimes, they just dropped their gear and walked off. Ultimately, this might depend on not only the price they offered but also the treatment and respect given to the men. By all accounts, Tappan Adney was respected, not only for his skills as an outdoorsman but also for his respect for the First Nations, though his writing does indicate some of the general bias and prejudice of the time.

Chapter 3 – Lakes, Rivers, and Rapids

Dyea and Skagway trails

Chilkoot and White Pass Trails to Lake Bennett, where they merged. From there, much of the journey was by boat. The railroad, as you read, was not built until after the gold rush was over.

In hindsight, the term "rush" to describe the hunt for gold in the Yukon might be a bit of a misnomer. Yes, over 100,000 people "rushed" to the north from New York, Toronto, Quebec, Chicago, and many other places, but once they got to Alaska and then Canada, things slowed to a crawl.

For us today, it's almost impossible to understand the monotony, not to mention the backbreaking labor, of the journey to the Yukon. There were no phones; any contact with the outside world came from the occasional telegraph message to a Mounted Police post or a town like Dawson City. Even then, it might take days or even weeks for news to reach the people on the trails. Newspapers were prized. In Pierre Berton's *The Klondike Fever*, he relates that one man who had lived in the Klondike for some time as a trapper had saved about fifty old newspapers from months and even years before the rush, which he loaned out to miners who were desperate for something to read.

The monotony was matched by the anticipation of finding gold. In some ways, the men of the Klondike Gold Rush were similar to men at war, except in reverse. In war, most men think the next man on the line will "get it," but not him. In the Klondike, many men believed they would surely find enough gold to come out of the adventure ahead of the game, while their neighbors would find nothing. Even the wisdom of experienced prospectors did not dissuade them—no one wants to believe they gave up everything they had for a *slim* chance at finding gold. Thus, they were willing to suffer the privations, hard work, and monotony of the trails.

Once they made it to Long Lake (on the Chilkoot Trail) or Lake Bennett (on White Pass Trail), most Stampeders chose to make boats by hand. The men often carried oakum, which the *American Heritage Dictionary* describes as "loose hemp or jute fiber, sometimes treated with tar, creosote, or asphalt, used chiefly for caulking seams in wooden ships and packing pipe joints." The men also had to carry pitch, which is essentially tar or sometimes pine resin. These items were used in the making of wooden ships and boats. They also carried nails, not just for odd jobs that might come up but to build the boats that would hopefully take them to their destination near the Klondike. At the southern ends of Long Lake or Summit Lake, large settlements went up, and trees by the hundreds (possibly thousands) came down.

Boat- on Bennett Lake during the Klondike Gold Rush.
https://en.wikipedia.org/wiki/File:Boat_on_the_Upper_Yukon.jpg

Tappan Adney, who had some experience building boats and canoes, was amazed at the good quality of some boats and the exceedingly poor quality of others. He also described the scene at the foot of the lake as extremely busy, with people and animals moving by the hundreds and the noise of sawing, yelling, swearing, neighing, and barking as being almost deafening at times. The Northwest Mounted Police estimated that close to three thousand boats were built to pass over the lakes on the Chilkoot Trail alone. Not everyone had to build their boats, though. A minority of men brought prefabricated vessels in an effort to save time or because they had no faith in their own boat-building abilities.

Tappan Adney went on to describe the boats he saw being made and launched, including his own, which he made with one of his four partners (a man named Al Brown from Stockton, California, who grew up on stories about the California Gold Rush of 1849, which was not far from his birthplace). The others brought up the rest of the gear.

The boats ended up being able to carry five to ten men each. Different men and crews made different types of boats, although not all of them were "seaworthy," for lack of a better word. They could weigh upward of two to three tons and could be thirty-five feet long. A variety of sails were used; sometimes, they only used one, but sometimes a boat would be festooned with sails.

Most of the parties sent two men with some woodworking knowledge ahead to begin building their boat. The work was intense. The men would have to cut down trees, float them downriver, and then either build or rent a saw pit to create their planks. Most of the trees used were spruce, which was soft and not very reliable. Experienced boat-builders like Tappan Adney and his partner would use harder wood, though this wood was tougher to work with.

Once the boat was constructed, the pitch and oakum brought all the way up the trails would be used to caulk the boat. When it came time to launch, virtually all the boats leaked, at least at first. If good wood was used, it swelled up and tightened the planks together. If not, well, the men nearby helping to launch the boats would get a good laugh if they sank. Those who could not build a sea-worthy vessel were asking for trouble. Few men lost their lives on the lakes, which could sometimes become very rough, but many boats got swamped and sunk, mainly due to poor and hasty workmanship. A boat might sink with an entire party's outfit. When that happened, their dream of "striking it rich" was likely over, though quite a few of those unfortunate men traded work for a place with a more successful party or found work on the trail, earning money for the trip back home.

Those who made it over the first lake had to use sleds or figure out a way to carry their boats, which weighed at least as much as their original outfits, as they needed them for the next lake and possibly another after that before they could make the long, relatively easy voyage on the Yukon River to their ultimate destination.

The trips on the lake, most of which were made in daylight, did give some respite to the men and women. They had hiked thousands of miles (again, considering the staging of goods and the repeat journeys required), but weather, rocks, and other factors made the journey even more difficult. Occasionally, they would stumble across the camps of First Nations people eager to "make a deal" for the prospectors' goods or, failing that, steal them either openly or covertly. Adney describes being overwhelmed by First Nations children while attempting to trade with an elder, only to find that some of his goods had been pilfered. Though he was wary of stopping at another First Nations camp, he did not hold the children's actions against them, citing the treatment the tribes had received by many white men since the opening of the Canadian West.

Once the prospectors made it across the lakes, they were confronted with the Yukon, the Klondike, and the smaller rivers leading into them. The Yukon is just under two thousand miles long and flows southward into the Bering Sea in southwest Alaska. The river picks up more water and more force from the mountain streams and melting glaciers along its route. It is not easy to sail or paddle, as the river can change with the tides and the weather. Along the route, there are rapids to navigate. While some men drowned in their attempts to navigate the rapids, most made it through. However, this did not always mean that their outfits did. Boats were overturned or swamped, or the party's outfit was not lashed right. Those who were smart, like Tappan Adney and Al Brown, emptied their small vessels, carried their outfits to the end of the rapids, and then returned to their now empty boats and sped down the rapids.

On the cliffs lining one particularly dangerous set of rapids, prospectors gathered at the edge to see what they would be facing and to place bets and/or cheer for those who made it through. A writer captured Adney's voyage through these rapids, which were the roughest on the trail.

"As I came down the sandy hill-side to the lake, I saw at the landing two men unloading a trim-looking double-ender boat of distinct individuality that it needed only a glance to show was vastly superior to the ordinary Yukon type. One of the men was a slender six-footer, with a face wind-tanned the color of sole-leather. He wore weather-stained clothes that, judging from the general suggestion, no doubt still carried a little of the smoky smell and balsam aroma from camps in the green woods of New Brunswick ... Not only was his rig suggestive of the aborigine, but his every action proved him to be so thoroughly at home in his untamed environment that it is little wonder that at first glance I took him to be an Indian, and that it required several minutes after his jolly smile and voluble greeting to dispel the illusion ... Adney was an expert at river navigation; and his companion, though inexperienced in this kind of work, was a champion oarsman, cool-headed and gritty ... I ran across just in time to see the [Adney's] boat swept by with the speed of a bolt from a crossbow, leaping from wave-crest to wave-crest, and drenching its occupants with sheets of spray. Adney and Brown were standing erect in bow and stern, each wielding a single oar used as a paddle, and from their masterly course it was evident that they had their boat well under control. It was all over in a very small fraction of time. They had avoided by the narrowest margin jagged bowlders [sic] that it seemed impossible to pass, and in a slather of foam shot out into the smooth water below."

At the end of the trail was Dawson City. Most of the Stampeders launched themselves into the final leg of their journey from the city.

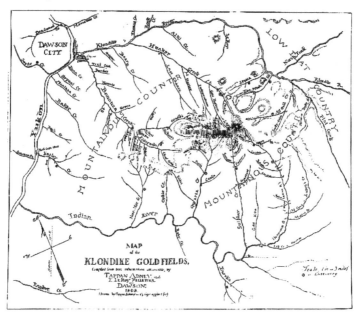

Tappan Adney's map of the goldfields and Dawson City.
https://commons.wikimedia.org/wiki/File:Map_of_Klondike_gold_fields,_1898_(AL%2B CA_785).jpg

Chapter 4 – "Eureka!"

The word "Eureka" comes from the Greek language. It means "I have found it!" The mathematician Archimedes was said to have exclaimed "Eureka!" when he found a method for discovering the purity of gold. The miners hoped to shout it from the top of their lungs when they made a gold strike. Then, they just might get drunk on hooch (or hootch), distilled whiskey that was popular among both First Nations and the men looking for their fortunes. This whiskey was called hoochinoo ("hooch" for short), so the next time you're out camping and ask one of your friends to "pass the hooch," raise your glass to the men of the Klondike who went on an adventure they'd never forget.

Most of them returned home, or to "civilization," disappointed. For many, that disappointment set in almost right away when they found that most of Bonanza Creek and its neighbor, Eldorado Creek (the site of even bigger strikes than those in the original area), had been claimed. There were two or three things that a miner might do: buy a claim, buy a portion of a claim, or venture off to the many other streams in the area, hoping he might find his own strike there.

As you can imagine, those men who were selling their claims were doing so because they had not struck gold—or at least *they* hadn't. These claims could be bought more cheaply. "Cheap" is a relative word, though; a claim near a strike, even a small one, could run someone five thousand dollars or more. One farther away would sell between 1,500 to 2,500 dollars. Some sold for much more, with the owners likely taking the newcomers (derisively called "cheechakos," meaning "tenderfoot") for suckers. If they were lucky, these cheechakos might ask for the help or advice of a kindly "sourdough," an "old-timer." The name "sourdough" came from the fermented flour that was used to make more filling and longer-lasting bread. A "sourdough" might be kind, but he also might lead the men on or help them for a share in any find. However, for the most part, the new miners were on their own.

Many who tried to find gold on their own soon tired of the frustration and signed on to work for successful strikes for an hourly wage, which could have been fifteen to twenty dollars an hour depending on the owner, the strike, and whether the rush was still on. For many men, twenty dollars an hour was more than they had ever dreamed of; today, that twenty dollars would be worth almost seven hundred dollars. Still, many miners preferred to be on their own or with their party, hoping to make thousands of times that.

Some men did find gold after they left their claim to be worked by others. For instance, Ulysses "Uly" Gaisford from Tacoma, Washington, tired of the hard labor and became a barber in Dawson City. Later in the year, miners working for him struck it rich. Uly began making fifty thousand dollars a year for years to come.

Others sold their claims, convinced they had found nothing, only to tragically discover they had not dug deep enough or didn't pan in the one spot on their claim that would have led them to the gold vein all men hoped to find. This was absolutely crushing, as Pierre Berton relates. "Trudged up Bonanza as far as Twenty Above, then shrugged his shoulders. 'I'll leave it to the Swedes,' he said, using the classic term of derision, for Scandinavians were alleged to work ground that no other man would touch. A companion drove his stakes into the neighboring Twenty-One [the number of the claim], then decided not to record. He wrote a wry comment on the stakes: 'This moose pasture reserved for Swedes and Cheechakos.' Along came Louis B. Rhodes of Fortymile, put his own name on the stakes, and wondered why he had bothered. For two bits, he told his friends, he'd cut it off again. Nobody had two bits, and so Rhodes stayed on and thanked his stars he had. By spring he was worth more than sixty thousand dollars and had staked all his cronies to mining properties."

These stories repeated themselves many times over in the Yukon.

How did men find gold? You read about George Carmack and Skookum Jim, who somewhat casually panned for gold and found four ounces by just straining the dirt from the streambed. They rotated their gold pans so that the dirt and water slowly spilled over the edge while the heavier gold (in dust or nuggets) remained in the pan.

Typical gold panning. This picture was taken in Colorado at the time of the Klondike Gold Rush
https://en.wikipedia.org/wiki/File:Postcard_of_unidentified_man_panning_for_gold_in_F air_Play,_Colorado_taken_in_the_early_1900s_-_DPLA_-_36c572e8b910b25a531ec110232def2e_(cropped).jpg

If one's claim ran downhill or over a small waterfall, then sluicing might be used. To do this, a long, slowly descending gutter-type box would be placed to allow the water to run through. At the bottom of the sluice box were wooden rods placed lengthwise next to each other to fill the width of the box. As the water ran through the box, gold would drop down in between the rods to be collected later. The key to sluicing, besides being lucky enough to have a good claim, was the box's elevation. It could not be so steep that gold dust would run out of it, but it had to be steep enough for most of the dirt to pass through yet hold the gold.

Sluice boxes leading from underground to rocker boxes, which help filter gold dust.
https://en.wikipedia.org/wiki/File:Klondike_mining,_c.1899.jpg

Another way to find gold was to dig by hand, usually downward into and along the banks of sunken streams. After about five feet, depending on the location and weather, one would hit the permafrost layer, which was hard as a rock year-round. The only way to get down into the permafrost to look for that hidden vein of riches was to construct a large fire or fires to melt the permafrost. Then, one would dig, light another fire, and so on. Some men dug to about a hundred feet or maybe a bit more, but this was time-consuming and backbreaking. Cave-ins were not much of an issue since the surrounding soil remained frozen.

The last way was dredging. Toward the end of the rush, corporations or groups of outsiders brought in equipment in an attempt to construct an efficient dredge, which simply chewed up the soil on a gigantic scale. To make the dredging operation cost-effective, a working claim or claims had to be bought, and a lot of money had to be invested. Some of those who had made a fortune in the Klondike invested in dredging machinery and employed perhaps a hundred men working around the clock.

The largest nugget ever found in the Klondike Gold Rush was an astounding seventy-seven-ounce nugget found in 1898, oddly enough in a place called Cheechako Hill. At the time, that nugget was worth 1,500 to 1,600 dollars, which is over 50,000 dollars today!

Most of the men who went to the Yukon never made it to the goldfields. Of the twenty-five thousand to thirty thousand who did, most went home with empty or near-empty pockets. So, who did "strike it rich?"

One of the most famous was Alex MacDonald, a Nova Scotian who had tried finding gold in Colorado before moving on to the Klondike. At its height, his find was making over five thousand dollars a day. He made millions and, for a time, was the biggest employer in the Klondike, but he gave much of his fortune away and spent the rest of it buying more and more claims, all of which were worthless. For many of them, he paid much more than they were worth. He died of a heart attack in his cabin in the Yukon. He was virtually penniless. His wife, however, made out like a bandit; she bought a life insurance policy on MacDonald at the height of the rush and became a rich woman upon his death.

Anton Stander was an Austrian who immigrated to New York in 1887 and moved west and then north to seek his fortune. In 1896, he went to the Yukon on a hunch and found the first huge claim with three friends, which they dubbed "Eldorado Creek." Within a year, he was one of the richest men in the Yukon. He built a hotel in New York City but continued to prospect for gold. Due to hard times, alcoholism, and a bad business sense, he died broke in 1952.

Probably the most successful of the Stampeders was Clarence Berry (or, as he was known to friends and family, CJ). CJ had gone broke as a California fruit farmer a few years before the Stampede but made his way to the Yukon in 1894 due to rumors of gold. After building a cabin deep in the woods, Berry began to prospect with little luck. He returned briefly to California, married his long-time girlfriend Ethel, and returned with her to the Yukon for their "honeymoon." She worked as a bartender in the mining camp at Forty Mile, south of Dawson City (both of which were, at the time, nothing more than mud, a few cabins, and tents). Forty Mile closed up for all intents and purposes when gold was found in the Klondike area. Berry was in the crowd at Dawson City when George Carmack announced his find. Berry and his brother Fred were among those who struck out for the Klondike that very evening. The pair arrived at Rabbit Creek a few days later and staked out their claims. Though there is much more to the story, for our purposes here, suffice it to say that Berry ended up with a half-claim on Bonanza Creek and another half on Eldorado Creek—the two richest areas of the rush—and became fabulously rich. Unlike many of those who did cry "Eureka!" Berry wisely saved and invested his money, eventually starting Berry Petroleum Company, which is still in existence today and traded on NASDAQ.

Hundreds of other men struck it rich to one extent or another. Some went home and lived a comfortable life. Many, however, were besotted by "gold fever" and believed they had luck on their side and could find more gold when they wanted or needed to. These men spent literally hundreds of thousands of dollars (millions in 2022) on bottles of champagne, the finest imported beef, diamond stickpins, and much more. At the height of the rush, the steamers carrying the Stampeders also carried luxury goods from all over the world via Seattle, San Francisco, and other major cities. Fifty thousand dollars was lost on a hand of poker or another popular card game called faro. Most of these men went home completely busted—a true "rags to riches to rags" story.

The Women

Many of the women who "went Klondike" went home the same way. Some, like the "Queen of the Klondike," Irish immigrant Belinda Mulrooney, made a fortune from the Stampede. Mulrooney brought whiskey and hot-water rubber bottles to the Yukon and built her fortune gradually, eventually building a deluxe hotel and buying stakes in over a dozen mines—all this by the age of twenty-seven.

Some women did mine, but they were generally looked down upon and not treated well by the other miners. Some bought a stake in the mining operations and did the cooking, cleaning, sewing, and other domestic duties for their parties and others for a share. Unfortunately, many of the women who went to the Yukon ended up as sex workers, either full-time or occasionally. These women were often exploited by the men there, who, despite "polite" accounts by Tappan Adney and Pierre Berton, were often abused in a land with no real law to speak of and plenty of whiskey. Violence, including gang rape, was common, and most women had no recourse in regard to justice. Unfortunately, this book is only an introduction to the Klondike Gold Rush and has to limit the details of this relatively newly studied and horrible aspect of the Stampede, but in the bibliography, you will find a great book by Brian Castner that includes much detail about the *real* lives of women in the Klondike.

Conclusion

The Klondike Gold Rush was essentially over by 1900, if not the year before. Most of the productive areas had seemingly been claimed. Dawson City became a sort of "Paris of the North," filled with luxury hotels, gambling halls, and much else. However, the city became filled with underemployed or unemployed men, which led to trouble. Most of the latecomers either filed north to search for gold in other areas or made their way back home. Some of the more successful miners, as well as many newcomers, had come not only for gold but also to get away from "civilization," the crowded, often disease-ridden cities of the United States and eastern Canada. They simply cashed out if they were wealthy and left to find another adventure. Many newcomers did the same, as they were often broke and could not return home or perhaps could not return home due to being wanted by the law or having to face angry wives and families.

Like today's media, the newspapers of the day soon got bored of the Klondike. The story had been told, and in 1898, a new story captured the minds and imaginations of Americans: the start of the Spanish-American War. Many miners went off to join the armed forces, but similar to their journey north, they arrived too late, as the war was over in less than four months.

The Klondike Gold Rush still remains a fascinating tale. We hope that you enjoyed this short volume and encourage you to read more on this exciting and often tragic topic. A bibliography follows that will lead the way!

Part 4: History of Quebec

A Captivating Guide to the Largest Province in Canada and Its Impact on French History

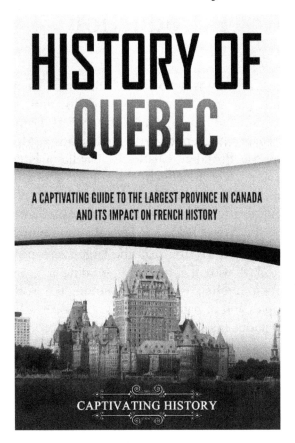

Introduction

Montreal, 1967

Place Jacques-Cartier was an ocean of electrified people, French tricolors, and placards bearing fleurs-de-lis and sovereigntist slogans. Cries swelled into the air, and cheers erupted for the stocky Frenchman who stepped onto the balcony at Montreal's city hall. The man was President Charles de Gaulle of France. He was tall, standing at six feet, four inches, and bore a long face marked by sharp features. De Gaulle was known for his stern and serious expression but also for his unmistakable charisma and command. He nodded to the crowd, acknowledging their excitement.

Gaulle had arrived in Montreal (the largest city in the province of Quebec today) with the intent of sending a message to the Quebecois about the necessity of unity among the world's French-speaking peoples and of national identity. However, what would be remembered about his speech was the historic pro-independence sympathies that he spoke into the microphone.

"Great emotion fills my heart as I look before me, out at the French city of Montreal. In the name of the old country, I salute you with all my heart.

Today, I will share with you a secret. Tonight, and for the whole of my trip, I have found myself noticing a peculiar atmosphere, an atmosphere along the lines of *liberation*.

And for the whole of my trip, I considered what great progress and what great developments you are accomplishing here, and I must say it to you, Montreal, because if there is one city in the world leading by example with its modern successes, it is yours. I say *your* city but permit me to say that this is *our* city. If you only knew what confidence France has in you, if you only knew how much affection she feels for the French Canadians, you would know to what point she feels obligated to support your cause!

This is why France has concluded, along with the support of the government of Quebec, and with the support of my friend Johnson, that French people should work together to fulfill a French vision ... We know that you are establishing factories, enterprises, and laboratories that'll amaze us all, and that will one day help France. I am sure of it. And so, I came here tonight to tell you that our reunion with Montreal will be an unforgettable memory. The whole of France knows, sees, and hears what is happening here, and I can tell you, she wants better for you.

Long live Montreal! Long live Quebec! Long live a *liberated* Quebec! Long live French Canada, and long live France!"

The crowd erupted into thunderous applause. The French president had just uttered a pro-separatist slogan on an international stage. French and Quebecois associates standing behind him were only beginning to absorb de Gaulle's words when the crowd broke into chants of "*Le Quebec aux Quebecois!*" (Quebec belongs to the Quebecois). At the Canadian Parliament in Ottawa, Prime Minister Lester B. Pearson flared as he watched the broadcasted speech. According to him, the French Canadians were just as free as any other Canadian, and regardless of what they believed their identity might have been, the French Canadians were, in fact, Canadians. It's easy to imagine that the prime minister and most other Canadian politicians were embarrassed by de Gaulle's speech. Before the whole world, the president had revealed the Franco-Canadian tensions that had been straining the relationship between Quebec and Canada for centuries.

The fact of the matter was that the Quebecois' fight to maintain their identity as French Canadians distinct from other Canadians and their struggle to be recognized as a nation separate from Canada had been a point of contention between Quebec and Canada, dating back to the long-standing colonial conflict between the two nations.

This book traces the development of the Quebecois identity through the province's long and storied history. From the founding of New France to French-indigenous relations in the early 17th century to the province's economic struggles and the Quiet Revolution, this book will examine how major historical events shaped the province and Quebecois culture, language, and traditions.

A map of where Quebec is located today.

Chapter 1 – Pre-Contact Indigenous Civilizations

Indigenous creationism weaves a story of a Creator who, at the beginning of time, placed the first humans on the face of Turtle Island, what we today call North America. Archaeological evidence maintains that the first humans to inhabit North America traversed the Bering Strait, a vast sheet of ice that linked Asia to the Americas, approximately forty thousand years ago. These humans were hunter-gatherers who followed the migration patterns of deer, moose, and caribou.

Treacherous landscapes and harsh weather conditions made for strict seasonal limitations in the meat supply, so these humans' diets were supplemented by nuts and wild berries. Limitations in the meat supply also caused stagnant population growth for several thousands of years. However, these early generations of people managed to spread through the continent and develop into distinct societies.

It's estimated that humans only reached what we know as eastern Canada ten thousand years ago, just as the continental ice sheet began to recede from the Champlain Sea into the lowlands between the Laurentian and Appalachian Mountains. Throughout the pre-contact era, indigenous societies separated into bands and tribal systems and fostered their own cultural and linguistic subgroups. Three major indigenous linguistic groups developed in

Canada: the Iroquois (made up of nations like the Mohawk, Oneida, Onondaga, and Cayuga), the Algonquin (the Cree, Mohican, Delaware, and Shawnee), and the Inuit. These people were further split into two categories of subsistence: the Algonquin and Inuit semi-nomads of northern Canada and the Iroquois villagers of the south.

Semi-nomadic Societies - Algonquin and Inuit

In the Canadian Shield and the Arctic, Algonquian and Inuit tribes were bound to an unpermissive seasonal cycle and unrelenting weather systems. Poor soil and weather conditions, along with glacial temperatures, prevented the development of horticultural societies and limited significant population growth. Tribes survived the winter months by separating into small hunting bands. Bands would move inland and hunt for large mammals, beavers, and otters, which would keep them fed as the season dragged on. In Jesuit Pierre Biard's observations of nomadic indigenous societies, he remarked, "If the weather then is favourable, they live in great abundance, but if it is against them, they are great to be pitied and often die of starvation."

In the spring, as the warmer months drew near and the land began to thaw, hunting bands reunited by waterways: either lakes, rivers, or on the shores of the Atlantic. In the summertime, they subsisted on fish, migratory birds, fruit, nuts, and small game. With summer congregations came socialization. Groups bartered with one another and engaged in trade or play, and young people took summer gatherings as an opportunity to court.

The Algonquians and Inuit developed technologies that allowed them to adapt and thrive in their precarious environments. Birchbark canoes, transportable teepees, and toboggans allowed humans to navigate vast distances with relative ease, while moccasins, beaver robes, and snowshoes served as protective garb. They forged bows, arrows, and fishing nets to hunt and developed food preservation methods, such as drying and salting fish, meat, and berries. Pemmican, a jerky-like mixture of dried meat and fat, could be stored for long periods.

Sedentary Societies - Iroquois

The Iroquois settled in areas characterized by mild climates and nutrition-rich soil, such as the Saint Lawrence valley, where they could establish dependable horticultural systems. The Iroquois raised a triad of crops they called the Three Sisters: squash, beans, and corn. Through their practice of horticulture, the Iroquois created an intricate network of villages. They lived in longhouses: wooden dwellings that historians estimate were thirty meters (ninety-eight feet) long and seven meters (twenty-three feet) wide with few interior divisions. Each longhouse contained three to five fireplaces, and families slept, worked, and socialized there. Villages were made up of up to 1,500 people and occupied a stretch of land for up to fifteen years or until surrounding resources were depleted and relocation was required.

Iroquois societies were mostly, if not completely, matriarchal. Women were perceived to be the backbone of Iroquois communities, as they were the ones who grew and harvested crops, fetched firewood, and cared for the children in the community. Men were often drawn away from their settlements to hunt, trade, or take part in warfare. The Iroquois matriarchy was evident through the organizational structures of the longhouses, which were occupied by matrilineally related families, either by a mother and her daughters or by a group of sisters.

The Algonquians and Inuit were adept at crafting tools required for survival, and while the Iroquois did craft and use some of the same tools, such as birchbark canoes, they specialized in developing agrarian tools, such as hoes, axes, and woven baskets and mats.

Internal and external conflicts were a persistent issue among Iroquois tribes. Rapidly growing populations stoked the flames of competition over land and resources, and it fostered internal tensions among tribes. Iroquois communities could only be sustained with the implementation of sophisticated political structures. Clan-level governance was divided into two roles: the civil chief and the war chief. The civil chief led daily life affairs, such as religious ceremonies, trade negotiations, and village relocations. The war chief directed defensive and offensive strategies in times of war.

Warfare unified communities by directing collective aggression toward external adversaries. Rather than enlarging territories, indigenous warfare sought to capture members of foreign nations and subject them to ritualistic torture. The village chiefs occasionally met in tribal councils to discuss common issues and arrange joint war parties. The chiefs led with respect, and disputes were met by collaborative efforts to resolve conflicts. Executions were a rare form of punishment, as it was only used for the gravest of offenses, such as treachery or witchcraft.

European Contact

Upon their arrival, European colonists deemed the indigenous peoples of North America to be uncivilized "savages." Blinded by a Eurocentric perspective, it took several centuries for the Europeans to acknowledge the complex societies, technologies, and cultures that the indigenous peoples had developed during the pre-contact era, but that was not before the indigenous populations were decimated by the introduction of European warfare, disease, and marginalization.

Chapter 2 – European Contact and the Fur Trade

The 16th century marked the dawn of a new era, bringing with it Europe's first contact and subsequent connection to North America. John Cabot (1497), alongside the Corte-Real brothers' voyages (1500–1502), forged initial ties between the Old World and the New World. They discovered massive populations of cod off Newfoundland's Great Banks and established fisheries. The cod fisheries introduced North America into the European economic system. In 1524, Giovanni de Verrazzano, an Italian explorer contracted by the king of France, Francis I, landed in Newfoundland and deemed the land *La Nouvelle France*, or New France.

On Friday, July 24th, 1534, a crew of French seamen erected a wooden cross on the shoreline of the Gaspé Peninsula. The cross stood high above the foaming mouth of the Atlantic—an emblem of the New World facing the Old. The seamen were led by seasoned explorer Jacques Cartier, who had been commissioned by Francis I to find a new trade route to prosperous Asia through the New World. In Gaspé Bay, Cartier and his men encountered the Iroquois, who were upset about the Frenchmen raising their cross and claiming Iroquois land in the name of France. Cartier ordered the kidnapping of two Iroquois men and brought them back to France, presenting them to the king as proof of the "savages" that occupied New France.

A painting of Jacques Cartier.
https://commons.wikimedia.org/wiki/File:Jacques_Cartier_1851-1852.jpg

A year later, in 1535, Cartier returned to New France with the two kidnapped Iroquois in tow and returned them to their village. During his voyage, he discovered a river he had missed the previous year. Driven by his aim to discover a trading route to Asia, Cartier believed this river was the Northwest Passage. However, he hadn't discovered the Northwest Passage; instead, he had discovered the Saint Lawrence River.

He sailed up the river and debarked at several Iroquois villages in the Saint Lawrence Valley. Cartier traded French goods such as knives and animal skins for beaver pelts. Cartier may not have known it at the time, but he began the fur trade that would be integral to the development of Quebec as a French colony.

While cod had initiated trading relationships between North America and Europe, the European market for furs, namely beaver pelts, strengthened the trade ties between the continents. The North American beaver supply increased European felt production, which resulted in the wide-brimmed hat becoming a fashionable item among the Parisian bourgeoisie during the late 16th century. By the 1630s, the wide-brimmed hat had become a standard part of military attire and had gained widespread popularity among all classes of men.

As French settlements and trade posts cropped up in the Saint Lawrence Valley,

the fur trade became increasingly dependent on native labor. Newly arrived French missionaries hoped to convert the indigenous people to Christianity. The natives were hesitant to adopt Christianity due to its imposition on traditional native customs and ways of life. Policies created by French colonizers aimed for assimilation through language, education, and agricultural settlements, but these policies ultimately proved unsuccessful when they were met with resistance from the natives. The Jesuit missionaries introduced a version of Christianity that made relative accommodations for native traditions and culture, and they found some success in converting native groups.

Conversion rates increased significantly throughout the 1640s because many indigenous leaders perceived Christianity as a way of gaining power and prestige within their communities. The religion offered a new set of beliefs and practices that could be used to challenge and replace traditional spiritual systems. Christianity also provided a means of obtaining material goods, such as guns and tools, which could be used to gain power and prestige within communities. Christianity was often presented as a "civilizing" force, and many indigenous leaders saw conversion as a means to gain access to European technology, education, and other benefits. Furthermore, converting to Christianity could help them form alliances with Europeans, which, in turn, could help them in their struggles against other indigenous tribes.

Indigenous culture never made a lasting impact on the European settlers in the Saint Lawrence Valley. The French held an unshakeable belief in their supposed religious superiority and therefore incorporated aspects of indigenous life into their lifestyles while remaining Christians. A *coureur des bois*, for example, wore traditional native clothing, traveled with the use of snowshoes and toboggans, and even took indigenous wives, all while maintaining a firm commitment to Christianity.[98]

The Beaver Wars

The Beaver Wars, also known as the Iroquois Wars, were a series of conflicts that took place in New France between the 17th century and the mid-18th century. The wars were fought between the Iroquois Confederacy, which was made up of five indigenous nations—the Mohawk, Oneida, Onondaga, Cayuga, and Seneca—and other tribes who were involved in the fur trade. The Iroquois Confederacy sought to control the fur trade. They attacked their rivals, destroyed trading networks, and controlled access to beavers and other furry animals. By doing so, they aimed to become one of the dominant powers in the region. The Iroquois also sought to assert their dominance over other tribes and exert their influence over the other indigenous nations in the region.

French traders were caught between the warring parties. They formed alliances with the Huron to maintain their access to the beaver supply, maintain their influence in the region, and counterbalance the growing power and influence of the Iroquois Confederacy. The French had a strategic interest in maintaining the power balance among the indigenous tribes, as they did not want any tribe or confederacy to become too powerful and dominate the region.

The Beaver Wars shattered the tribes of the Great Lakes region. The Huron, Algonquin, and Erie, among others, were forced to flee their ancestral lands as the Iroquois dominated the region and gained control of the fur trade. However, the weakening of these tribes allowed European colonizers to gain a foothold in the region, as the tribes could no longer effectively resist the colonizers' military and economic power, and the subsequent

---

[98] More on the coureurs des bois can be found in Chapter 3.

displacement and subjugation of indigenous people created a power vacuum for the colonizers to fill.

Chapter 3 – Colonial Life and the British Conquest

The birth of New France and colonial settlements brought a new economic landscape. Those immigrating from France seeking economic opportunities had two paths to choose from: participate in the fur trade as a voyageur or coureur des bois or farm and cultivate land as a habitant. Working in the fur trade involved supplying furs for transport to the colonies in Montreal and Quebec while providing sustenance to the coureurs des bois and indigenous hunters.

An image of a coureur des bois.
https://commons.wikimedia.org/wiki/File:La_V%C3%A9rendrye.jpg

Young male settlers also had the option to become *coureur des bois* (French for "runner of the woods"). The coureurs des bois were traders and adventurers who traveled through the interior of North America, mainly in the Great Lakes and Mississippi River regions, during the late 17th and early 18th centuries. They navigated the wilderness and engaged in trade with indigenous tribes. They also engaged in other activities, such as hunting, trapping, and smuggling. The *voyageurs*, on the other hand, engaged in the fur trade but operated in the Great Lakes region and the Saint Lawrence River.

The coureurs des bois lived independently and lawlessly, as they operated outside of the French government's control and were not subject to the strict regulations that governed the activities of the fur trading companies. French settlers who chose to live as farmers lived on seigneuries. The seigneury was a feudalistic form of property distribution that was structured around the relationship between lords and peasants. The lord, on behalf of the king of France, granted land in exchange for annual rent and levies when the properties were sold. Their tenants had to clear the property and farm it. If tenants didn't meet their landlord's obligations, they risked eviction or civil punishment.

In exchange for work, the seigneur received privileges, such as having a reserved seat in the front pews at church and first rights when receiving Communion. Moreover, the seigneur's authority extended beyond spiritual matters, as each had the right to set up manor courts for legal disputes among the habitants, which provided an economical alternative to the royal courts, which charged higher fees. These courts served as a source of administrative power and community benefit.

Religious Influence

In France, the king was considered to have his authority granted by God, and the church enjoyed a high social status. In New France, the state distributed civil responsibilities to religious orders. The church oversaw education and health care. The church ran two schools, two hospitals, and a college before the creation of the first parish. The seigneurial system funded the clergy and its institutions. Nuns began arriving in the colony in 1639, and they undertook educative responsibilities and organized the colony's health care. The first nuns to arrive were the Ursulines, who established schools to educate young native girls. Later on, they founded three schools for colonists' daughters in Quebec City, Montreal, and New Orleans, where they taught domestic work and manners.

In 1642, Jeanne Mance founded the Hôtel-Dieu hospital. This was the first hospital in the colony that cared for both the colonists and indigenous people. In 1658, Marguerite Bourgeois founded the Congregation of Notre Dame, an order that set up elementary schools throughout New France. Children typically began their schooling at six or seven years old and stayed for three or four years. These schools taught the basics of reading and writing. Children were taught their places in society, and the schools reinforced patriarchal standards. General hospitals were built to segregate and care for the poor and the elderly. Many daughters of the colonial elite joined the nuns and the nursing orders. In her book *La Noblesse de Nouvelle France,* Lorraine Gadoury writes that 20 percent of all noblewomen in the colony were nuns.

In 1764, the Jesuits of New France were expelled from the colony for several political and economic factors. One of the main reasons for their expulsion was a growing concern among French officials that the Jesuits were becoming too powerful and independent. The state also accused the Jesuits of being too sympathetic to the indigenous peoples and not being sufficiently supportive enough of French colonial interests. Furthermore, the French government saw the Jesuits' vast wealth and landholdings as a potential source of revenue. The French government ordered the Jesuits' expulsion in 1763, and the order was implemented the following year.

The expulsion was met with some resistance among members of the colony, including some of the indigenous people who had converted to Christianity under the Jesuits' guidance. The Jesuits were ultimately forced to leave, and most of their missions and schools were left in the hands of the Catholic Church. The Jesuits' expulsion resulted in a decline in the number of conversions to Christianity among indigenous peoples, and it contributed to the eventual erosion between the French and Iroquois. Since the Jesuits had founded several educational institutions within the colony, their expulsion took a toll on the cultural and intellectual life of New France as well.

Legal System in New France

In New France, the legal system was based on the Napoleonic Code and the Coutume de Paris (Custom of Paris), which was a set of legal customs specific to the governance of Paris. These laws were intended to uphold the social order and maintain the authority of the French government. However, this legal system was not always successful in providing fair and just treatment for all inhabitants.

The highest court in New France was the *Conseil Souverain*, or the Royal Council, located in Quebec City. The council was made up of appointed members, such as the governor, the bishop, and the chief justices. It heard appeals from lower courts and made decisions on important legal matters. The council was often criticized for being too closely tied to the government and for being more interested in maintaining order rather than administering justice. The lower courts in New France were the Courts of Justice and the Courts of Peace. The Courts of Justice heard criminal and civil cases, while the Courts of Peace were responsible for resolving disputes between individuals and enforcing local laws and regulations. These courts were often the first point of contact for people seeking justice, but they were also known for being slow and inefficient and for lacking in resources.

The legal system in New France also had a difficult time dealing with the unique social and legal issues that arose from the interactions between the colonizers and the indigenous people. The indigenous people were often treated unfairly in the courts, and the legal system was not able to protect them from the violence and exploitation they suffered at the hands of the colonizers. Additionally, the legal system did not recognize the indigenous people's traditional laws, customs, and governance, which further marginalized them.

While the legal system in New France was implemented to maintain French authority and the social order, it was not well equipped to deal with the colony's unique challenges and often failed to provide the protection and justice that the settlers needed.

The Arrival of the Filles du Roi and Lives of Colonial Women

Between 1663 and 1673, Quebec's population witnessed an unprecedented surge, with an influx of over four thousand men and women settling in the colony. This rapid growth was due in part to unmarried male soldiers coming into service in the colony for three-year periods. As a result, there were six times more single men than single women. To even out the colony's gender discrepancy, King Louis XIV sent hundreds of marriageable girls to the New World. These girls earned the name *filles du roi*, French for the King's Daughters. The *filles du roi* would be equipped with dowries so they could find partners to marry among the French soldiers living in Quebec. Altogether, 850 new inhabitants arrived by ship, thanks largely to this royal initiative.

A painting of the King's Daughters arriving in Quebec by Eleanor Fortescue-Brickdale.
https://commons.wikimedia.org/wiki/File:Arrival_of_the_Brides_-_Eleanor_Fortescue-Brickdale.png

Louis XIV believed that couples should marry as soon as possible, so on April 5th, 1669, he signed an edict that pressured the colony's couples to wed. His decree imposed hefty fines upon fathers who failed to marry off their sons by the age of twenty and on fathers who failed to marry off their daughters by the age of sixteen. By 1673, the colony, now holding a population of 6,700 people, achieved a gender equilibrium. France stopped exporting marriageable girls.

Women's lives in New France were shaped by the patriarchal society and traditional gender roles of the time. Marriage was considered to be the most important aspect of a woman's life, and most women were expected to marry and bear children. Women were also responsible for domestic tasks, such as cooking, cleaning, and childcare. If a woman's husband was absent or deceased, she was responsible for maintaining the household's finances and running her husband/late husband's farm or business. Upper-class women, such as the daughters of wealthy merchants or government officials, had more opportunities and autonomy than lower-class women. They were often educated and could be involved in business and politics. However, upper-class women were still subject to the legal and social restrictions placed on all women in New France.

Women in New France had very few legal rights. They were not allowed to vote or hold public office, and their property rights were limited. In marriage, the husband held legal authority over his wife and children. Women were barred from testifying in court, which further restricted the autonomy and agency of colonial women.

It should be noted that the experiences of colonial women varied depending on social class, ethnicity, and religion. Some women held more privileges than others.

New France's Expansion

With the invaluable aid of their indigenous allies, French adventurers undertook a series of expeditions to discover new lands for France and to continue their centuries-long search for an alternative route to East Asia. As they explored west and south of New France, they encountered no resistance, at least not immediately. Indigenous guides led explorers south. During the 17th and 18th centuries, French explorers left their mark across North America. From Detroit, Michigan, to Des Moines, Iowa, the French presence in today's United States is still apparent in city and state names, regardless of if those names have been Anglicized or not.

This period was growing ever-tumultuous for New France when Governor Jacques-René de Brisbay de Denonville captured forty Iroquois chiefs as a response to escalating tensions between France and the Iroquois Confederacy. The Iroquois retaliated by continuously raiding the trading port of Lachine, a port essential for maintaining the shipping routes across Canada. Meanwhile, another threat loomed on the horizon: England. England thirsted for territorial expansion, and the 160,000 British colonists hoped to conquer the much smaller and weaker colony of New France, which had a population of no more than 10,700 people to protect it.

The British Conquest and the Seven Years' War

The British conquest of New France, also known as the conquest of Canada, refers to the gradual process of territorial expansion in Canada that occurred over several decades. The conquest was a series of major battles and smaller fights that occurred between 1746 and 1760 and were fought primarily in the Great Lakes and Saint Lawrence regions. Led by General James Wolfe and Admiral Charles Saunders, the British were able to defeat the French, who were led by General Louis-Joseph de Montcalm, and take control of New France.

Historians point to the British army's naval superiority and their ability to recruit the Iroquois Confederacy as allies to fight the French as the most pertinent reasons for a British victory. The British navy's capture of the Saint Lawrence River led to the Battle of the Plains of Abraham in Quebec City, a decisive battle that ultimately ceded victory to the British. The British victory marked the end of French colonial rule in North America and the beginning of British rule. British dominance in North America would last until the American Revolution.

The Seven Years' War was a global conflict that occurred during the British conquest of New France. In North America, the war took on a new shape and is often referred to as the French and Indian War. This theater of the Seven Years' War was fought primarily between the British and the French, who both desired to expand their global influence. The British, who had been rapidly expanding their global territory, conflicted with the French over control of the Ohio River Valley and the Mississippi River Valley, lands rich with opportunities for trade and resources. But the French had already established profitable trading posts there and sought to maintain control of their territory.

The French and Indian War began in 1754 with the Battle of Jumonville Glen and continued for several years, with the French and the British fighting one another alongside their respective indigenous allies. Britain's victory in the Seven Years' War (and the French and Indian War) contributed to its success in its conquest of New France. In 1763, the Treaty of Paris officially ended the war. All of New France, including Quebec, was ceded to the British Empire. The British had officially become the imperial power of North America.

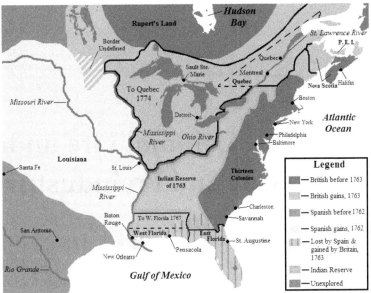

The territorial gains of the British after the French and Indian War

Jon Platek, CC BY-SA 3.0 <https://creativecommons.org/licenses/by-sa/3.0>, via Wikimedia Commons; https://commons.wikimedia.org/wiki/File:NorthAmerica1762-83.png

The conquest of New France had a significant impact on the habitants, the majority of whom were living in Quebec. The Treaty of Paris did not protect the preservation of the French language, the practice of Catholicism, or French culture. Many habitants felt lost and alienated within the British colony. However, many chose to assimilate into British culture to maintain their social and economic status. Others chose to maintain their cultural identity and resist assimilation.

Chapter 4 – Colonial Life under British Rule and Preindustrial Economy

Due to Britain's successful conquest of New France, it inherited the Province of Quebec, which was inhabited by French Catholics who were unfamiliar with British culture, traditions, and the English language. The British government believed that it could transform Quebec into a British colony, one ruled by British laws and largely populated by Britons. It also created a reserve for indigenous people located within the continent.[99]

The British government requested that Governor James Murray establish British law through the Anglican Church and English schools, but Murray realized that installing such institutions would prove unsuccessful in assimilating the French Canadian populace. Of the seventy thousand French Canadians, 85 percent lived in rural environments and lived remotely from Briton immigrants and British institutions. Only a few British settlers had arrived in the colony, and most of them settled in Quebec City or Montreal. A surge of British immigration in the near future proved unlikely.

---

[99] Tousignant, Pierre. 1973. Problématique pour une novuelle approche de la constitution de 1791. *Revue d'histoire de l'Amérique* française 27 (septembre): 181-232.

The Test Act, a law passed in Great Britain in 1673, made matters more complicated for Murray. The act prevented Catholics from holding public office. French Canadians couldn't hold positions in government, nor could they sit in the colony's assembly. However, Murray had origins in the Scottish landowning class and had more in common with the aristocratic and clerical elite of Quebec's *ancien régime* than with the newly settled British merchants who sought power within the colony. In an effort to prevent the British merchants from coming into power, Murray never held elections for the assembly, preferring to rule through a council sympathetic to the French Canadians.

However, Murray's attitude toward Catholicism wasn't as sympathetic. He tried to get members of the French Protestant clergy to immigrate to Quebec to convert the French Canadians, and he managed to impose his authority over the Quebecois Catholic clergy. Murray's refusal to call for assembly, his sympathy for the Quebecois elite, his relative tolerance of Catholicism within the colony, and his unwillingness to let British merchants develop their commercial empire in Quebec angered the British merchants, who accused his administration of being oppressive and unconstitutional.

Murray's successor, Sir Guy Carleton, who descended from the Anglo-Irish elite, also sympathized with the French seigneurial and clerical aristocracy. He viewed them as the inherent leaders of the French Canadians. Carleton followed Murray's policies, further enraging British merchants.

It was clear by the 1770s that government efforts to assimilate the French Canadian population through the establishment of British institutions would prove fruitless without a steady influx of British immigrants. Rising tensions with the Thirteen Colonies south of Quebec proved to the British government that concessions were necessary to earn the loyalty of the French Canadians. The Quebec Act was enacted in 1774, and it allowed Catholics to exercise their religion to the fullest extent. The Test Act was supplanted by an oath of loyalty that allowed Catholics to hold office.

The Quebec Act also established a dual judicial system. British criminal law was maintained, but French law was implemented in civil cases. The seigneurs and Catholic clergy were satisfied with the Quebec Act, as it recognized their elevated social status within the colony. But Anglophone merchants remained angry, as the act reinforced French institutions and refused to grant an assembly. The act changed very little for the rest of Quebec's population.

In the Thirteen Colonies, the Quebec Act was considered to be one of the many "intolerable acts" the British enforced. The act set new boundaries for the Province of Quebec, and in doing so, it excluded merchants based in New York because Albany was cut off from the fur trade. It prevented settlement in the Ohio Valley, and the act offended the Puritans in New England because it protected the Catholic Church.

As the colonists in the Thirteen Colonies inched closer toward revolution, soon-to-be Americans expected support from the French Canadians. The Continental Congress addressed the people of Quebec and accused the Quebec Act of violating the tenets of liberty. The address only appealed to Montreal's Anglophone merchants and was largely opposed by the clergy and seigneurs. Since Quebec was relatively inconsequential to the Quebecois peasantry, they remained indifferent to the Continental Congress's address.

French Canadians' attitudes toward the American colonists were unclear and varied at best. The elite, including seigneurs and the clergy, were supportive of the British, and Quebec's bishop, Jean-Olivier Briand, demanded that French Canadian Catholics be loyal to the British king. Most of the peasantry remained neutral. When American forces invaded Quebec in 1775 in an attempt to drive out the British, five hundred militiamen took up arms to defend Quebec, but none enlisted to join the British army to attack the American colonies in the Revolutionary War.

The Peace of Paris, signed in 1783, united the remaining colonies south of the Great Lakes into the United States. While Quebec did lose some of its territories to the United States, French Canadian merchants continued to trade in American territories until the end of the 18th century. The formation of the United States also signified the arrival of British loyalists in Quebec, who would come to challenge the inherent French culture and traditionalism of the colony.

The Quebec Act was no longer offensive only to Anglophone merchants in Quebec; it also proved unsatisfactory to the newly arrived British loyalists, who urged the governor to allow for an elected assembly. While the seigneurial elite continued to campaign against an elected assembly and for the Quebec Act to be retained, a budding Franco-bourgeoisie made up of merchants, notaries, and lawyers stood alongside the Anglophones in their petition to have the Quebec Act repealed and to establish an elected assembly.

The Constitutional Act, enacted in 1791, repealed the Quebec Act and maintained imperial control in Quebec. The British believed that democratic excess had been responsible for the American Revolution, so they held an interest in maintaining executive power through a governor, an executive council, and a legislative council. The three councils established the British Crown's alliance with Quebec's clergy, seigneurs, and powerful merchants—an alliance made of groups that would ultimately be known as the Château Clique.

Quebec's first legislative assembly was created, and all property owners and their tenants were eligible voters. However, voters had to be at least twenty-one years old and could not have been convicted of treason. Few women were eligible to vote, as property was usually in the name of the woman's father or husband, so mostly unmarried women and widows were qualified to vote. The act also separated Quebec into Upper and Lower Canada, which led to conflicting legal systems between the regions. Lower Canada used French civil law, while Upper Canada used British common law.

The late 18th century saw the rise and emergence of a new breed of French Canadian nationalism under British rule. The new legislative assembly that had been established under the Constitutional Act simply created a new forum where Anglophone and Francophone elites would fall into conflict with each other while trying to pass legislature on their respective interests. Francophone efforts to have French be recognized as the assembly's official language garnered opposition from the Anglophones, while attempts to control the Catholic Church within Quebec and to create an Anglophone education system throughout the colony were resisted by the Francophones.

Despite ethnic tensions, the Francophone elite were loyal to Britain when the Americans started a war in 1812. This was due in part to the church's call for loyalty to Britain. It reminded Francophones of Britain's good governmental policies, which allotted religious freedom to French Canada.

Chapter 5 – Preindustrial Society

Throughout its early development, Quebec's economy was dependent on the metropolitan centers of England and France. However, the colony's population grew rapidly as agricultural production increased. Quebec's abundant and nutritionally rich land, which allowed families to settle and reproduce on dependable farmland, and its staple-based exports made it extremely different from England and France.

Merchants and Artisans

Harold Innis's staple theory dominated the study of Canada's economy until very recently. Innis pointed out that Canada's long-standing dependence on foreign trade and its trade in staples such as cod, beaver, wheat, and timber drove Canada's social and economic evolution. However, Innis's staple theory neglects the importance of the colony's local markets and the peasant economy (Sweeny 1994).[100]

During the preindustrial period, merchants profited off the international markets (trading cod, fur, and timber) and the local markets. While merchants were usually confined to urban areas for

---

[100] Sweeny, Robert. 1978. *A Guide to the History and Records of Select Montreal Businesses before 1947.* Montreal: Centre de recherche en histoire économique du Canada français.

most of the 17th century due to the colony's small population size, they eventually moved to rural areas as the population grew. Rural merchants typically sold imported textiles and hardware, and in return, they bought alcohol, wheat, and other agricultural goods.

Merchants contributed to the colony's economy by exchanging goods, while the artisans' contribution was crafting those goods. Canadian artisans enjoyed more freedom than European artisans since there were no corporations within the colony to control standards and since market forces directed the development of trades. The rapid population growth quickly overwhelmed the supply of immigrant artisans, so an apprenticeship system was essential in producing labor for a given trade. Boys were apprenticed to trade masters for up to seven years. Girls were apprenticed to a lesser extent for specialized trades, such as dressmaking. The apprenticeship system was a way to adjust the labor supply to suit the needs of the marketplace.

Artisanal shops were usually small family businesses where a trade master and his wife worked alone or in the company of an apprentice. A trade master's wife's work included handling sales, keeping records, and home-keeping.

The Peasant Economy

During the preindustrial period, most of the population were farmers who practiced agriculture for home consumption or for local trade. By the 18th century, Canada was producing enough agricultural surplus to export to neighboring colonies or to western trading posts.

Preparing land for agricultural use was an arduous process. Settlers in the Saint Lawrence Valley were granted land by the seigneurs, and it took approximately two years to clear a hectare of dense forest to build a cabin, and it took up to five years to clear three hectares, the minimum amount of land for self-sufficiency. During the time it took to clear the land, families subsisted off locally produced food, which was sometimes bought at the market but was usually offered to them by relatives.

Peasant families could never truly be self-sufficient, as they needed to buy goods, such as cloth, salt, tea, tools, and kitchenware. The average peasant family owned an iron stove, which was a major expenditure, and even the poorest families still bought copper pots and pans, as well as iron tools. Richer peasant families owned an abundance of copper and iron kitchenware and perhaps some china and silverware.

Wheat was the major crop grown in Canada. Although newly developed land bore wheat almost exclusively to profit off its commercial value, oats, peas, and beans were also raised on well-developed farms to promote self-sufficiency. Other crops that were often grown by the peasantry included hemp, flax, corn, salad vegetables, and fruit. Surplus produce could only be sold in areas near urban markets.

Livestock herds were kept small as a result of the emphasis on wheat over feed crops and the relatively small market for meat. Since livestock had to be sheltered from the winter and be fed, farmers usually slaughtered their herds and kept a few animals for breeding purposes. This guaranteed a winter meat supply but proved to be an insufficient strategy to fertilize fields properly. Over time, yields would decline, as the fields lost their fertility.

Rural and Urban Daily Life

Rural life was heavily dictated by the seasons. In the spring and summer months, people plowed, planted, weeded, and harvested. In the late fall and winter months, people threshed grain, sold their surplus, and worked on clearing new stretches of land. Agricultural life demanded an efficient division of labor among families. Men and adolescent sons performed the heaviest and most arduous tasks, such as plowing, cutting wood, and clearing stumps. Women and older girls cared for children, cooked, cleaned, sewed, gardened, and attended to livestock. All family members, even the young, participated in familial labor.

Rural houses were akin to log cabins, and most properties included a barn and stable. Relatively prosperous farms consisted of specialized buildings, such as sties, coops, and sugar shacks. The interiors of peasant homes were minimalistic. Parents slept in large beds, and children slept on straw mats. Other furnishings usually included a chest, table, benches, and utensils.

Living conditions throughout the seasons weren't ideal. In the summer, families had to adapt to fly and mosquito infestations, and in the winter, families huddled around an iron stove or fireplace for warmth.

Urban housing and living conditions were dictated by class. Rich merchants, clergymen, and administrators lived in luxurious stone houses furnished with wall tapestries, expensive silverware, and fabric chairs. Parents slept in their own private bedrooms, and most children slept on real beds. Artisans' homes were similar to those of the rural peasants; however, fire regulations ruled that all houses be built of stone, which added to artisans' housing costs.

Urban towns were dirty, unsanitary, and unsafe. While garrisons were hired to keep peace and order, they were often the perpetrators of criminal activity. In the 18th century, more than 20 percent of criminals in Canada were from the military.[101]

Bread was a staple food in the colony, and bakeries were monitored so that they sold loaves at government-set weights and prices. Meat, typically smoked or salted pork, was consumed in the winter, and root vegetables, such as onions and cabbage, were stored in cellars for when the fresh fruit and vegetable supply ran out. Most men drank French wine and brandy, although as the colony continued to integrate into the British Empire, rum began to replace wine and brandy among workingmen. Tea also became a popular drink. Some beer had been brewed in the colony prior to the British conquest, but British interest expedited beer production. John Molson established his famous brewery in 1786 using local produce.

Daily Life of Women

In preindustrial societies, the rights and responsibilities of the family were viewed to be more important than those of the individual. Therefore, a woman's role in preindustrial Quebec was wholly centered on the maintenance of her family. Her primary responsibilities were bearing children, raising children, tending to the household, and working for little to no pay for family enterprises.

Women were subordinate to their male familial leaders, either their husbands, fathers, or oldest brothers. Women couldn't marry or meet with a male from another family without permission from a male relative. Once a woman married, she was under the control

---

[101] Lachance, André. 1978. *La justice criminelle du roi au Canada au XVIIIe sciècle. Tribunaux et officiers.* Quebec: Presses de l'Université Laval.

of her husband. She and her children were obligated to respect his authority. Men were obligated to care for their families, but they were legally permitted to beat their wives and children as punishment. Battered wives could only seek a separation from the court if they could provide proof that their lives were in imminent danger.

Although a woman's estate or property fell under her husband's control, property that she inherited through a familial death or through marriage could not be mortgaged without her permission. Occasionally, a woman would seek a legal separation of her and her husband's estates if her husband was beating her severely or if he was mismanaging her affairs. Divorce was prohibited by the church and the court, and legally separated couples were still considered to be married.

Older single women and widows were granted more freedoms and autonomy than their younger and married counterparts. They were allowed to manage their properties and run their own businesses. Widows were integral to Quebec's economy, as they often inherited businesses, factories, and land. Widows from lower classes often became domestic servants and occasionally sold out their children as laborers.

Education and Cultural Life

In the preindustrial era, most of Quebec's population was illiterate. Literacy was prevalent only among the wealthy elite and some artisans. Printing presses were imported into the colony after the British conquest, and Quebec's first newspaper, the *Quebec Gazette*, started publication in 1764. Because of the high rates of illiteracy, the initial sales of the *Quebec Gazette* were low, and the newspaper had to rely on government advertising to survive. Eventually, more newspapers emerged, including the bilingual *Montreal Gazette* and the *Montreal Herald*. Political journalism only truly emerged in Quebec after 1805, when publications with well-defined political affiliations came to print. *The Quebec Mercury* represented the Anglophones, whereas *Le Canadien* represented the Francophones.

The exile of the Jesuits under the French regime presented a serious blow to Quebec's education, as the Jesuits had dominated male education within the colony. Postsecondary education only began to recover at the beginning of the 19ᵗʰ century with the creation of colleges across Quebec. Those who sought to become specialized professionals, such as lawyers or notaries, attended these colleges before becoming apprentices. The sheer cost of attending a classical college, along with finding a professional willing to train an apprentice and having the resources to establish one's own practice, cemented Quebec's bourgeoisie by ensuring that boys from lower classes could not enter specialized professions.

Bourgeois culture in most of Europe was defined by theater, opera, and Enlightenment literature. Since the church opposed most of these, bourgeois culture in Quebec was severely underdeveloped. Plays were sometimes staged by college students, but professional theater did not develop until the Molson Theatre opened in 1825. Musical productions existed in the colony, but they were centered on church ceremonies. Dancing was popular among both the Anglophone and Francophone elites. French garb, including "scandalous" low-cut dresses, were imported into Quebec for winter balls and dinners thrown by members of the colony's administration.

In rural communities, French oral and folkloric traditions were maintained by fiddlers and storytellers. Feast days were held for religious processions and socializing. Peasants and artisans generally did not own books, and libraries of all social classes were dominated by pious literature. Local literature would not become important until the mid-19ᵗʰ century.

Crime and Protest

While all facets of Quebec were bound to the Catholic Church's influence and strict morality, criminal activity abounded during the colony's entire history. In the preindustrial era, bar and tavern fights accounted for half of the cases presented in criminal courts. Theft was the second-most prevalent crime after physical violence. The most prevalent form of property crime was breaking and entering into homes and stores. Crimes against the church included blasphemy, witchcraft, and several sexual offenses, such as seduction, rape, and adultery.

The colonial government tried to prevent protests by only allowing people to congregate to discuss social issues in the presence of a judge. Protests did occur in the form of petitions and demands for an elected assembly. Sometimes, social protests erupted into riots. The government was always quick to intervene, though. For example, in 1714, the townspeople of Saint-Augustin, a small community southwest of Quebec City, made their way to the colonial capital. Armed with muskets, they protested poverty and the high cost of imported goods. State troops barred their entry into Quebec City and forced them to retreat.

Chapter 6 – Industrial Revolution: Economy and Society

Throughout the course of the 19th century, Quebec would see major societal and economic shifts as the Industrial Revolution trickled over the Atlantic from Great Britain. At the beginning of the century, Quebec was a preindustrial society with an economy dependent on agricultural and artisanal production and trade in local markets. Despite it being a commercial center, Montreal was relatively pastoral in the first half of the century but would soon metamorphize into a major economic hub within the colony. Quebec's 19th-century development would be marked by the ever-growing importance of money and eventual urbanization.

Population

British immigration rates rose quickly in the 19th century, but Quebec's population maintained its Francophone majority. The colony's population quadrupled from 340,000 in 1815 to 1,359,027 in 1881. Urbanization was mostly to blame for this demographic shift, as immigrants flocked from Europe to settle in Montreal, chasing urban employment rather than the agricultural lifestyle they were used to back home.

Historians point to stable birth and death rates for the increase in Quebec's Francophone population. Immigration was responsible for the rise in the Anglophone population, but the immigration rates began a slow decline in the latter half of the century, keeping the Anglophone population a minority in Quebec.

Immigrants traveled in the overcrowded holds of cargo ships heading to Canadian ports. Infectious diseases, such as cholera, typhus, and measles, ran rampant on the ships. Thousands died on the journey or in the quarantine camp near Quebec City. Six cholera epidemics spread throughout Lower Canada between 1832 and 1867. The worst of them was the spread of Asian cholera in 1832, which killed around 2,700 people in Quebec City, 2,550 in Montreal, and an unknown number of people in rural areas.

Anglophones grew in economic importance. They often worked as contractors, bankers, and industrial producers and were often favored by the British government for government and military contracts. The increasing number of Anglophones taking on positions of power in Quebec's economic and social institutions contributed to Francophone nationalism, which had been growing over the previous century.

Francophone nationalists were particularly frustrated with imperial land companies that preferred to assign land to British settlers. They accused the British of infiltrating Lower Canada with cholera-ridden immigrants. The Catholic clergy retaliated against the British land companies by forming colonization societies through the colonization roads program in 1848, which subsidized the cost of land and established colonization societies, such as the Société générale de Montreal, which promoted Catholic and Francophone immigration and settlement, especially in the Anglophone-dominated Eastern Townships (southeastern Quebec).

The new forms of labor, overcrowding, and disease that arose because of industrialization deeply impacted family life and social dynamics. The rates of illegitimate births rose quickly, and couples began to postpone their marriages for economic reasons. Hospitals began to take care of an increasing number of abandoned infants. These infants were placed in the care of midwives but often died.

It is unclear how many native people lived in urban centers, as census data regularly underestimated or ignored indigenous populations. We know that in Montreal, Iroquois people lived with white communities, but most indigenous people lived in hunting bands scattered throughout Canada.

Transportation in Industrial Quebec

Quebec's industrialization was due in part to the rapid and complex development of transportation. Shipping between Montreal and Quebec City was improved by Canada's first steamboat built in North America, *Accommodation*, which was funded and launched by wealthy brewer John Molson in 1809.

Steamships and newly built railways promoted increases in industrial production, capital, and labor. Unlike steamships, railway networks allowed for the transportation of cargo throughout the year.

Notable Producers

The companies and industries founded by John Molson and John Redpath demonstrate Quebec's shift from dependence on artisanal production to industrial production. John Molson's business empire was rooted in the brewery he opened in 1785. He and his sons used the brewery's profits to buy into the steamship building and steamship industries and into foundries, whiskey distilleries, sawmills, warehouses, banking, and railways. By the second half of the 18th century, the Molsons owned the most land in Montreal.

John Redpath, a Scottish immigrant, became a well-reputed stonemason in Montreal during the 1820s and 1830s. He accumulated his wealth through the construction of large projects. Redpath oversaw the construction of canals and churches and used his profits to open Canada's first sugar refinery. His influence is still felt today, as Redpath Sugar can be found on Canadian grocery store shelves.

Although there is much evidence of Francophone participation in the construction of railway and industrial institutions, the Anglophone elite owned most of the production centers. This was because they had certain advantages: most of the control of the fur and timber trade; the transatlantic network of friend and family connections that offered powerful positions to British immigrants; and the use of Britain and the United States as sources of immigration, technology, and industrial professions.

Organization of Industrial Production

Effective industrial production required changing the way work was organized. Work organization refers to the management, discipline, work relations, or work dynamics that differed wildly from the way work was organized in artisanal shops or on the farm. Industrial producers could employ more laborers than artisanal producers and could maintain higher standards. As a result, artisans suffered a loss of status.

Apprenticeships underwent a transformation after 1810. Masters took on less responsibility over their apprentices and paid them higher wages instead of offering them room and board as they had in the past. An increased number of apprentices per master meant larger shops, more division of labor, and an apprenticeship that focused less on the acquirement of skills than on the completion of a labor contract.

The changes in work organization were widely resisted. Though organizing strikes and other forms of resistance was difficult, some laborers were determined. The workers in the leather, construction, and transportation sectors were particularly vocal. They opposed their poor salaries, dangerous work conditions, and arduous hours. Riots and strikes often occurred and sometimes turned bloody. In Beauharnois in 1843, twenty strikers working in construction were murdered by British troops.

New forms of work and working conditions and changes in the link between capital and labor were evident in the creation of unions across crafts and trades. Unions became prevalent among tailors, shoemakers, bakers, carpenters, printers, firemen, mechanics, painters, and milkmen.

The Knights of Labor, an organization formed to unite workers, spread from its origins in Philadelphia to Quebec. The organization strongly appealed to Quebec's workers. It promoted class solidarity, collective principles, and a nine-hour workday. It emphasized symbolism, secret rituals, self-help, picnics, galas, and parades to encourage the unity of classes and the spirit of community. The organization attracted both Francophone and Anglophone workers, and it remained a strong force in Quebec until the end of the 19th century.

Financial Institutions

Open access to capital was integral for industrial producers. Banks, therefore, created lending and saving facilities that allowed bank owners to collect money. The Montreal Stock Exchange was established in 1874 and legitimized the raising of capital within Quebec. Life insurance increased in popularity in the 1870s. Sun Life was founded in 1871 and would eventually become Canada's largest insurance company. It quickly gathered large sums of insurance premiums. This money was initially invested in mortgages but became increasingly invested in public utilities.

French-speaking entrepreneurs faced difficulty in competing with their Anglophone counterparts, many of whom had familial ties to financial and political interests. However, they were aware of the importance of banks and investment capital. Francophone-founded financial institutions included the Banque du Peuple, which was established in 1835. Francophones also established several smaller banks.

Social Life

Bourgeois housing in Montreal consisted of single-family homes that were made of higher-quality materials and built on larger lots than housing in lower-class neighborhoods. The Francophone bourgeoisie lived in greystone houses along Saint Denis and Saint Hubert streets, while the Anglophone bourgeoisie moved into villas and rowhouses along Mount Royal.

Cultural life and social activities were also ways for one to embrace their class. In Montreal and Quebec City, the bourgeoisie created curling, cricket, and hunting clubs. The daughters of the elite spent their free time horse riding, socializing with friends, going to parties, crafting lace, and studying piano. Urban working-class men engaged in sports like lacrosse, hockey, and baseball. Wrestling, boxing, and horseracing were also quite popular.

The 1880s saw the opening of public swimming pools. Previously, those looking to swim had to wade the freezing and dangerous waters of the Saint Lawrence River. Ice skating was another popular pastime, and by the 1870s, private rinks were scattered across cities.

Other popular activities among all classes included parades, sledding, picnics, fireworks, and circuses. Taverns were hubs for men to gamble, play billiards, and engage in political debate.

Working-class Women and Industrial Society

Women faced new responsibilities in industrialized Quebec. An industrialized society meant crowded living conditions, wage labor, and consumerism, which posed challenges for women who continued to be responsible for caring for their families and households. A working-class family couldn't survive on a man's wage alone, so women and children had to contribute to the household.

Urban families continued to keep farm animals, such as horses, cows, pigs, and poultry, for some time. City regulations made it difficult for families to keep their animals, and families were encouraged and eventually forced to buy meat rather than produce it.

Widows and unmarried women without significant capital were especially desperate. They found work where they could use their domestic abilities, such as cleaning, washing, and cooking. Sometimes, they ran taverns or boarding houses.

Chapter 7 – Expansion of Industrial Capitalism

In 1867, a new confederacy was established. The Canadian Confederation locked Quebec into a federal state in which power was granted to a central government in Ottawa, Ontario. Industrial capitalism in Quebec was subordinate to Ottawa's control, but it continued to mature between the 1890s and 1930s. Energy came into use, which quickly expanded manufacturing. After World War I, American capital became particularly important to Quebec's economy. Industrial capitalism brought new methods of organizing labor, manufacturing, management, and cost regulation.

Up until the 1880s, small artisanal shops remained important, but by the dawn of the 20th century, industry became large and mechanized, leaving little to no room for economic dependence on artisanal shops. Farming lost its place as Quebec's largest employment sector, as young people traded farming for work in mines, forests, and factories. In Montreal, the opening of major companies, such as Bell Telephone and MacDonald Tobacco, allowed for new forms of work, especially for women.

Changes in production and ownership reflected changes in culture and consumerism. Automobiles, cigarettes, radios, and movie theaters brought moral challenges to a society that had long been dominated by religion and conservatism. While these new products were mostly consumed in urban areas, by the 1930s, they had spread across the province.

Consumerism and Social Relations

Shifts in social relations were brought on by rapidly increasing literacy rates, new forms of rail, telegraph and telephone communications between cities and the country, the changing form of consumerism, and the growing influence of capital and of the state.

The Anglophone bourgeoisie expanded its institutions that separated it from the rest of Quebecois society. In the wealthy Anglophone towns of Westmount and the town of Mount Royal, municipal services like libraries and parks were meant to exclusively serve the Anglophone community. This cultural segregation was prevalent in smaller towns across Quebec. Separate neighborhoods provided fashionable Tudor-style homes and clubs for the local Anglophone elite.

Labor Standards

During and after World War I, increases in hourly wages and buying power improved the poor urban working conditions of the 19th century. However, there were still critical issues facing public health. Class inequality manifested, and there was a high infant mortality rate among Francophone working communities, high unemployment rates, and a general struggle for survival during the Great Depression.

Adolescents from the working class entered the workforce and were usually restricted to low-paying jobs. Young women were increasingly encouraged to work in nursing or teaching or perform clerical work. Midwives were eradicated from the workforce since the professionalization of medicine decreased the importance of the position, and clerical work was increasingly feminized during the labor shortage of World War I.

Work remained seasonal for many workers despite industrialization. Many worked in forests during the summer and fall months and worked in urban centers in the winter. Longshoremen, construction workers, and even sailors didn't expect to work for more than eight months of the year.

Quebec's per capita income in 1926 was $363. Many Quebecois workers had achieved the fifty-hour workweek their predecessors had been fighting for throughout the 19th century, but women and children often worked up to sixty hours a week. A provincial law passed in 1912 aimed to reduce the legal working hours to fifty-five hours a week in the textile industry, but the law wasn't widely applied.

Child labor was an important part of the labor force in the first quarter of the 20th century. Corporal punishment and fines were used to discipline child laborers. Children were fined for working too slowly or for talking during working hours. Factory inspections were irregular and completed with little effort. Factory inspectors were overworked and had little power to make any significant changes to a factory's ventilation, sanitation, or safety.

Industry Expansion

Popular journalism became especially profitable at the turn of the century, and pulp and paper became an important facet of Quebec's economy. The largest paper mills were founded in the Canadian Shield and Appalachians, where dense forests abounded. A series of pulp-and-paper towns cropped up along the Ottawa, Saint-Maurice, and Saguenay rivers.

Mining also became important in the first half of the 20th century. By the end of the 1920s, Quebec's gold and copper became world-renowned, as a plethora of mines opened in the Abitibi region near Rouyn-Noranda. The Great Depression triggered a rise in gold prices, which stimulated Quebec's gold production.

Aluminum was a critical element in the electrical, war, and automobile industries. Alcan, a branch plant of the Aluminum Company of America, was founded as Canada's major aluminum producer in 1902. Alcan partially funded the development of hydroelectric dams along the Saguenay River in the 1920s.

Food and beverage processing remained Quebec's most important manufacturing sector during the 20th century. It had undergone a sharp transition from agricultural to industrial processing, and the creation and expansion of transcontinental railway systems ensured that the products of sugar refineries, mills, breweries, and canneries could be distributed across the country. Quebec's brewers made record profits in the first half of the century, and they were determined to protect the market. The Molson, Dawes, Dow, and Ekers breweries grouped together to defeat the Anti-Alcohol League in the 1919 referendum to enact prohibition. When the nation voted against prohibition, Molson experienced a record-breaking 22.5 million liters sold in a year.

Unlike food and beverage processing, agriculture became less central in Quebec's economy. The percentage of Quebec's agricultural labor force declined from 45.5 percent in 1891 to 19 percent in 1941. The dairy industry was the only agricultural sector that maintained its importance. Butter production tripled with the introduction of new manufacturing technology, refrigerated rail transportation, and an increase in domestic demand.

Working Women

Women continued to be responsible for childcare and domestic work, although their contributions to the workforce became increasingly significant. The labor shortage brought on by the First World War led to women moving into labor sectors that had traditionally been exclusive to men, such as munitions and steel production and transportation. Female labor was perceived to be cheap labor, as men were expected to be the breadwinners, and women's labor was less significant to the household. Women were paid half a man's wage.

Women typically became elementary school teachers, nurses, telephone operators, and office and store clerks. Private secretarial schools were established to teach office tasks like typing and stenography to young women. Males also attended these schools, but they were taught more valuable skills, such as accounting and bookkeeping.

Female elementary school teachers in Quebec were underpaid and blocked from professional advancement. They worked in poorly ventilated, mal-equipped, and crowded classrooms. Above teaching, rural teachers were expected to clean classrooms, shovel snow, and light fires.

Nursing, another feminized role, became professionalized in the 1890s through probationary training, diploma programs, and residences for trainees. Quebec's first nursing school opened in 1890 in the Montreal General Hospital. French nursing courses were offered at Notre-Dame Hospital in 1897.

Labor Groups

Until the end of the Great Depression, Catholic ideology defined the framework of workers' rights. Catholic social activists stressed that Quebec's language, culture, and religion needed to be protected against unions. Their labor reform efforts were centered on peace, temperance, accessible and improved education for the working class, and restricting work in mills and factories on Sundays.

At the beginning of the 20th century, Catholic authorities participated in the Quebec labor movement. Early confessional unions saw priests acting as chaplains and united the Catholic authorities and Francophone trade union activists in defending their property rights, projecting a corporatist view of the workplace over that of class struggles, and choosing arbitration over strikes. Labor organizers did not doubt the role of the church, as it provided ideological support to the influence of capital rather than mediating between capital and labor.

International unions grew rapidly in Quebec in the years before World War I. Many of the organizers were Jewish, and some became particularly radical after the war, occasionally promoting communist ideals and condemning capitalism. Though they created influential and revolutionary unions, they were unable to stop the spread and influence of older American unions. The Great Depression had a negative impact on international unions, even the most powerful among them, such as the United Mine Workers and the Amalgamated Clothing Workers, both of which suffered massive financial losses and eventually fell into ruin.

Although there was an active communist party in Quebec based in Montreal, it was not a significant force among labor groups. Though the party managed to draw 1,500 members to Montreal to commemorate Vladimir Lenin in 1926 and 1927, it continued to have difficulty influencing Francophone unions, and many union members were expelled based on their communist ties. Fear of governmental reprisal and a growing insistence on defending the Soviet Union lessened the party's appeal among working men and women.

Women's unions were prominent in the labor resistance. The textile and garment sectors, both of which depended heavily on female labor, saw frequent strikes. Despite the Catholic Church's opposition, Francophone women working in the garment industry joined hands with their Jewish coworkers during strikes. In 1924, the female workers at the Eddy Match factory in Hull went on strike for over two months over the management's attempt to reduce salaries in the company and to replace female managers with men.

Culture Shifts

Despite the rise of new consumable goods, such as the telephone, radio, and film, traditional culture maintained itself in the daily lives of the Quebecois. Church and family held the most influence, and many social activities were centered around the parish, including Mass, bazaars, choir singing, dinners, processions, and service clubs. People only traveled for major occasions, such as weddings and funerals, or to visit one of the several religious shrines in the province.

In urban areas, taverns played an important role as centers for male socialization. With the creation of the Quebec Liquor Board in 1921, independent taverns could be licensed. Until then, they were restricted by law to being located in inns, where they provided food and drink. Independent taverns held a monopoly on the sale of draft beer. Taverns were restricted only to male patrons until 1979. Most taverns were found in working-class neighborhoods.

The expansion of industrial capitalist society allowed for the development of new leisure forms for the working class and the elite. The rapid growth of literacy created a new market for local literature. Newspapers could be published cheaply with the advance of printing technologies, such as the Linotype machine. Newspapers like *La Presse* featured political illustrations that appealed to the public. Small weekly editions like *La Bibliothèque à cinq cents* (the five-cent library) provided readers with excerpts of French and Canadian literature for a nickel. The increase in the popularity of newspapers led to specialized editions. The first women's journal, *Le Coin du feu* (*The Fire Corner*), appeared in 1893.

Quebec's elite sought to raise the population's cultural awareness by opening specialized museums. The Art Association of Montreal was established in 1860. It held many exhibitions, but a permanent gallery was built in 1879. By the 1890s, the gallery attracted more than twenty thousand visitors each year. In 1883, the city of Montreal purchased the Château Ramezay, the previous home of New France Governor Claude de Ramezay, and turned it into a history museum. It opened to the public in 1896 and saw massive success, drawing sixteen thousand visitors in its first month.

In the 1920s, two new cultural activities influenced leisure among all classes. Cinema garnered immense popularity, and by 1933, Quebec was home to 134 movie houses. Radio began in Montreal in 1922 with the founding of two Montreal stations: CKAC for Francophones and CFCF for Anglophones.

The rise of public transportation gave the urban working classes access to new forms of leisure. Amusement parks satisfied the people's need for entertainment, music, food, and drink. Mount Royal Park opened in 1876 and provided natural space in the heart of Montreal. Sohmer Park, located in Montreal's east end, received up to ten thousand visitors a day. The park included attractions such as magic shows, giants, dwarfs, firework displays, circuses, puppet shows, and vaudeville shows. The park often held shows by famed Quebec strongman Louis Cyr.

—

Quebec's economy became increasingly based on electrical power and factory production in the first half of the 20th century. The era also saw the creation and growth of great corporations. Most of Quebec's economic power was controlled by Montreal's Anglophone capitalists. The Francophone bourgeoisie did not control much capital but maintained its power over regional financial, commercial, and industrial power.

Chapter 8 – Church, State, and Women in the 1890s to 1940s

Conservatives had a strong hold on Quebec's society and culture up until the 1930s, when provincial leadership fell mostly under the conservative leadership of the provincial Liberal Party (yes, it sounds contradictory, but the Liberal Party was more conservative than liberal). The party earned comfortable relationships with the Anglophone elite, the Catholic Church, and the Liberal Party of Canada. While religion, class, and gender usually divided the party's opponents, it used the church's influence and its nationalistic ideologies to its own advantage.

Elements of potential reformation were greatly suppressed by clerics, nationalist politicians, and journalists. In this era, the church held the most power over education and social life. As a result, progressives, feminists, and political radicals were forced into marginalized political groups and ethnic ghettoes.

Familial paternalism in the family, workplace, state, and church continued to bind women to their marginalized economic and social positions in Quebec. The church maintained its influence over women's reproductive, domestic, and labor activities.

The Church

In 1941, Quebec's population was 86 percent Catholic, and the Quebecois remained subject to the church's influence in all aspects of daily life. The clerical authorities also retained their power over social and intellectual life. The church governed regulations over theaters and cinemas, and it governed Sunday activities.

Quebec's Catholicism wasn't simply symbolic. Its institutional presence was omnipresent and accompanied by ideological rigor. The church continued to insist that the Quebecois attend Mass, and they emphasized the importance of confession. Patients at church-run hospitals were obligated to attend the chapel three times a day. In 1912, urban parishioners took Communion an average of twenty-two times; rural parishioners took Communion an average of twenty-eight times.[102]

The church extended its influence on morality through fraternal self-help societies and publications. These societies and publications used their platforms to warn against the dangers of urban consumerism, and they stressed the importance of traditional values, such as the centrality of the family unit.

Clerical strength was also apparent in the daily lives of those who lived in the countryside. Families placed religious images in their bedrooms and held daily prayers. Family pews were regularly crowded for Sunday Mass. Holy days and feasts were observed, and attendance at Mass was customary on Easter. Priests intervened, especially in rural parish life. They imposed their views on crop rotation, disciplinary approaches to children's misbehavior, cleanliness, and the village's appearance.

Farming organizations and *caisses populaires* (popular banks) provided the clergy with more influence over the countryside's social and economic life. The Union catholique des cultivateurs (the Catholic Union of Cultivators) was formed in 1924. The power of the movement's chaplains ensured that the movement would focus on social and moral reforms rather than secular politics.

---

[102] Hamelin, Jean. Gagnon, Nicole. 1984. *Histoire de catholicisme Québécois: le xxe sciècle.* Vol. I: 1898-1940. Montreal: Boréal Express.

The oldest bank in Canada was built in 1845 in Montreal.

Dickbauch, CC BY-SA 3.0 <http://creativecommons.org/licenses/by-sa/3.0/>, via Wikimedia Commons; https://commons.wikimedia.org/wiki/File:Bank_of_Montreal_1_db.jpg

Pilgrimages were sanctioned. The three most important pilgrimage sites in Quebec were in Saint-Anne-de-Beaupré, Cap-de-la-Madeleine, and Saint Joseph's Oratory in Montreal. All three sites had been established in the early days of French colonization.

Quebecois society relied on religious philanthropy to provide social services before Quebec's welfare state emerged. Sick Catholics were cared for in medical institutions run by female religious orders. The Protestant elite subsidized institutions, such as the Montreal Ladies Benevolent Society, which provided care for poverty-stricken women.

Over the course of the 20th century, a divide hardened between Catholic and Protestant ideologies. Asylums, orphanages, schools, hospitals, and cemeteries were defined by the ethnicities and religions of their clientele. Differences in ethnic attitudes were also apparent in approaches to smoking and cremation.

Catholic and Protestant educational institutions weren't welcoming of non-Christian communities, especially the ever-increasing Jewish community. Montreal Jews opted to pay their school taxes to the Protestant education system, where their presence was at least tolerated. However, their place in the Protestant school board was that of second-class citizens.

Racism toward immigrant groups was prevalent in both English and French Montreal. Chinese laundromats were regularly subject to physical attacks by youths. In Montreal's male sporting and gambling clubs, English, French, Jews, Italians, and Greeks were welcomed as members. However, the Chinese were not. The only segregated clubs in Montreal were Chinese clubs. The Chinese community was sold a grave lot at the back of the Protestant Mount Royal Cemetery next to the section for the poor. They were barred from holding cultural or religious ceremonies on the cemetery's property.

Clerical Intellectualism

The clergy always held an interest in higher education. Under the pressure of the chamber of commerce, the École des hautes études commerciales de Montreal (known as the HEC Montreal) was founded in 1907 as Quebec's first business school. The archbishop of Montreal, Premier Gouin, promised that the school would be independent, although it would be run as an offshoot of the Université de Laval and be subordinate to its religious authorities.

Classical colleges remained at the core of Quebec's secondary school system. Clerical authorities retained their tight hold on the founding of these colleges, their curriculum, and their faculties. Classical colleges reflected Quebec's changing demography. The colleges had previously been established in small communities, but between 1920 and 1939, thirty-nine colleges were established in Montreal and Quebec City. Fifteen of these colleges were for women.

At the time, Quebec's most important intellectual was Abbé Lionel Groulx. He was a conservative who was completely dedicated to the family and church. He struck a nerve in Quebec's political and ideological culture by questioning the value of industrial capitalist society and by defining the dangers of the decline of rural Quebec. He appealed to Francophones by emphasizing an idyllic, preindustrial past absent of the increasing influence of Anglophone wealth.

Groulx questioned the Canadian Confederation during the First World War's conscription crisis when thousands of conscripted Francophone men resisted what they viewed to be forced participation in Britain's war. He suggested that Quebec's Catholic values had been lost in the British conquest through compromises with the British and through the Francophone bourgeoisie's betrayal of traditional French values.

He emphasized racial homogeneity and moral purity, which appealed to the right wing's attacks on the Jewish community and Jehovah's Witnesses in the 1930s. Groulx promoted his nationalistic and fascistic ideologies from his chair at the Université de Montreal and through his monthly publication, *Revue de l'Action française*

Despite the institutional strength of Catholicism in Quebec, clerical prerogatives fell under the threat of bureaucratization and the growth of state power in the 20th century. The Great Depression also threatened clerical power through the newly installed Canada-wide social programs.

Quebecois Minority in Canada

The Canadian Confederation turned Quebec into a larger political state than it had ever been before, but its vulnerabilities were clear within the federation. Quebec had held a vision of developing a viable French Canadian presence in western Canada; however, this vision would never materialize. Furthermore, growing anti-Catholic and Francophobic attitudes in Ontario and New Brunswick would emphasize Quebec's minority position within Canada.

Up until the 1880s, conservative politicians held control over Quebec at the provincial and federal levels. Ethnic and racial tensions, political scandals, and a newfound acceptance of liberalism in the Catholic Church created a new, powerful generation of Quebecois liberals. Quebec's own Wilfred Laurier was elected as Canada's prime minister in 1896. Historians point to Laurier's faith in British institutions and the goodwill of his Anglophone allies as the reason for the election of a liberal Quebecois at the head of Parliament.

An image of Wilfred Laurier.
https://en.wikipedia.org/wiki/File:PAC_-_Sir_Wilfrid_Laurier_(1869).jpg

Despite having a Quebecois prime minister, there was no question that the majority of Canada was English-speaking, and Quebec's views would ultimately be subordinate to the views of the majority. It was clear that from the perspective of Canada's Anglophone majority, the Canadian Confederation had not created "two nations" as its supporters had promised. Instead, it had created a federation in which Quebec was one soft voice among the other English-dominated provinces.

Canada's role in the British Empire displayed another challenge in establishing the image of French Canada as an equal partner within the Canadian Confederation. By the 1880s, Great Britain was expecting Canada's support in imperial issues. In 1897, Laurier was pressured to contribute Canadian military forces to Britain's Royal Navy. Throughout the Boer War (which lasted from 1899 to 1902), French Canadian nationalists opposed a British motion that would have allowed the Canadian military to suppress South Africa's Boers, a European minority with whom French Canada sympathized. Furthermore, Canadians of British descent insisted that Canada support the British military in World War I, while French Canada resisted the war efforts.

A recruitment poster used in Canada during World War I.
https://commons.wikimedia.org/wiki/File:I0016902.jpg

In the early days of the 20th century, Quebec failed to establish a French school system in the new western provinces of Alberta and Saskatchewan. This presented a serious blow to any hopes of French expansion in Canada and was worsened by the enaction of

Ontario's Regulation 17 in 1911. The law restricted the teaching of French as a secondary language in the first two years of elementary school and the teaching of French to one hour a day at higher levels of education. Ontario school officials viewed the teaching of French as a necessary but temporary issue that must be tolerated in exchange for the goal of a uniform and unilingual education system.

The issue of World War I, specifically the issue of mandatory military service, created the biggest rift between Quebec and Canada in the first half of the 20th century. A decline in volunteer recruits and a rising casualty cost overseas placed more and more pressure on the Canadian government to enact conscription. Most military recruits had been British immigrants and British decedents who were eager to defend the empire. French Canadians were the least willing to participate in a European war. The Canadian military further alienated potential Francophone recruits by maintaining its resolutely British traditions.

In June 1917, Robert Borden's conservative government proposed the Military Service Act to raise 100,000 recruits. Most liberals joined the conservatives in a Union Government created to implement conscription. French Canadians' resistance to conscription manifested through anti-conscription riots. Forty percent of conscripted French Canadian men failed to report for duty, and in 1917, only three Union government supporters were elected to seats in the House of Commons.

An anti-conscription parade in Montreal.
https://commons.wikimedia.org/wiki/File:Anti-conscription_parade_at_Victoria_Square.jpg

Push for Provincial Autonomy

A sense of isolation within the Canadian Confederation, paired with the worry of Quebec's institutions and language being under attack from the Anglophone majority, led to a cultural and ideological separateness of Quebec from the rest of Canada. Between the 1880s and the 1920s, Quebec's politics were defined by growing attention to the minority status of the Quebecois within Canada, the enaction of provincial rights, and the role of Quebec's government in the pursuit to defend Quebec's linguistic, religious, and cultural traditions. French Canadian resistance to the linguistic and cultural majority of Canadians led to the hardened attitudes of the Quebecois elite toward immigration and the ethnic pluralism that was developing, especially in Montreal.

In the post-Confederation era, the Quebec government was caught between two forces: the conflicting interests of conservative Catholicism and maturing industrial capitalists. Quebec's politics were, therefore, characterized by instability, political division between centrists and Catholic conservatives, and increasing provincial debt to subsidize railways. The attacks of Quebecois politicians, scholars, and intellectuals on Canadian federalism created repercussions in the law and politics of the province.

In 1918, jurist Pierre-Basile Mignault was appointed to the Supreme Court of Canada. From his seat on the federal bench, he rejected federalism and the pro-common law of earlier Quebecois judges. Not only did he attack common law principles in areas concerning the Civil Code of Quebec, but he also placed his interpretation of the law within the framework of the theory of the Canadian Confederation. He stated that "The provinces were not created by this charter [the British North America Act]. Confederation is only the legalization of a pact concluded between the four provinces. It seems then that one can conclude a priori that the provinces acted like merchants who form a corporation. They put together a part of their property but kept the rest."[103]

Provincial separateness of language and culture, along with the power of conservative institutions within Quebec, frustrated the

---

[103] Dickinson, John. Young, Brian. *A Short History of Quebec.* Fourth Edition. Montreal: McGill-Queen's University Press, 2008.

reformers who sought to achieve solidarity throughout Canada. Although Quebec farmers faced the same problems as farmers in the rest of Canada (for example, issues with the costs of running a farm, credit, and effective political representation), Quebec farmers did not join the Canadian agrarian protests that resulted in the United Farmers' associations in Ontario and Alberta. With the conscription crisis still at the forefront of Quebecois consciousness, Quebec voted for liberal politicians in both provincial and federal elections throughout the 1920s.

The fight for women's rights was also characterized by the lack of solidarity between Protestant and Catholic reformers. By 1922, women in all provinces but Quebec had secured the provincial vote. In Quebec, Francophone suffragists were unable to successfully ally themselves with their Anglophone counterparts, even though a successful alliance would have advanced their cause.

Similarly, Quebec maintained its sheer refusal to accept Protestant social values concerning the issues of smoking and prohibition. Francophones were less likely to contribute and participate in campaigns led by women reformers that aimed to prevent the sale of cigarettes to children. In a 1989 prohibition referendum, Quebec was the only province to vote "no." Over the next few decades, Quebec continued to resist the prohibition movement.

Notable Governmental Administrations: Gouin and Taschereau

Lomer Gouin and Louis-Alexandre Taschereau both ran provincial liberal administrations that aimed to unite conservative nationalists and industrial capitalists. Across their three decades of power, the liberals described "progress" as the foundation of their administrations. In this case, progress meant the rapid exploitation of natural resources, the sustainment of low taxes, ensuring minimal state interference with business, and bearing a paternalistic attitude toward labor. Taschereau was particularly keen on attracting American capital, stating the province's need to "develop ourselves with the gold of our neighbours."[104]

---

[104] Jones, Richard. 1972. *Community in Crisis: French Canadian Nationalism in Perspective.* Toronto: McClelland & Stewart.

The alliance between consecutive liberal governments and major financial and industrial corporations was secured with cronyism, legal business, sinecures, and political contributions. Even indigenous communities, which were being increasingly marginalized through Quebec's power structures, felt the impact. For example, the Hurons on the Lorette reserve saw a portion of their territory expropriated and their ways of life threatened through the creation of the Lake Saint John Railway.

Both Gouin and Taschereau made efforts to maintain the liberal tradition of positive political relations with the church hierarchy. In their commitment to industrial expansion, economic growth, and social peace, church and state officials shared an ideology that was reinforced by their respective hierarchies. To the benefit of the liberals, the church had proved itself a reliable force in suppressing public unrest. In fact, Taschereau's uncle, Cardinal Elzéar-Alexandre Taschereau, had condemned the Knights of Labor in 1885. In 1903, Archbishop Paul Bruchési responded to a series of strikes in Montreal with a letter that rejected a labor theory of value and called on workers to be moderate in their demands concerning wages. From his perspective, strikes caused money to stop flowing in and resulted in cheap immigrant laborers replacing the Quebecois labor force.

The church-state alliance could be seen most clearly in education. In 1875, the Education Act gave every bishop in Quebec a seat on the Catholic Committee of the Council of Public Instruction. The act resulted in the significant growth of clerical influence to the point that most Francophone Catholic leaders submitted completely to the power of the Catholic hierarchy, clergy, and community. Despite some state centralization of education that oversaw financing and inspections, the church was successful in opposing demands for the establishment of a ministry of education. It continued to have complete control over curriculums and textbooks, and it resisted an extension of mandatory education that would have reduced the responsibilities of the family and increased state power.

In 1908, the budget was less than fifty cents for each child enrolled in elementary school.[105] Costs were kept low through the cheap labor of nuns and brothers, who made up 48.3 percent of elementary teachers and 85 percent of secondary and post-secondary teachers. A labor force composed of clerics ensured that the salaries of teachers, most of them women, remained low. Although Quebec invested little in its educational system, its literacy and attendance rates were comparable to the other provinces.

The church-state collaboration did not completely eliminate tensions. Protestant and Jewish constituencies mounted pressure on state authorities to increase educational subsidies and change the curriculum. The state eventually assumed the financing of male education in 1897, although women's education remained under the financial control of the church. In 1900, Quebec's fifty female boarding schools received state aid that was the equivalent of one classical college. In 1908, the Congrégation de Notre-Dame was permitted to open Quebec's first female school of higher learning, but it only received the status of a classical college in 1926.

There were also tensions in the social sectors, where clerical control and Catholic ideology were often at odds with the realities of urban society. Quebec's reported illegitimacy rates were slightly lower than the rest of Canada, varying between 2.9 and 3.4 percent of live births. As attitudes toward work and family life shifted in industrial capitalist society, the vocation of many Catholic institutions changed. Daycare centers became necessary for working-class families. The Grey Nuns opened a slew of daycare centers in the latter half of the 19th century. The number of children admitted to these daycare centers peaked at the turn of the century and then declined, which suggests that many of the centers were turned into hospices for the children of poor families. Faced with wartime separation, unemployment, or the imprisonment or illness of the family head, parents had no choice but to abandon their children at hospices.

---

[105] Ryan, William F. *The Clergy and Economic Growth in Quebec (1896-1914)*. Quebec: Presses de l'Université Laval, 1966.

Nationalist and religious sensitivities were impacted by the state's financial participation in social affairs. In 1924, the Taschereau administration passed the Child Adoption Act, which relieved crowding in orphanages by finding homes for illegitimate children and provided legal safeguards to adoptive parents. Clerics protested the act, particularly against the act's provision that allowed for Roman Catholic children to be placed in non-Catholic households. The clergy described the act as part of an anticlerical campaign that sought to eliminate and systematically displace the church's maternal influence.

Populism in Montreal (1900–1950)

Through the development of Montreal's industrial capitalist society, the proletarianization of Montreal's working class resulted in urban populism. In the 1880s, working-class communities in Montreal's East End, such as Hochelaga and Saint-Jean-Baptiste, were annexed by the city, adding the weight of Francophone laborers to Montreal's proletariat. Francophone laborers became increasingly important in the politics of a city that saw rapid industrialization, monopolies, persistent strikes in the transportation sector, and serious public health crises.

Riots broke out after the smallpox epidemic of 1885 claimed 2,500 lives. In 1913, an eighteen-meter-long crack in the city's water circuit cut off the water supply for four days. The 1918 influenza epidemic hit Quebec the worst of all the provinces. A reported 530,000 cases resulted in 14,000 deaths in the province. Montreal achieved the worst infant mortality rates in North America when an impure milk supply caused tuberculosis and diarrhea.

It can be argued that the most shocking disaster to hit the city was the Laurier Palace Theatre fire of 1927. During a Sunday showing of the children's film *Get 'Em Young*, a fire broke out at the one-thousand-seat Laurier Palace Theatre. Seventy-eight children died, almost all of them having asphyxiated in the theater's four stairwells. An investigation showed that the theater was operating without a permit and that safety inspections had been shoddy at best. The theater's exits had been blocked by heavy ropes and snowbanks. The law stated that parents were required to accompany children under seventeen for all viewings. Almost none of the children had been there with their parents, and none of the victims were over the age of sixteen.

Until 1914, Montreal's mayors exclusively represented the city's elite. This changed with the mayoral victories of Médéric Martin (mayor 1914–1924, 1926–1928) and Camillien Houde (mayor 1928–1932, 1934–1936, 1938–1940, 1944–1954), both of whom were able to garner strong working-class support through patrician leadership and by attacking the city's powerful corporations.

In 1914, Médéric Martin ran against George Washington Stephens. Martin was a cigar maker from the working-class borough of Sainte-Marie. Stephens graduated from McGill University and was the dominant shareholder of the Canadian Rubber Company. He lived permanently at Montreal's Ritz-Carlton Hotel. Although Stephens's "City Beautiful" campaign had been supported by almost all of Montreal's newspapers and the Trades and Labor Congress, he was defeated by Martin, who campaigned against "the millionaires and rich men pretending to be working in the public interest." Instead of appealing to progressive ideas, Martin promised pavement, patronage, and the expansion of public works projects in working-class neighborhoods. These promises, along with his working-class image, kept Martin in office for a decade. The Laurier Palace Theatre fire and the influx in infant mortality rates that stemmed from poorly pasteurized milk led to his defeat by Camillien Houde.

Houde's background was similar to Martin's. Houde was born into a working-class neighborhood. He worked as a store clerk, a bank clerk, and eventually became a bank inspector. Throughout his campaign, Houde exploited the fears of the Montreal proletariat with a message that linked the monopolies of the great banks, tramways, and electrical companies to paganism, which would "lead to the disappearance of our western civilization." His campaign also centered on what he believed to be the profound and wholly negative implications of women's participation in the labor force. He suggested that "the man at home in a bathrobe while the woman is in a factory in pyjamas, the husband taking care of the children while the wife is out fighting for their daily bread and perhaps her honour, that is the world upside down."

Evolution of Women's Rights in Industrial Capitalist Quebec

The social dimensions of industrial society for women are revealed in early daycare centers, maternity centers, and hospices for the children of poor families, as well as in the economic effects of widowhood. The church symbolized female subordination to men, but it also protected female autonomy and provided legitimate alternatives to domestic life and working-class labor.

Bourgeois women, in particular, were unable to take social and political action, as they were barred from doing so by the state and corporations. A census taken in 1911 shows that there were no female engineers and architects and that fewer than 1 percent of domestic servants in Quebec were women. Of the two thousand licensed doctors in Quebec, only twenty-one of them were women, none of whom had been permitted to study in Quebec. Women were only admitted into the practice of law in 1941 and to the collective registry of notaries in 1956. Not only were women restricted access to higher education, but they were also subjected to the ideological symbol of the "woman" and her purpose within Quebecois society.

By the end of the 19th century, Anglophone women participated in a variety of newly established women's organizations. These included the Montreal Local Council of Women, the Young Women's Christian Association, the Montreal Suffrage Association, and the Women's Temperance Union. Women's organizations demanded social and legal reforms for equality in the workplace.

However, these English-based organizations were soon superseded by the Fédération nationale Saint-Jean-Baptiste. The federation was created in 1907 as a women's offshoot of the Saint-Jean-Baptiste Society. Its Catholicism and Quebecois nationalism predominated over its ideals of progressive feminism. Despite its conservative restrictions, the federation called for an extension of women's civil rights, access to higher education, and legal protection for female workers. One of their most vicious campaigns sought a reform of the Civil Code of Lower Canada of 1866, which displayed blatant discrimination against women. One of the civil code's passages ruled that while a husband could obtain a legal separation from his wife in the event of adultery, a wife could only obtain a separation if her husband brought his mistress into his home. In 1902, the manual *Traité de droit usuel* (*Concerning Common Law*) explained the law in lay terminology and demonstrated how it restricted women's civil rights.

Despite its demands, the federation was pressured by patriarchal institutions to focus on sectors that were traditionally of female concern, such as children's hospitals, workers' housing, familial courts, and alcohol abuse. Conservative rhetoric often surfaced. For example, a pamphlet the federation published for nurses declared that hospital training "prepared women admirably for their duties in family and society."

Most rural women and nuns worked within the boundaries of traditional Catholic attitudes. In rural newspapers, Françoise Gaudet-Smet encouraged women to value traditional domestic skills in a society that placed growing weight on consumerism and wage labor. Church authorities already perceived the importance of the developing field of household science or home economics. It was a way of training women while separating them from "male" fields, such as agriculture. By the 1880s, nuns in rural regions had already been teaching domestic skills to young girls who were destined to become farm wives. In 1905, the Congrégation de Notre-Dame founded Ecole ménagère Agricole de Saint-Pascal de Kamouraska. A year later, Montreal's first home economics school was opened.

During the First World War, urban society began to concentrate on teaching urban-born girls and women domestic skills. Under the watch of parish priests and the Fédération de Saint-Jean-Baptiste, ten thousand women a year enrolled in courses that taught sewing, cooking, and other domestic skills. Night and summer courses were established so that working women could access domestic education.

However, women were not blind to their circumstances. Married women were aware of the restrictions imposed on them by society, religion, work, and family. Anglophone companies preferred to hire English-speaking women who had significant connections within their communities, so most French-speaking women were turned away. On the other hand, English companies often made language exceptions for men. Gender-based obstacles were also observed in rural communities. Implicit sexism was present in almost all fields of employment, and women made a fraction of a male's salary based solely on their gender.

The clerical hierarchy opposed female campaigns for civil reformation. The Dorion Commission (1929), a provincial commission that was established to consider the demands of female-led campaigns, rejected the demand that married women should have jurisdiction over their own salaries and that there should be equal ownership between husband and wife over communal properties. The commission also didn't believe that female family members should be granted extended rights to act as their children's legal guardians. The commission's rejections were based on the idea that the individual rights of married women should be subordinate to a "superior law" of the family. They stated that once a woman willfully chose to enter a marriage, she was no longer free to reclaim her individual rights, as the superior law of the family dictated her duties.

Although the federal government granted women's suffrage in 1919, women did not obtain the right to vote in Quebec's provincial and municipal elections until 1940 under the Godbout administration. In 1921, Quebec's suffrage movement was revitalized with the creation of the Provincial Franchise Committee. The committee found it to be politically advantageous to claim that the goal of women's suffrage was not to change a woman's station in life but to inspire social life in general.

In 1928, Thérèse Casgrain became the president of the Ligue des droits (League of Rights). For fourteen years, she led the struggle for women's equality and civil rights. In this regard, Quebec lagged far behind the other Canadian provinces. The federal government maintained that Quebec did not allow women to exercise their public rights.

A political cartoon about women's rights in Quebec. Women were granted the right to vote in Turkey in 1930.

The suffrage movement faced severe hostility and criticism from clerical and political authorities. In 1922, the Episcopal authorities asked Quebec's premier to oppose women's suffrage, as it would represent "an attack against the fundamental traditions of our race and of our faith."[106] In 1940, the province's most important cleric, Cardinal Villeneuve, insisted on the opposition to women's suffrage, claiming that it would violate the principles of family unity and hierarchy and that it would tempt women with the "passions and adventures" of electoral politics. He also held his steadfast insistence that women didn't really want the right to vote and that

---

[106] Hamelin, Jean. Gagnon, Nicole. 1984. *Histoire de catholicisme Québécois: le xxe sciècle.* Vol. I: 1898-1940. Montreal: Boréal Express.

most of the demands called for by women's organizations could be achieved by groups outside the parliamentary system.

—

Quebec's industrial capitalist period was characterized by a combination of economic liberalism and social conservatism. Both the church and state remained dominant forces committed to the upkeep of traditional values, though foreign investment and corporations were increasingly given incentives. For their part, the church and state were able to muffle the demands of labor progressives, reformers, moderate Catholics, and suffragettes. In their struggle for educational reform, legal equality, the right to vote, and improved living conditions, labor and political reformers, along with feminists, suffered from ethnic and religious divisions in society.

Chapter 9 – La Grande Noirceur

La Grande Noirceur ("the great darkness") defines the period between the Great Depression and the Quiet Revolution that began in 1960. It's marked by the strengthening of conservative influence and ideology and clerical power. Politicians like Maurice Duplessis presented a portrait of Quebec as a calm Catholic population that doubled as an unaggressive labor force. The people were always respectful of the hierarchy and the "natural order." Of course, the reality of Quebecois society was much more complex. Quebec continued to modernize, and the population began to have a stronger awareness of class and ethnic realities.

Jewish, Slav, and southern European immigrants reignited ethnic and linguistic tensions in Quebec, which consequently led to a resurgence of Quebecois nationalism. Labor grew more organized, secular, and vocal. The newly increased presence of women in the workforce during the war legitimized paid and domestic work for married women. Feminism weighed heavy in the public consciousness, as more women demanded an extension of their political rights and increased social services.

Catholicism remained a dominant force in Quebec. It manifested itself through widespread piety, shrines, and devotions and through the presence of Catholic ideology in family life and morality. At the same time, industrial growth in the mining, transportation, and chemical industries promoted the expansion of manufacturing. American corporations became more important than ever in Quebec's economy, which was consistently integrating itself into North American markets.

Demography

The postwar "baby boom" refers to the sharp increase in Quebec's birth rate. The birth rate continued to rise until the early 1960s when birth control methods became widely available in the province. The increase in the population and steady immigration maintained Quebec's position within the country, which was home to approximately 29 percent of the total population by 1970.

The increase in marriages at a younger age was partly responsible for the postwar "baby boom." Thriving economic conditions allowed young men to feel comfortable marrying around the average age of twenty-five, while women were around twenty-three when they married. Quebec's infant mortality rates remained the highest within Canada, but they fell from 130 deaths per thousand births to 50 per thousand by the early 1950s.

The era after the Second World War is considered to be the golden era of the nuclear family in Quebec. Most couples married relatively young and had many children. Parents typically remained married and lived long enough to watch their children marry and leave home. Women usually took on the role of the stay-at-home wife. Separations and divorces were rare, and few marriages were interrupted by death.

While Quebec's population experienced a steady increase in births, its migration patterns were significantly altered by the Great Depression. Immigration rates fell, as there were fewer prospects of employment in Canada, and the tightening of American immigration laws slowed Francophone emigration to industrial centers in the United States. Post-Depression prosperity did little to reestablish old migration patterns. However, a new exodus of rural families benefited Quebec's industrial centers. Most emigrants who left Quebec headed to Ontario. Between 1956 and 1961, about three-quarters of the 74,000 Quebecois emigrants migrated to Ontario.

Although foreign immigration declined during the Great Depression and World War II, it increased sharply after 1945.

More than 420,000 immigrants settled in Quebec between 1945 and 1961, significantly altering Quebec's non-Francophone population. Italian, Greek, Polish, and German communities expanded, especially in Montreal. Italians increased from 4.6 percent of the non-Francophone population in 1931 to 12.4 percent in 1961. Two out of three immigrants sent their children to English schools, regardless of whether those schools were run by Catholics or Protestants. Anglophone Montreal was perceived by newly arrived immigrants as a more welcoming and receptive society and gave the English language much respect. They viewed Quebec as the gateway to North America's English-speaking North American culture.

An important development witnessed during the 1940s was the rise of the indigenous population. By the end of the decade, indigenous population levels were that of the pre-contact era; historians estimate that up to 200,000 indigenous people lived in Canada before the French began to settle in New France. The establishment of social programs, such as welfare, family allowances, and universal health care, was especially helpful in the recovery of vulnerable and materially poor indigenous communities.

However, indigenous subsistence patterns were disrupted, as resource extraction spread to traditionally indigenous and remote territories, such as Montreal's North Shore. The Algonquian Montagnais that lived on government reservations became increasingly dependent on government financial support, as the development of railway, lumber, and mining industries intruded on their hunting territories. As a result, the Montagnais settled in villages, and their population increased more than 50 percent between 1941 and 1961 since they had access to better health care.

Postwar Agriculture

Quebec's agriculture underwent a profound transformation in the years after the Second World War. As agriculture's importance to Quebec's economy lessened, the farming population fell dramatically after 1951. Technological advances in the timber industries reduced the seasonal employment that farmers depended upon in the winter months. As a result, many farm properties and farm towns in Abitibi, the Laurentians, and the

Eastern Townships were abandoned. In Saguenay, most of the agricultural land was exhausted by the 1950s, and in the Montreal and Quebec City regions, new suburbs were settled on nutritionally rich farmland.

Agriculture in North America was rapidly modernized in the 1940s and 1950s, and the effects of modernization were dramatic in Quebec. One significant change was the substitution of draft animals for tractors. In 1931, fewer than 2 percent of farms in Quebec had tractors, but by 1961, more than 63 percent had at least one. Tractors were commonly found in the Montreal region, where over 85 percent of farms had tractors, while in rural areas like Charlevoix, most farmers continued to rely on animals.

The Duplessis administration brought electrification to farms between 1945 and 1960. Commodities like refrigerators and mechanical milking machines became widespread in rural communities by the end of the 1960s.

By the 1930s, specialized farming was restricted to the Montreal region, the Eastern Townships, and Lac Saint-Jean. Otherwise, the mechanization of agriculture allowed for mixed agriculture and subsistence farming in most agricultural communities. At the end of the Second World War, farms were still small and independent. By 1960, they had become small capitalist enterprises dependent on new technological advancements, such as tractors, electricity, fertilizers, imported feed supply, and large corporations to market crops. A series of government-sponsored marketing boards and educational programs for farmers popped up in the 1950s. While agricultural cooperatives flourished and became increasingly prosperous, they faced internal conflicts between maintaining their traditional socio-democratic principles and meeting the demands of industrial management and big business.

Post-Depression Economic Expansion

The Great Depression rendered millions of Canadians unemployed and homeless. The nationwide unemployment rate reached 19.3 percent in 1933. While Quebec and Ontario experienced high unemployment rates, they were among the provinces least affected by the Depression due to their variety in industrial production, unlike the prairie provinces of Alberta, Saskatchewan, and Manitoba, which relied heavily on wheat production and which suffered from both the Depression and a catastrophic drought.

The country recovered in the decades between 1930 and 1960, which were marked by sharp fluctuations in the labor market. The years after the Great Depression were characterized by the strong demand for labor during World War II and then by a thriving postwar economy driven by consumerism. Between 1941 and 1951, manufacturing replaced agriculture as the most important occupation for males in Quebec. The number of men working as farmers dropped from 44.7 percent in 1901 to 17 percent in 1951. In 1931, women represented 21.3 percent of the labor force in Quebec, and by 1951, they represented 24.5 percent. The service sector held the most female employment, and office work was the fastest-growing female profession. The number of women working in manufacturing fell after the war, and by 1951, manufacturing accounted for 28.5 percent of the province's female labor.

Despite the affluent postwar economy, the Great Depression left scars on the collective psyche of the working class. During the Depression, in some Montreal neighborhoods, 40 percent of the working population was unemployed, while in remote regions such as Chicoutimi, unemployment reached 60 percent. Government incentives drew twelve thousand people to land-clearing and colonization projects in Abitibi and Gaspé.

The *caisse populaire* movement (communal banks), which were started by Alphonse Desjardins and his wife Dorimène in 1900, served low-income communities as a cheap alternative to banks. The Abitibi and Gaspé regions were highly receptive to the *caisses populaires*. In these newly colonized areas, the clergy and the local bourgeoisie, which partially financed the *caisses*, held great economic and social power and influence. Between 1934 and 1945, eight hundred *caisses* had been established across Quebec, and by 1945, the *caisses'* assets reached $90 million.

The war increased production and employment across Quebec. Military demand for aluminum led to sharp increases in the populations of towns centered on the aluminum industry. The chemical industry experienced exponential growth too. The industry accounted for around 5,800 laborers in 1939 and over 46,500 in 1943. Wartime demand for beef, powdered milk, and other foodstuffs offered work to farms and dairy factories. Montreal especially benefited from war production, especially in its aircraft and armament factories. Although Ontario held the largest amount of war contracts in the country, Montreal bore the largest number of laborers working in war production. Quebec City was in third place behind Toronto.

Until the 1920s, Montreal bore the title of Canada's metropolis. It had the most active stock exchange and the largest number of corporate offices and served as a communication and transport hub. In the 1920s, Toronto challenged Montreal's place, as it developed prosperous retailing, wholesaling, and banking industries. Eaton's and Simpsons, two Toronto-based department store chains, had the most catalog sales of all of Canada's department stores. By 1930, Montreal had lost much of its financial dominance to Toronto, and by 1960, it could barely compete. Between 1941 and 1961, twenty-one insurance companies moved their head offices from Montreal to Toronto, as did the massive American Prudential and New York Life insurance companies. By the 1960s, American capital was concentrated in Toronto. In 1961, over 660 American-based companies were in Toronto, leaving only 99 in Montreal.

Demand for Quebec's natural resources powered Canadian consumerism, postwar reconstruction in Europe, and the American demand for steel during the Korean War. Iron ore, aluminum, and asbestos were in especially high demand. The value of production in Quebec's mining industry rose from $59 million in 1945 to just over $246 million in 1960. Industrial regions that suffered serious blows during the Great Depression developed rapidly, thanks to high industrial demand.

In this same period, government policy favored Montreal as a hub for Canadian-based air travel. Montreal's major airport, Dorval, was named by the federal government as the Canadian point of entry for inbound flights from Europe. In 1957, Canada's national airline, Trans-Canada Air Lines (now Air Canada), based itself in Montreal.

Prosperity in the postwar period ensured low unemployment rates until the recession in the late 1950s. Unemployment rose from 5 percent to 10 percent in 1960 before dropping again.

Quebec's industrial structure at the end of World War II provided clear evidence of its phases of industrialization. The oldest and most critical sectors of the economy—food, clothing, leather, wood, textiles, and tobacco—relied on cheap immigrant and rural labor. These essential industries accounted for almost half of Quebec's labor force and 48.6 percent of the total value of industrial production in 1950. Hydroelectric industries founded at the turn of the century continued to play an important role in the economy, and the pulp and paper and chemical industries were crucial to postwar industrial growth. Rapid growth also occurred in industries like petroleum and electronics because of growing demands.

Quebec did not benefit from the booming automobile industry. Ford, Chrysler, and General Motors opted to build their factories in southern Ontario. Quebec's economy benefited mostly from the new dominance of the tertiary (service) sector. Consumerism sparked the expansion of retail shops, consumer credit, insurance companies, advertising, entertainment, tourism, and recreational industries.

Women and Paid Labor

While women in Quebec had historically lived in a Catholic and natalist society, the female labor reserve was beneficial to Quebec's economy. It was useful in times of labor demand and could be dispensed with in times of labor surplus. Women continued to make half of what a man did, and they remained susceptible to the domestic and maternal ideals imposed upon them. However, women's wartime labor did legitimize the place of married women in the labor force and eventually allowed women to combine paid labor with their traditional roles as mothers and homemakers.

The provincial right to vote was obtained in 1940 as a culmination of a three-decade struggle by feminists against the patriarchal idea that men had exclusive access to the public arena. In the post-suffrage era, women's influence was felt through universal programs and changes in educational laws. However, within unions, farms, and cooperative movements, women still struggled to ascend to power, as leaders maintained their patriarchal ideologies. In hospitals, offices, schools, and other institutions, women continued to be subject to the traditional authority of male doctors, priests, and male administrators.

Women were reminded of their place in the labor market as reserved labor pools during the Great Depression. Liberal leader Henri Bourassa was quick to remind women that their primary duty was to stay in the home. He stressed the importance of women leaving the factory work to the male heads of their families. Troubled by the increased presence of women in the wartime labor market, political leader Hervé Brunelle addressed the House of Commons, telling them that the "infiltration of women" into the male-dominated labor market would "create an overwhelming afterwar problem." However, the medical profession idealized the "caring" role of women and stressed their importance in health care.

Of course, the Second World War transformed Quebec's labor market. At the beginning of the war, in Montreal alone, there was a shortfall of nineteen thousand workers. As a result of patriotic appeals, the federal government recruited women into war factories. The Cherrier munitions factories offered daycare services, and an amendment to the income tax act in 1943 allowed husbands to claim a married-status tax exemption, regardless of their wives' income.

The number of working women doubled during the war. In 1945, 20 percent of female workers were married. After the war, working women were expected to cede their positions to returning soldiers or to their male family members. Despite this, fundamental cultural changes had occurred through female participation in the workforce, and by the mid-1960s, the number of female workers in Quebec had returned to wartime levels.

Education and work opportunities that were granted to women were not only dependent on gender but also on region, ethnicity, and social class. Before 1954, there was no network of public secondary schools. Catholic girls attended private boarding schools run by religious communities. Throughout the 19th century, opportunities for boys to attend school expanded with classical colleges, commercial schools, and universities. While a girls' college opened in 1908, it would only be deemed a classical college in 1926. Female religious communities, such as the Ursulines, the Congrégation de Notre Dame, and the Grey Nuns Hall, continued to open classical colleges for girls throughout the first half of the 20th century. Eighty percent of students at girls' colleges were from families of the elite. Women graduates of colleges had limited opportunities, and most ended up marrying young, working unpaid jobs, or working in philanthropy. Some continued their education in music, secretarial, or nursing schools, while others entered religious orders to fulfill central roles in education, social services, schools, and hospitals.

Throughout the 1920s and 1930s, Thérèse Casgrain, Idola Saint-Jean, and other suffragettes fought for the provincial right to vote in the press, at party conventions, before parliamentary committees, and in suffragist organizations like the Alliance Canadienne pour le vote des femmes du Quebec (the Canadian Alliance for the Female Vote in Quebec). The opposition to suffrage claimed that the world of women should remain "private" and be characterized only by family and the home. Thus, the participation of women in juries or politics would subject women to passions that were intrinsically opposed to their nature. None of the thirteen suffrage bills brought before the National Assembly between 1919 and 1940 was admitted for a second reading. Two decades passed before the first woman was elected to the National Assembly. Marie-Claire Kirkland-Casgrain was elected in 1961. She became Quebec's first female cabinet minister, fought for women's rights, and was the first woman to serve as a provincial court judge in Quebec. Women were only recognized as equals under Quebec civil law in 1964.

During World War II, the health and social service sectors expanded rapidly, and new professions became available to women. Women could now work as physiotherapists, nutritionists, and social workers. In 1925, the Université de Montreal created its public health program, the Ecole d'hygiène social appliquée, and it created its school of social work in 1940. By the midpoint of the century, the number of women enrolled in professional programs at the Université de Montreal increased from ninety to two thousand. Still, women continued to be subjected to male authority in their newfound professions.

Unions, cooperative movements, and municipal governments did not easily cede power to women. For example, the few female employees working for the city of Montreal were all single and employed as stenographers or librarians. Unions often undercounted the number of their female members. As late as 1942, the Confédération des travailleurs catholiques du Canada (Confederation of Catholic Workers of Canada) called for prioritizing the employment of men over women.

Changes in the Role of the State

Quebecois society between 1930 and 1960 is often described as rural and reactionary and under the complete control of the Duplessis administration. However, under closer examination, the era shows serious social conflict and an emerging desire for democratic and universal rights among unions, women's groups, and farm organizations. Clear signs of this can be detected in this period from the weakening influence of conservatism and a decline in the church's power over the state and society. The church was largely challenged and opposed by Quebecois youth, agricultural cooperatives, and progressive clerics.

These thirty years were characterized by two separate policies from two levels of government. Ottawa grew increasingly dominant as it settled the pillars of the welfare state. The Duplessis government remained relentlessly critical of federal intervention in provincial matters.

During the 1930s, the federal government and the municipalities stepped in to provide social services for victims of the Great Depression. Expansion of the technocratic and centralized state during the 1930s to 1960s had many elements: the creation of federal corporations, such as Central Mortgage and Housing (1946); wartime measures, such as conscription and the recruitment of female workers; the Saint Lawrence Seaway project; and the institution of universal social security programs, such as the family allowance program and government pension plans.

Much of this changing state power was federal. The federal government used the Rowell-Sirois Royal Commission report (1940) as an intellectual and economic rationale to extend government influence into family relations, work, family size, and education. The report called for a Canadian unemployment insurance plan and for the federal government to undertake the costs of all old-age pensions. The welfare state was introduced in 1944 when Ottawa established the family allowance.

Throughout the postwar era, federal-provincial conflicts over jurisdiction were relevant political issues. Ottawa gradually took control of sectors that had traditionally been under provincial authority, such as the expansion of highways and university programs, and other projects in social, regional, and educational sectors. In 1929, the Royal Commission on Radio Broadcasting suggested a national broadcasting service capable of creating a national spirit and interpreting national citizenship. In 1936, the Canadian Broadcasting Corporation (Société Radio-Canada) was created as a federal crown corporation. In 1939, the National Film Board was created, which reinforced the sense of federal expansionism.

Quebecois nationalists were further offended by federal intervention in culture and education when Ottawa gave $7 million to Quebec's universities. As a result of the Royal Commission on National Development in the Arts, Letters and Sciences (also known as the Massey Commission), Ottawa established the Canada Council for the Arts. The mission of the Canada Council was to encourage the study and enjoyment of the arts, humanities, and social sciences. The creation of the Canada Council was accompanied by increased federal funding for cultural institutions, such as museums and galleries.

The National Research Council grew in the postwar era as a crown corporation to fund science and research; by 1951, two thousand people were working at the council. Although government funding played an essential role in encouraging universities and cultural organizations, Quebecois nationalists were offended.

It was difficult for the provincial government to resist federal intervention because of the structure of government finances. In 1933, almost half of the taxes in Quebec were collected by the federal government. By the end of World War II, the federal government collected 82.8 percent of taxes in Quebec, the province received 7.3 percent, and the municipalities only collected 9.9 percent.

Although the Duplessis administration opposed social security programs, it wasn't hostile to the development of civil services. In fact, there was an increasing demand for civil services in Quebec.

In 1933, there were over eight thousand civil servants active in Quebec, and by 1960, there were almost thirty-seven thousand government employees.

The Duplessis Effect

In 1933, a reform program, *Le programme de restauration sociale* (Program for Social Restoration), was published by a coalition of social activists, the Catholic farmers' union, and the Catholic labor unions. They agreed upon the need for increased state intervention in relief programs, for the breakup of powerful trusts, and for electoral, labor, and agricultural reforms. Progressive liberals like Paul Gouin and nationalists like Philippe Hamel and René Chaloult were attracted to the Program for Social Restoration, and in 1934, they established a new political group, the Action libérale nationale (ALN), which would later serve as one of the founding parties of the Union Nationale.

During the 1930s, the Conservative Party of Quebec was revitalized under the leadership of Maurice Duplessis. Duplessis was the son of a conservative politician, and he worked as a lawyer in Trois Rivières. Duplessis's greatest political forte was his profound understanding of the history, culture, and ideologies of rural and small-town Quebec. He was well aware of the needs of his constituents, he was familiar with the local elites, and he understood their conservative traditions and deep-rooted beliefs. Although Gouin and other progressives were suspicious of Duplessis's reform credentials, the ALN and the Conservative Party established a common front: the Union Nationale.

An image of Maurice Duplessis circa 1940.
https://commons.wikimedia.org/wiki/File:L%27honorable_maurice_duplessis.jpg

Charges of corruption, tired leadership, and complicity with the monopolistic electrical trusts in Quebec, such as Montreal Light, Heat & Power, led to the downfall of the Taschereau government. In Quebec's 1935 election, sixteen conservatives and twenty-six ALN members who participated in the Union Nationale front were elected to Parliament. In the following months, Duplessis displayed parliamentary dominance in the face of Taschereau's forty-eight liberals. In June 1936, he became the leader of the Union Nationale, and he forced an election in August. Campaigning for a breakup of monopolistic trusts and for rural electrification, Duplessis defeated the liberals and won the electoral majority.

The Union Nationale quickly broke up with its progressive constituents and aligned itself as a strictly conservative party. Duplessis built his electoral base in rural Quebec by enacting policies that extended agricultural credit, created agricultural schools, brought in rural electrification, and created rural roads. Duplessis did not fight for workers' rights. He prohibited the closed shop, passed anti-labor bills, and took the sides of factory owners during the textile strikes of 1937.

Duplessis's campaign against communism earned him increased conservative and clerical support. The Act Respecting Communistic Propaganda (1937) was particularly hard on civil libertarians. Also known as the Padlock Act, this policy permitted the police to lock any building suspected of being used for communism or Bolshevism. Because the definitions of communist or Bolshevik acts were so broad, political authorities and the police used the act against unions, political groups, and religious minorities, such as the Jehovah's Witnesses.

The act was resisted by civil libertarians for decades; it was only declared unconstitutional by the Supreme Court of Canada in 1959 through the *Roncarelli v. Duplessis* case. Frank Roncarelli was a Montreal restaurant owner who had his license revoked in 1946. The official reason for his revoked license given by state authorities was for liquor violations, but the court found that his license was revoked in retaliation. Roncarelli had supplied bail to Jehovah's Witnesses and had distributed pamphlets attacking the Catholic Church.

As the Second World War began to ravage Europe in 1939, Canadians were just as divided on the matter of Canadian participation in the war as they had been during the First World War. The Quebec government continued to accuse the federal government of dragging Canadians into the "king's war," and conscription remained a controversial topic. In the end, 160,000 Quebecois voluntarily enlisted in the army, representing 20 percent of the Canadian Armed Forces fighting overseas. In 1939, Duplessis called an election regarding possible conscription. With the support of Quebec ministers in Mackenzie King's federal liberal government, who threatened to resign if Duplessis was reelected, Adélard Godbout's provincial Liberal Party was elected. Godbout was now faced with the crisis of war, and he left the matter of centralized economic planning to the federal government. When Ottawa established the family allowance program in 1944, Godbout did not fight to preserve provincial jurisdiction in social services.

However, Godbout did respond to demands for reform in social and economic provincial matters. In 1940, Quebecois women earned the right to vote in provincial elections. Labor relations were regulated by a new law that acknowledged the workers' right to join accredited unions and negotiate collective agreements. Schooling was deemed mandatory for children between the ages of six and fourteen. Hydro-Quebec was created in 1944 through the nationalization of Montreal Light, Heat & Power.

Despite installing these measures, Godbout's government was defeated by Duplessis's use of nationalism and the conscription controversy in 1944. His association with the federal liberals also played a role in Godbout's defeat. Since the World War I conscription crisis, Quebec had been consistent in returning liberal members to Ottawa, and the province expected Prime Minister Mackenzie King to stand by his 1939 commitment against conscription for overseas service. The prime minister, faced with a dramatic loss of life on the war front and pressure from other provinces, announced a plebiscite on April 27th, 1942, to release his administration from its anti-conscription promise. This left Canada sharply divided. The Quebecois voted 27 percent "no" in the conscription referendum, while the other provinces voted 79 percent "yes." The creation of Bill 80 allowed the federal government to introduce conscription.

Quebec reacted to the bill with anger and riots. In the provincial election of 1944, Duplessis benefited from this province-wide resentment by illustrating himself as a defender of provincial autonomy, language, and tradition.

Dawn of the Quiet Revolution

The 1956 Tremblay Report, which spanned four volumes, was a publication that gave ideological and statistical support to provincial autonomy and to the concept that Quebec's government should step in as the primary defender of a threatened culture. Conservative nationalists interpreted the Canadian Confederation in terms of provincial rights (an idea referred to as the compact theory) and argued that the Confederation had always been a pact between Canada's two founding peoples:

"The 1987 Constitution made the Province of Quebec, which was already historically its national focus, the French Canadian civilization. It also applied indirectly, insofar as it constituted the cultural focus of the French minorities of the other provinces and to the extent that its influence was exerted on all-over Canadian policy. No other Canadian province is, as a political unit, charged with any such high and difficult mission."[107]

The commission declared that provinces had the right to impose taxation to finance programs exclusive to their jurisdiction. Quebec used the report to justify the establishment of a provincial income tax in 1954.

By the 1930s, Quebec's intellectual and cultural life had become rich and pluralistic. Aging nationalists, such as Edouard Montpetit, continued to stress the importance of traditional values like frugality, anti-consumerism, maintaining a rural lifestyle, and peaceful coexistence within the Canadian Confederation. Meanwhile, the Bloc populaire (Popular Bloc) was an urban movement that grew out of opposition to conscription and federal centralization. It pressed for nationalization in areas that had traditionally been dominated by the church, for an extended

---

[107] Dickinson, John. Young, Brian. *A Short History of Quebec.* Fourth Edition. Montreal: McGill-Queen's University Press, 2008.

cooperative movement, and for long-term credit plans. The Bloc populaire used radio, weekly newspapers, and local meetings to promote finding a middle road between socialism and capitalism and to promote the welfare state. It also attacked the monarchy, old-line parties, and Duplessisism. The Bloc populaire elected four members in the provincial election of 1944 and two in the federal election of 1945.

By the end of the war, Quebecois intellectuals were divided between the left wing and the right, between liberal and conservative Catholicism, between Catholic ideologies and humanist ideologies, and between those who advocated for collective rights and those who emphasized the supremacy of individual rights. Abiding by social Catholicism and liberalism at Université de Laval's faculty of social sciences, intellectuals like Jean Charles Falardeau, Léon Dion, Fernand Dumont, and Georges-Henri Lévesque emphasized that the work of social scientists should be put at the disposal of the people and that they carry their scientific knowledge into social action. In Montreal, writers for the *Cité Libre* newspaper, such as Pierre Elliott Trudeau and Gérard Pelletier, attacked the clergy, conservatives, and the insularism of Quebecois society.

Social struggles did not only manifest themselves as battles between intellectuals. The urban working classes were increasingly ignoring traditional culture and institutions, especially the church.

The Decline of Religious Influence

Quebec's struggle between conservatism and modernism is best evidenced by the shifts in public attitude toward religion and culture. The power, influence, and strength of the Roman Catholic Church peaked in Quebec in the 1950s. With a clergy comprised of over eight thousand priests and approximately fifty thousand members of religious communities, the church held a stable presence in the lives of the Quebecois through its power over Catholic education, health care, and parish life.

Clerics, such as Abbé Groulx and members of the École sociale populaire, ensured that Catholicism held a strong influence over nationalist ideals and social values. Despite its seemingly secure position within Quebecois society, the church was vulnerable. In the 1930s, a significant number of clerics began to question the church's social policies and traditional values. The Dominicans, who had always been known for their liberal values, founded two institutions that stressed a scientific approach to knowledge rather than a religious one: the Institut d'études mediévales at the Université de Montreal (1942) and the École des sciences sociales at Université de Laval (1938).

At the end of World War II, new university departments were created that were out of the control of theology faculties. Quebecois publishers and booksellers had traditionally depended on clerical patronage for textbook purchases, and large-volume sales added to the church's censorship clout.[108] Albert Pelletier's publication of *Un homme et son péché* (written by Claude-Henri Gagnon) marked the beginning of independent publishing in Quebec. The 1935 creation of the Société des écrivains canadiens-français (Society of Canadian Writers) signaled growing literary freedom and autonomy in the province.

Up until World War II, clerical censorship meant that Quebecois publishers were forbidden from printing books listed on the Index—a list issued by Roman authorities in the 16th century that named literary works that Catholics were barred from reading. When France fell to Nazi occupation in 1940, Quebecois publishers began publishing French works, and clerical control over literature began to slip.

Quebecois had long stopped parroting the dominant conservative ideologies. Quebecois rural novels, such as *Un homme et son péché* (*A Man and His Sin*, 1933), *Trente arpents* (*Thirty Acres*, 1938) by Ringuet, and *Le survenant* (*The Outlander*, 1945) by Germaine Guèvremont, moved away from the traditional idealizations of rural life. Instead, these novels illustrated the tensions between rural and urban traditions and values, as well as intergenerational conflict.

Female voices also played an important role in modern Quebecois literature. *La chair décevante* (*The Disappointing Flesh*, 1931) by Jovette Bernier and *Chaque heure a son visage* (*Every Hour Has Its Face*, 1934) by Medjé Vezina illustrates the

---

[108] Dickinson, John. Young, Brian. *A Short History of Quebec*. Fourth Edition. Montreal: McGill-Queen's University Press, 2008.

challenges that faces traditional nationalism, duty, and patriarchy.

Opposition to intellectual repression reached its climax in 1948 when Paul-Émile Bordua published his manifesto, *Refus global*, which denounced the successive colonial regimes of Paris, London, and Rome, accusing them of alienating the Quebecois. Author Gérard Bessette also displayed hostility to church censorship in his 1960 novel *Le libraire*. Claire Martin's autobiographical novels cast a spotlight on the patriarchy, authoritarianism, and the suffocating religious climate that prevailed in Quebec. The most important literary attack on Quebec's traditional order came from Jean-Paul Desbiens, who, under his pseudonym Frère Untel, published *Insolences du Frère Untel* in 1960. The book attacked the clergy's hold on education, especially the anachronistic curriculum taught in schools and the use of ultraconservative literary works in French education. The book sold 100,000 copies in only four months, and it became an important element of the intellectual turmoil that took place throughout the 1960s.

Quebecois publishers flourished during the war when new markets opened in railway stations, drugstores, and newsstands due to the absence of competition with French publishers. However, the postwar era brought new challenges to publishers, with French magazines going back into publishing and the introduction of American pocketbooks and comic books. Fierce literary competition reduced the number of Quebecois publishers from twenty-seven to four between 1945 and 1960.

A new standard of living, advertising and media, and the popularity of the automobile homogenized Quebecois culture and weakened regional variations. Radio and television played an integral role in the spread of urban values to every corner of the province. The establishment of the Canadian Broadcasting Corporation (Société Radio-Canada) was of particular importance, as it produced most of the popular entertainment in the country. It had a distinctive Montreal flavor to its programming. Americanization would soon permeate Quebecois culture through the Anglophone community, which lived in the same cultural bubble as their American and Ontarian neighbors. People developed a taste for fast food, rock and roll, American television programs, and Hollywood films.

—

The period between 1900 and 1960 was characterized by significant societal shifts. The rise in labor was accompanied by the growing importance of American capital, the expansion of wartime industries in Montreal, and the growth of other resource industries. The era was also marked by a growing presence of women working outside the household and widespread questioning of traditional structures by intellectuals. The conscription crisis, linguistic tensions, postwar immigration, labor strikes across Quebec, and the activist reform movements within the church proved that, behind popular Duplessis conservatism, class and ethnic relations were boiling well before the Quiet Revolution launched in 1960.

Chapter 10 – The Quiet Revolution

Maurice Duplessis passed away at Schefferville in September 1959. His death, along with the election of Jean Lesage's provincial liberals in the spring of 1960, signaled the end of the Grande Noirceur that had plagued Quebec for decades. The 1960s and 1970s proved to be an era of rapid change in Quebec, as old institutions and attitudes were swapped with transforming ideas of the state, economy, family, and society. These drastic political, economic, and societal changes were brought about without violent revolt, so the era is referred to as Quebec's Quiet Revolution.

In the 1960s and 1970s, Francophone intellectuals rose to political power in both the provincial and federal governments. These doctors, teachers, journalists, and public administrators were the products of classical colleges. They rejected Catholic values and embraced secularism and statism. They accelerated modernization and developed structures to deal with the demands of mass education and the welfare state. These measures flitted the state closer to private life than it had ever been before, and issues like divorce, abortion, health insurance, rent control, consumer protection, state-run automobile insurance, and state sponsorship of cultural productions raised concerns about societal rights versus private rights.

Language was the central element in the process of widespread state intervention on behalf of collective interests. Protection of the French language was at the center of nationalism. Bill 101, or the Charter of the French Language, was passed by the Quebec National Assembly in 1977. The bill was central to the fiery language debate that spanned these decades.

A linguistic map of Quebec. The blue is where a large Francophone majority lives, the green a small Francophone majority, the red a large Anglophone majority, and the yellow a small Anglophone majority. The grey areas are where an indigenous language holds the majority.

Piotron, CC BY 3.0 <https://creativecommons.org/licenses/by/3.0>, via Wikimedia Commons, https://en.wikipedia.org/wiki/File:Quebec_langues.png

Reforms like Bill 101 were part of the "national question." Varying concepts of Quebec as a society were revived, and so was the concept of a "nation" being synonymous with the physical territory of the Province of Quebec. These imperatives presented a new dilemma to Anglophones and non-Francophones, whose assimilation into the Quebecois people had been implied. These imperatives also isolated the federal government as foreign and hostile to the hopes of the Quebecois.

Debates over nationalism, the role of the state, and the future of Canada were fiercely present in Ottawa, which was now headed by Prime Minister Pierre Elliott Trudeau, and in Quebec City, which was headed by Premier René Levesque. From the federal Royal Commission on Bilingualism and Biculturalism in the late 1960s to the 1980 sovereignty referendum to the creation of the Charter of Rights and Freedoms in 1982, Quebec's association with sovereignty and aspirations for independence were examined from every angle. Quebec's political direction was shifted by the failure of the referendum in 1980, the barring of Quebec from the constitution in 1981 when Quebec opposed the transfer of constitutional control from Great Britain to Canada, Trudeau's resignation in 1984, and the defeat of the Parti Quebecois in 1985.

Throughout the 1960s and 1970s, trade and farmers' unions, women's and social action groups, and municipal reformers struggled beyond the national question of political interference in issues such as housing, violence, education, and abortion. For example, in 1972, Quebec's teachers' union (the CEQ) published a manifesto that accused the education system of mirroring a capitalist society, which could not be maintained without the exploitation of the majority by a rich and powerful minority. Reform groups increasingly viewed Quebec's independence from Canada as essential to achieving their social aspirations.

As Montreal continued losing its pan-Canadian economic power to Toronto, Quebec's regional economy amassed more importance for Francophone entrepreneurship and the state. Quebec began to focus on controlling its own economy rather than gaining outside capital. Francophone control over manufacturing increased from 47 percent in 1961 to 60 percent in 1987.[109]

---

[109] Langlois, Simon, Jean-Paul Baillargeon, Gary Caldwell, Guy Fréchet, Madeleine Gauthier, and Jean Pierre Simard. 1990. *La société Québécoise en tendances,* 1960-1990. Quebec: Institut Québécois de recherche sur la culture.

While companies like Bombardier increased the perception that Quebec was moving into international markets rather than Canadian markets, the truth was that the international market was growing increasingly American. Quebec's exports to the United States increased from 66 percent in 1968 to 77 percent in 1987. For this reason, Quebec was the most enthusiastic province in Canada over the 1988 Free Trade Agreement with the United States.

Quiet Revolution and Demographic Evolution

Quebec's demographic evolution throughout the Quiet Revolution was triggered by four factors: a sharp decline in the natural birth rate, an aging population, the decline of the traditional family, and increased immigration.

Quebec's birth rate had been one of the highest in the West, but it dropped to one of the lowest by the 1980s. The decreasing influence of the church and the introduction of the birth control pill impacted Quebec's fertility index, which fell from 3.4 children per woman in 1960 to 2.0 in 1970. Before 1960, only 30 percent of women were limiting their fertility, but by 1970, that number rose to 90 percent. A variety of contraceptive methods grew popular in the 1970s. Vasectomies and ligatures largely replaced the pill. Reports show that by the mid-1980s, 40 percent of Quebecois couples over the age of thirty were voluntarily sterilized.

The Canadian birth rate had been declining as well, but the drop in Quebec was more severe and would eventually lead to a decline in Quebec's share of Canada's population from 29 percent in 1950 to 26 percent in 1981. The decline in Quebec's birth rate gave legitimacy to fears for the survival of the Francophone population. It was a core cause for the tightening of linguistic tensions within Quebec and for the heightened pressure on immigrants to assimilate into Francophone society as quickly as they could.

Another detriment to Quebec's birth rate was the legalization and province-wide access to abortion, which had been a central demand of the feminist movement for decades. Abortions had initially been performed in specialized private clinics, but they became increasingly available in hospitals and public health clinics referred to by the acronym CLSC (centres locaux de services communautaires). In 1971, there were only 1.4 abortions performed for every hundred births, but that number rose to 18.9 by 1986. A common misconception at the time was that the vast majority of abortions were performed on teenage girls. In actuality, most abortions were performed on women between twenty and twenty-nine years old, proving the determination of Quebecois women not to be forced into giving birth to unwanted children.

The combination of a declining birth rate and the stable adult mortality rate made for an aging population. Male life expectancy increased after the end of the war, rising from approximately 60 years in 1945 to 72.2 in the mid-1980s. Women's longevity increased during this period as well, rising from 63 years to 79.7. Province-wide increases in longevity meant increased dependency on disability and the loss of autonomy after the age of sixty. There was, of course, the component of class affecting these mortality rates. In 1987, the lifespans of wealthy Montrealers exceeded those of the poor by ten years. The increasing participation of women in the workforce meant fewer women were available to care for the elderly, and the Quebec government was forced to establish a network of residences for the aged.

There were important consequences to the changes in the age profiles of the Quebecois. The school-age population decreased after 1960, hence the sharp decline of young adults entering the workforce after 1980. The demand for health care and pensions rose. In 1961, Quebecois who were fourteen years old or younger represented a third of the population but only a fifth in 1987. During those same years, the population of sixty-five-year-olds went from 5.8 to 10 percent of Quebec's total population.

Changes in the family structure were an important change in Quebec's demographics as well. A sharp decline in religious practices during the 1960s and changes in moral attitudes contributed to marriage no longer being the norm for the Quebecois, especially among educated Francophones. By 1987, 27 percent of females between twenty and twenty-four and 42 percent of those aged between twenty-five to twenty-nine opted for common-law relationships rather than marriage. In 1986, 487,000 couples in Quebec declared themselves as having common-law relationships.

There was a growing tendency for people to live alone or in single-parent families. In 1961, 4.9 percent of Quebec's population lived alone, and by 1989, this figure had risen to 24.5 percent. In 1961, 8 percent of households with children were headed by a single parent, who were usually widows, but as divorce became less taboo, that number jumped to 26 percent by 1986—double the Canadian average. The structure of the average family changed as well. In 1961, the average size of a household was 4.53 people, and by 1989, it had decreased to 2.59 people. Of all home buyers in 1986, 42 percent did not have any children in the home.

Heavy immigration into Quebec changed the population profile and led to emigration out of the province starting in the 1960s. The emigration rate reached its highest following the October Crisis of 1970 (the kidnapping of important political figures) and the election of the Parti Quebecois government in 1976. The majority of those who emigrated during this period were Anglophones. Between 1971 and 1986, almost 200,000 Anglophones left Quebec.

Immigration to Canada decreased after 1974, and so did Quebec's share of immigration. The majority of immigrants settled in Montreal. In the 1950s and 1960s, most immigrants came from Europe or the United States. In 1986, most came from Asia, North Africa, the Middle East, or Latin America. The concentration of immigrants from different corners of the world in Montreal neighborhoods, such as Côte-des-Neiges, brought racial tension, violence with the police, and difficulties in schools.

Quebec's indigenous population was growing at a faster pace than it had in years. It's generally accepted that census figures from this time are incorrect since the 1876 Indian Act decreed that indigenous women who married whites were barred from band membership, so the descendants of these interracial marriages could not be counted as indigenous.

Quiet Revolution and Economy

Like most facets of Quebecois society, the economy underwent fundamental changes during the Quiet Revolution. Postwar economic expansion allowed the Quebecois to enjoy prosperity they had never seen before. This expansion halted during the first oil crisis in 1973, and economic growth thereafter was slow and accompanied by high unemployment rates, high taxes, regional disparities, and the introduction of a post-industrial economy.

Fingers are often pointed to the 1976 election of the Parti Quebecois as being the cause for Montreal's downfall, but as we've seen, the city had long ceded its place as *the* metropolis to Toronto. The construction of the Saint Lawrence Seaway hurt the city's port and rail traffic, and the decision to divert international flights to Mirabel airport and keep Dorval open only to North American flights put an end to Montreal's position as the main hub for Canadian air traffic. Cultural factors after 1960, such as rising nationalism, FLQ terrorism (Front de libération du Quebec; more on them later), and debates on limiting access to English schools, contributed to undermining the city's financial position.

Historians in the 1950s and 1960s denounced Quebec's economic inferiority in Canada. The provincial government adopted the slogan *Maîtres chez nous* ("our own masters"), and starting in the 1960s, it became an active player in the economy and contributed to the economic advancement of Francophones.

The 1963 nationalization of private electric companies (becoming part of Hydro-Quebec) was a spectacular economic move by the government. Massive hydroelectric power developments along Montreal's North Shore in the 1960s and in the James Bay drainage basin in the 1970s created thousands of jobs. Furthermore, it created an energy surplus fit enough for exportation to New England. The creation of a welfare state at the provincial and federal levels and the expansion of educational and medical facilities that were free from religious control created new opportunities for Francophones.

Postwar growth in Quebec was thanks partly to the rapid expansion of the natural resource extraction industries. However, after 1975, this sector suffered. Successive recessions in the American economy; the relocation of international corporations to developing countries, where they could capitalize off cheap labor; and the discovery of health hazards associated with asbestos fibers led to the closure of copper, iron, and asbestos mines. The downfall of the iron ore market after 1985 was a massive blow to the once-important mining towns of Schefferville and Gagnon, and it put an abrupt end to Sept-Îles's shipping activity. The population of Sept-Îles fell from thirty thousand to twenty-five thousand between 1976 and 1986, and it never recovered.

While Quebec's manufacturing base decreased, its profile was the same. Food, textiles, leather, wood, and tobacco remained as important as ever, and these industries continued to rely on immigrant and female labor. However, the growing awareness of the health hazards associated with tobacco use and competition from Asian textile producers threatened these industries and led to sharp declines in employment in Montreal and Quebec City.

As we've seen in previous chapters, Quebec didn't play a large role in automobile manufacturing. Despite efforts to create new automobile factories by attracting companies like Peugeot and Renault in the 1960s and Hyundai in the 1980s, only the General Motors plant at Sainte-Thérèse remained in occupation during these decades. Ontario continued to dominate auto assembly and the supply of auto parts.

Montreal refineries were severely impacted by the energy crises of 1973 and 1979 since they used imported crude oil rather than Canadian crude oil. Several refineries closed. However, the oil crisis proved beneficial to the aluminum industry, as automobile companies opted to construct their cars with lighter metals to increase fuel efficiency. Hydroelectric resources also helped Quebec's aluminum industry to lead the world in aluminum production. Quebec also became a leader in rail and transit technology, with Bombardier playing an important role in international markets. Despite Montreal's success in some projects, such as the Canadair water bomber and the Challenger executive jet, the city's aeronautics industry never regained its wartime prominence.

The rise in prosperity and consumption led the average family income to rise from $22,120 in 1961 ($216,832 today) to $37,282 in 1986. Most new jobs were in retail and services. The grocery sector experienced dramatic changes with the advent of the supermarket. Supermarkets had a variety of services and enlarged parking lots, and they soon dominated the sector. Supermarket chains, such as Metro and Provigo, provided their own baking, canning, and transportation networks. Their small convenience store affiliates were successful in lowering prices enough to eliminate most of the small independent grocery stores in Quebec.

The government monopoly over the sale of beer, certain wines, and lottery tickets kept small convenience stores (*dépanneurs*) alive. When the large supermarket chains were allowed to start selling beer, wine, and lottery tickets, the *dépanneurs* survived by selling cigarettes and other tobacco products, which were barred from being sold in grocery stores and supermarkets.

Part-time employment became an important feature of Quebec's labor market, and it had both a gender and age dimension.[110] Women represented 70 percent of part-time workers. Many company pension plans and government incentives that invested in retirement savings plans allowed men over fifty-five to progressively leave the labor market by working part-time.[111] A third of people under twenty-five, who faced a staggering absence of full-time work opportunities, worked part-time in the tertiary sector. The flexibility offered by part-time work benefited people but rarely made up for the loss of job security and career advancement that was available with full-time work. Part-time work also often benefited employers, as it provided them with flexibility, reduced costs, and minimized union strength in the face of ever-changing economic conditions.

One of the goals of the Quiet Revolution was to allow Francophones to thrive in business. By breaking free of the Catholic Church's chokehold and by democratizing education, Quebec began producing qualified professionals who could compete with Anglophones. Montreal's fall from being Canada's shining metropolis, along with the government's promotion of the French language in the workplace, created a small but strong Francophone business-based bourgeoisie. Pierre Péladeau of Quebecor (a media and telecommunication company) is a prime example of the power and influence held by members of this new group.

---

[110] Dickinson, John. Young, Brian. *A Short History of Quebec.* Fourth Edition. Montreal: McGill-Queen's University Press, 2008.

[111] Langlois, Simon, Jean-Paul Baillargeon, Gary Caldwell, Guy Fréchet, Madeleine Gauthier, and Jean Pierre Simard. 1990. *La société Québécoise en tendances, 1960-1990.* Quebec: Institut Québécois de recherche sur la culture.

By the late 1980s, almost two-thirds of employment was in companies run by Francophones. For the previous two centuries, Francophones had always had a strong presence within smaller companies, but now they were increasingly heading massive corporations in banking (National Bank), engineering (SNC), transportation (Bombardier), and food processing and distribution (Culinar).

Quiet Revolution and Politics

Jean Lesage was viewed as a pragmatic politician who assumed leadership with the intent to modernize government structures and implement institutions that would be useful for the development of Quebec. The Lesage administration exercised its leadership by analyzing and adopting reform measures one by one based on the circumstances in which the province found itself.

Armed with the slogan *Maîtres chez nous*, the Lesage government used the state to effect change. The creation of a ministry of education was essential to this process. The school curriculum and power over schools and teachers were ripped from the church and put in the trust of a generation that embraced secularism, nationalism, and modernism.

In 1965, Lesage created the Caisse de dépôt et placement du Quebec (the Quebec Deposit and Investment Fund). The fund acted as a deposit for the Quebec pension fund and fifteen other public agencies, such as the state-owned automobile insurance fund (Société de l'assurance automobile du Quebec). Its access to large amounts of capital and the *caisse*'s mandates of "achieving an optimum financial return" and making a "sustained and durable contribution to the Quebec economy" made a strong impact on the Quebecois and Canadian economies. By 1985, the *caisse* held assets of over $20 billion and became one of the largest investors in the Canadian stock market.

One of the most notable acts of the Lesage administration was to spark dramatic expansion in the public sector. It created departments for provincial-federal relations and communications, cultural affairs, family and social welfare, and natural resources. The number of public sector employees rose from 60,980 in 1961 to 141,468 in 1987.[112]

Revolutionary factors in the working class during the 1960s rejected democratic ideals as a means of gaining social justice and independence. People were bitter about unemployment rates, which were outside the control of Quebec's economy, and conflicts over the language of education. Many embraced Marxist ideologies or the developing world's liberation models supported by leaders like Che Guevara. In 1968, Quebec CEGEPS (College of General and Professional Training) was forced to stop classes over a network-wide strike, and in January 1969, a protest at Sir George Williams University (Concordia University today) inflicted millions of dollars' worth of damage to the university's property.

One of the most prominent Marxist figures of the 1960s in Quebec was Pierre Vallières. Born to a Montreal working-class family, he yearned to politicize the Quebecois with his influential book *Nègres blancs d'Amérique* (*White Negroes of America*, 1971) by comparing them to other colonized people throughout history. His ideology took form with the creation of the future terrorist group called the Front de libération du Quebec (FLQ). The FLQ was committed to overthrowing "medieval Catholicism and capitalist oppression" through revolution. The FLQ held particular resentment toward the federal government and the Anglophone bourgeoisie. It threatened to destroy all colonial symbols and institutions, the Royal Canadian Mounted Police (RCMP), and the Canadian Armed Forces; all the English informational media that "hold the Quebecois back"; all commercial enterprises that did not use French and, therefore, discriminated against the Quebecois; and all plants and factories that discriminated against Francophone employees.

In 1966, the Lesage government was defeated by a reformed and revitalized Union Nationale, one that sought to balance reform with nationalism and rural anxieties over statism. Daniel Johnson's Union Nationale bore the slogan *Égalité ou indépendance*, and it acknowledged the growing support for Quebec's exclusive control in certain fields. During this time, another group opted for a federal vision where Francophone aspirations would be integrated

---

[112] Langlois, et al. 1990. *La société Québécoise en tendances.*

into Canadian interests. In 1968, Quebecois Pierre Elliott Trudeau defeated Lester Pearson and became the liberal prime minister of Canada.

The latter half of the 1960s saw the fracture of the provincial Liberal Party. To many nationalists, Lesage and his government had refused to see the *Maîtres chez nous* mission due to its subordination to foreign capital and by refusing to consider independence. René Lévesque would be the one to draw the nationalists out of the party in 1967.

An image of René Lévesque.
BAnQ Vieux-Montréal, CC BY-SA 3.0 <https://creativecommons.org/licenses/by-sa/3.0>, via Wikimedia Commons
https://en.wikipedia.org/wiki/File:Ren%C3%A9_L%C3%A9vesque_BAnQ_P243S1D865.jpg

In the 1960s, the independence movement grew more significant thanks to the weakening position of Francophones outside Quebec, perceived federal intrusion in provincial affairs, and the emergence of a powerful and especially ambitious Francophone bourgeoisie.

Lévesque founded the Mouvement souveraineté-association, which eventually formed the Parti Quebecois in 1968. Using Quebec's possible independence as its banner, the Parti Quebecois won seven seats in the National Assembly.

While the formation of the Parti Quebecois was a legitimate political action, the revolutionary activities of the FLQ were not. The October Crisis of 1970 refers to the kidnappings of British consular official James Cross and Quebec Labour Minister Pierre Laporte. The Trudeau administration made a strong response to the FLQ kidnappings. It installed the War Measures Act, which suspended the public's civil liberties. It called out the army, and hundreds of Quebec's intellectuals, political activists, and labor leaders were detained. Pierre Laporte was murdered by his captors on October 17th after his attempted escape through a window in the house where he had been held. James Cross, on the other hand, survived his kidnapping. After being held hostage for sixty-two days, Cross was released by the FLQ once the Canadian government negotiated a safe escape to Cuba for his five known kidnappers.

Quebec's population was divided over the FLQ manifesto. Some appreciated its attacks on the church, corporate colonialism, and Anglophone racism, but most believed that the murder of Pierre Laporte discredited the movement.

Quiet Revolution and Culture

The strengthening and modernization of Quebecois culture are considered to be the most important themes of the Quiet Revolution. However, the decline in religious influence and the prevalence of American consumerism created a new problem in retaining the Quebecois identity within North America. For their part, Catholicism and the romanticization of rural values offered some level of certainty. As these disappeared, Francophones resorted to cultural defenses.

Quebec's artists had been some of the loudest voices demanding change since the 1930s. In the 1960s, artists were at the forefront of Quebec's nationalism. Novelists like Hubert Aquin, playwrights such as Michel Tremblay, and poets like Gaston Miron inspired nationalist feelings by expressing their pride in being Quebecois. Songwriters and singers aimed to do the same. Some rock and roll artists, such as Robert Charlebois and Diane Dufresne, attempted to add a Francophone flavor to the genre, but the traditional *chansonniers* (traditional Quebecois singer-songwriters) were able to make the biggest impact on the Quebecois cause through their music. Singers like Gilles Vigneault sang of Quebec's distinct character.

In the 1960s and 1970s, Quebecois culture was extremely present in literature, theater, and music. Pride in Quebecois literature grew as the traditional Catholic anthologies in high school and CEGEP curriculums were replaced with the works of authors like Jacques Godbout. Universities established Quebecois literature as a field of study in undergraduate, postgraduate, and doctoral programs.

The cultural revival in Quebec was triggered by the historically insufficient cultural infrastructure. By 1960, only 45 percent of the population had access to a municipal library. As part of Canada's centennial celebrations in 1967, government-funded halls, such as Place des Arts in Montreal (built in 1967) and the Grande Théâtre in Quebec City (built in 1971), were constructed. The erection of the Museum of Contemporary Art (built in 1965) and the expansion of the Musée des Beaux-Arts provided open access to culture. Private historical museums, such as the McCord Museum, Château Ramezay, and the David M. Stewart Museum, were run by local historical societies.

Despite the expansion of cultural infrastructure and activities, most cultural activities were a privilege reserved for the elite. A poll taken in 1979 showed that 77 percent of Quebecois had never been in a library, 50 percent had never been to a bookstore, and 44 percent had not read a book in the previous year. From 1979 to 1980, Quebec's minister of cultural affairs ordered the creation of libraries, museums, and concert halls. The next five years saw the opening of more than one hundred new libraries, and within the decade, floor space for cultural exhibitions tripled. Attendance at cultural events soared as a result.

Quiet Revolution and Women

Beginning in 1960, gender relations experienced tremendous change for the better. Women in the workplace were cemented thanks to the Second World War, and their access to jobs only continued to expand. Despite wage disparity, women's ongoing economic autonomy increased their options when faced with marriage and parenting. Now that their roles in public service were no longer restricted to the church or philanthropy, women earned increasing power in business, professions, unions, and politics.

Women's rights were not considered a priority in the early years of the Parti Quebecois. Even the FLQ, which mentions the exploitation of indigenous peoples in its 1970 manifesto, did not make specific mention of women's rights. The 1972 manifesto of the CEQ, a teachers' union with substantial female membership, made the status of women a major political issue by pointing out the treatment of female role models featured in textbooks and by noting that the female dropout rate in secondary schools was twice that of males. It directed its attacks against the bias in education that directed girls and young women to careers of unpaid maternal and wifely duties.[113]

The most important political force in changing attitudes toward the role of women was the Royal Commission on the Status of Women, a federal commission that was active between 1967 and 1970. Headed by Ontario-based journalist Florence Bird, the commission heard from a variety of women's organizations in Quebec, such as the Montreal Voice of Women and the Women's Federation of the Allied Jewish Community Services of Montreal. The commission set an agenda for the progress of women's rights in the following decades by insisting on gender equality and equity.

Despite the 1974 creation of the Conseil du statut de la femme (Council on the Status of Women), women only earned a real voice in the provincial cabinet when television personality Lise Payette became ministre d'état de la condition feminine (minister of state for the status of women). Her voice represented the feminists who believed political power should be the way to achieve rights in the public and private domain.

In 1989, twenty-three women held 18 percent of the seats in Quebec's National Assembly. Thirteen of Quebec's seventy-five seats in the federal House of Commons were filled by women. A

---

[113] Latouche, Daniel. Poliquin-Bourassa, Diane. Bergeron, Gérard. 1979. *1900 à 1959: manifestes Québécois.* Montreal: Boreal.

wide network of women's organizations played an essential role in women's ascension to power. The creation of the Fédération des femmes du Quebec (FFQ), an anti-confessional, multi-ethnic group, was key to the development and success of this network. Although women's associations were often divided over political and social issues, such as access to abortion and divorce, they played a crucial role in the struggle for maternity leave, daycare centers, battered women's shelters, and changes in marriage laws.

The first important step in the improvement of women's rights was Bill 16. Passed in 1964, it established equality between men and women in marriage. Thanks to this bill, women were allowed to leave the family home if their husbands physically threatened them, and they were allowed to make decisions regarding their finances independently from their husbands. The Quebec Charter of Rights and Freedoms determined that gender and wage equality, along with the equality of partners within a marriage, were fundamental rights.

Although Canada had signed the United Nations Declaration of Human Rights in 1948, Quebecois women experienced difficulty obtaining equality in salary and treatment in the workplace for decades to come. Wage discrimination was endemic in the Quebecois workforce.

Chapter 11 – Notable Events from 1989 to 2005

Protection of Sexual Orientation

Although homosexuality had been decriminalized in Quebec in 1969 as part of the Quiet Revolution and the protection of all sexual orientations was present in the Canadian and Quebec charters, homosexuality in Quebec remained taboo and "closeted" until the AIDS epidemic brought gay and lesbian concerns into the mainstream. In the 1980s, Quebecois society grew more accepting of homosexuality. Despite the loss of hundreds of people to AIDS, the LGBTQ community continued to grow. It centered itself around the bright and vibrant gay village east of downtown Montreal. Montreal had its first gay pride parade in 1990 and has since become one of the world's most gay-friendly cities.

An image of Montreal today.
AnnaKucsma at English Wikipedia, CC BY-SA 3.0
<http://creativecommons.org/licenses/by-sa/3.0/>, via Wikimedia Commons;
https://commons.wikimedia.org/wiki/File:Downtown_seen_from_Mont-Royal.jpg

A major demand throughout the 1990s was the legal recognition of gay and lesbian couples. In 2002, the Quebec government under Bernard Landry created a new legal category of partnership, the civil union, that allowed same-sex couples to be legally recognized as common-law couples. In 2005, a federal statute ruled that gay and lesbian couples were allowed to marry. That year, 452 homosexual couples were married, while only just over 60 chose to remain in civil unions.

Violence against Women, the École Polytechnique Massacre, and Social Inequalities Affecting Women

Violence against women has always been and continues to be a problem in Quebec. Feminist historians have attributed domestic violence in Quebec to men feeling as if their power is threatened by the participation of women in the workplace, which affects their patriarchal position in the home. The massacre that took place at École Polytechnique in Montreal brought violence against women to the forefront of public discussion.

On December 6th, 1989, Marc Lépine, a twenty-five-year-old man, entered École Polytechnique. He was armed with a semi-automatic rifle and a hunting knife. Lépine entered a classroom and ordered the men to leave. He then ordered the women to line up against the wall. He proceeded to open fire on the women, killing fourteen and injuring ten before turning the gun on himself. The victims of the attack were all women. They included students, staff, and faculty members of the university. Many of them were studying engineering, a traditionally male-dominated field. In his manifesto, Lépine wrote that the shooting was fueled by his belief that women were taking opportunities away from men in the workforce, which was why he sought to target women in his attack.

In the aftermath of the attack, Canadian gun laws went through significant reform. The Canadian government established the Canadian Firearms Program to regulate the sale and use of firearms. Policies and initiatives were enacted designed to address violence against women. December 6th is recognized as the National Day of Remembrance and Action on Violence against Women in Canada.

Women's groups took on the responsibility of creating women's shelters, and over time, domestic violence was dealt with more effectively by police and the courts. However, between 1982 and 1986, only 18 percent of men charged with killing their girlfriends, wives, or children were convicted of murder. Sixty-six percent had their convictions reduced to manslaughter. The figures in 1990 were more optimistic: 65 percent were convicted of murder and 29 percent of manslaughter. Four-fifths of all cases involved women who had left their partners or threatened to leave.

The dual responsibilities of motherhood and paid work outside the home placed many women in stressful and exhausting situations. Many employers displayed little to no sympathy for their pregnant employees or for the mothers of sick infants. Although more men participated in domestic activities than they had before, the burden of most household chores and childcare was placed on women, which placed limitations on their work lives, such as eligibility for higher pay or career advancement. Despite the enaction of a 1997 law that promised equity, salary inequalities were endemic. Women working in full-time positions made only about 75 percent as much as men.

Despite decades of struggle and lobbying, some professions still remain dominated by men. In 2001, 90 percent of engineers and 77 percent of surveyors were men. In 1998, women represented only 20 percent of students at Montreal's École Polytechnique. Social work, dental hygiene, and nursing are fields that remain dominated by women.

The Oka Crisis

The Oka Crisis was a seventy-eight-day conflict between the Mohawk people of Kanesatake and the Canadian government that occurred in the summer of 1990. The conflict centered around a dispute over land in the town of Oka, which the Mohawk people claimed as their ancestral territory.

The dispute began in 1989 when the mayor of Oka, Quebec, announced plans to expand a golf course on land that was traditionally used by the Mohawk people as a burial ground. The Mohawk objected to the plan, and after months of negotiations, the issue was not resolved. So, the Mohawk set up a barricade on the road leading to the disputed land.

The situation escalated in July 1990 when the Quebec Provincial Police attempted to dismantle the barricade, leading to a confrontation between the police and the Mohawk protesters. The conflict resulted in the death of a police officer and the subsequent deployment of the Canadian military to the area.

The military's involvement in the Oka Crisis was controversial, as it was seen as an extreme response to a land dispute that could have been resolved through negotiation. The conflict received widespread media attention and sparked a national conversation about the relationship between indigenous peoples and the Canadian government.

The Oka Crisis had far-reaching effects on indigenous peoples in Canada, as it brought issues of land rights and sovereignty to the forefront of public discourse. It also led to changes in government policies, including the creation of the Royal Commission on Aboriginal Peoples, which aimed to address the issues of indigenous peoples in Canada.

Conclusion

Two days after French President Charles de Gaulle's address to the people of Quebec in late July 1967, he cut his visit to Canada short. He boarded a French military jet and made the transatlantic journey back to France. A diplomatic uproar lingered in Quebec and France for some time. Pierre Elliott Trudeau, who had been appointed as minister of justice and had yet to become prime minister, made a remark, wondering what reaction the French would have if a Canadian prime minister cried, "Brittany to the Britons," noting both the perceived irrelevancy and absurdity of Gaulle's statement. Gaulle responded to Trudeau's statement, saying, "We have no concessions, nor any amicability to extend to Mister Trudeau, who is the adversary of the 'French fact' in Canada."

While federal authorities were quick to dismiss Gaulle's breach of international protocol, it may have very well been a turning point for the sovereigntist cause in Quebec. In the eyes of many French Canadians and of soon-to-be sovereigntist politicians like René Lévesque, Gaulle's speech legitimized the sovereigntist movement.

Twenty-seven years after Gaulle's speech and twenty-four years after Quebec's first failed referendum, Premier Jacques Parizeau won the 1994 provincial election on the promise that he would hold another referendum on the matter of sovereignty in 1995. The Act Respecting the Future of Quebec was a bill presented to the National Assembly by the Parizeau administration. It painted a picture of a mythical past through agrarian traditions:

"The time has come to reap the fields of history. The time has come at last to harvest what has been sown for us by four hundred years of men and women and courage, rooted in the soil and now returned to it ... At the dawn of the 17th century, the pioneers of what would become a nation and then a people rooted themselves in the soil of Quebec. Having come from a great civilization, they were enriched by that of the First Nations, they forged new alliances, and maintained the heritage of France.

The English community that grew up at their side, the immigrants who have joined them, all have contributed to forming this people which became in 1867 one of the two founders of the Canadian federation.

Because the heart of this land beats in French and because that heartbeat is as meaningful as the seasons that hold sway over it, as the winds that bend it, as the men and women who shape it;

We know the winter is in our souls. We know its blustery days, its solitude, its false eternity and its apparent deaths. We know what it is to be bitten by the winter cold.

Our language celebrates our love, our beliefs and our dreams for this land and this country ... We proclaim our will to live in a French society. Our culture relates to our identity, it writes of us, it sings to the world [...]

Staying in Canada would be tantamount to condemning ourselves to languish and to debasing our very identity."

The 1995 referendum amassed a public turnout of 93.5 percent of Quebec's eligible voters. The results were as close as they could have been: 49.5 percent voted "yes," and 50.6 percent voted "no."

The federal government, as well as the rest of Canada, was shaken by the close election results. Some Anglophones chose to emigrate from Quebec, while others proposed a potential partition of Quebec in which Montreal and other Anglophone-majority and native communities would remain in Canada should Quebec earn sovereignty. The reality was that young Anglophones who had been born into the language provisions of Bill 101 felt comfortable as a minority in Quebec and in an increasingly pluralist Montreal. Most chose to stay in the province.

Thirteen years later, in 2008, Premier Jean Charest appointed the Bouchard-Taylor Commission, which presented its report on the matters of accommodation surrounding immigration, secularism, and the Quebecois identity. It attempted to define a concept of Quebecois "interculturalism," where the French language and Quebecois culture would be given priority and might be considered distinct from Canadian multiculturalism so the majority and the English language weren't threatened. The report called on French Canadians to come to terms with their dual identities as members of a majority in Quebec and members of a minority in North America. Despite its call for less anxiety over identity, the report was criticized by the nationalist majority in the National Assembly. They accused the report of underestimating the challenges posed to the survival of the "French fact" in Canada and North America.

Anxiety over the protection of the French language, culture, and traditions is still prevalent today. It is an open sore in the public consciousness and a persistent issue of contention. Linguistic, ethnic, cultural, racial, and gender tensions are still prevalent as well, though to a lesser degree. Despite ongoing tensions, many organizations and social activists are working toward a greater understanding, inclusivity, and appreciation for diversity within Quebec while defending the importance of recognizing and protecting Quebecois heritage. With continued efforts toward an open societal dialogue, there is hope for a truly harmonious and equitable Quebec.

Here's another book by Captivating History that you might like

OHIO

A CAPTIVATING GUIDE TO THE HISTORY OF OHIO AND ULYSSES S. GRANT

CAPTIVATING HISTORY

Free Bonus from Captivating History (Available for a Limited time)

Hi History Lovers!

Now you have a chance to join our exclusive history list so you can get your first history ebook for free as well as discounts and a potential to get more history books for free! Simply visit the link below to join.

Captivatinghistory.com/ebook

Also, make sure to follow us on Facebook, Twitter and Youtube by searching for Captivating History.

Further Reading and Reference

A Traveler's History of Canada. Robert Bothwell. 2001.

How Canada Came to Be: A Brief History. Anna Jennings Steen. 2017.

The History of Canada. Kenneth McNaught. 1991.

Becky Little. "How 22-Year-Old George Washington Inadvertently Sparked a World War."
https://www.history.com/news/george-washington-french-indian-war-jumonville. Accessed November 1, 2021.

Freeman, Douglas Southall. (1948) George Washington: A Biography. New York: Scribner

Stull, Charlene. "Washington's Mission to Fort Le Boeuf."
http://paheritage.wpengine.com/article/washington-mission-fort-le-boeuf/. Accessed November 10, 2021

"Washington and the French & Indian War."
https://www.mountvernon.org/george-washington/french-indian-war/washington-and-the-french-indian-war/#_ftn17

Library of Congress. "George Washington's map, accompanying his 'journal to the Ohio,' 1754."
https://www.loc.gov/resource/g3820.ct000361/?r=-0.251,0.291,1.605,0.647,0

Parkman, Francis. (1910). Montcalm and Wolfe (Vol.1).

Lengel, Edward G. (2005). General George Washington: A Military Life. Random House.

Fowler, William. (2005). Empires at War. Walker & Company.

Axelrod, Alan. (2011). A Savage Empire: Trappers, Traders, Tribes, and the Wars That Made America. New York: St. Martin's Press.

Green, Karl R. (2002). The French and Indian War. Berkeley Heights, NJ: MyReportLinks.com Books.

Gard, Carolyn. (2004). The French and Indian War: A Primary Source History of the Fight for Territory in North America. New York: Rosen Central Primary Source.

"Braddock's Defeat." https://www.britishbattles.com/french-indian-war/general-braddocks-defeat-on-the-monongahela-in-1755-part-x/. Accessed November 12, 2012

Hannings, Bud. (2011). The French and Indian War: A Complete Chronology. Jefferson, North Carolina: McFarland & Company, Inc., Publishers.

Accessed November 15, 2021

November 14, 2021

"Fort William Henry, 1757: A Massacre of Misunderstanding." https://warfarehistorynetwork.com/2016/01/11/fort-william-henry-1757-a-massacre-of-misunderstanding/ November 15, 2021

David R. Starbuck. "The Massacre at Fort William Henry." https://www.penn.museum/sites/expedition/the-massacre-at-fort-william-henry/ November 15, 2021

"The Battle of Rogers' Rock." http://nyindependencetrail.org/stories-Battle-of-Rogers-Rock.html November 20, 2021

Dr. Joseph F. Meany Jr. "Frigid Fury: The Battle on Snowshoes, March 1758." https://museum.dmna.ny.gov/unit-history/conflict/revolutionary-war-1775-1783/frigid-fury-battle-snowshoes-march-1758 November 20, 2021

Photo: Fort Louisbourg during siege 1758 By Pierre-Charles Canot – http://collections.britishart.yale.edu/vufind/Record/3628336http://b03.deliver.odai.yale.edu/88/28/88283354-6eee-48bb-ac8f-da6b76d74d5d/ba-obj-47548-0001-pub-large.jpg, Public Domain, https://commons.wikimedia.org/w/index.php?curid=56023137 November 21, 2021

Stacey, Charles Perry. (1973). Quebec, 1759: The Siege and the Battle. London: Pan Books.

"Battle of Quebec, 1759." https://www.britishbattles.com/french-indian-war/battle-of-quebec-1759/. Accessed November 22, 2021

"French & Indian War: North American History." https://www.britannica.com/event/French-and-Indian-War. Accessed November 22, 2021

Adney, T. The Klondike Stampede. 1899.

Berton, P. Klondike: The Last Great Gold Rush, 1896-1899. Anchor Canada, 2001.

"British Columbian Siwashes. Lilloett, [Lillooet] B.C." Welcome - RBCM Archives. Last modified 1865. https://search-bcarchives.royalbcmuseum.bc.ca/siwash-first-nations-at-lillooet.

Castner, Brian. Stampede: Gold Fever and Disaster in the Klondike. New York: Doubleday, 2021

"Diamond hitch." Wikipedia, the free encyclopedia. Last modified September 20, 2012. https://en.wikipedia.org/wiki/Diamond_hitch?wprov=sfla1

Duncan, Jennifer. Frontier Spirit: The Brave Women of the Klondike. Anchor Canada, 2010.

"Gold discoverers." NPS.gov (US National Park Service). Last modified September 22, 2020. https://www.nps.gov/klgo/learn/historyculture/gold-discoverers.htm

"Journey to the Yukon: Passage Aboard the Steamships from Puget Sound to the Far North." The Filson Journal. Last modified January 31, 2020. https://www.filson.com/blog/field-notes/yukon-journey-from-puget-sound/

"The Mountie Films." The Old Corral at b-westerns.com. n.d. https://www.b-westerns.com/mountie1.htm

Watterson, B. "The Yukon song – Bill Watterson." A Poem a Day. Last modified August 7, 2011. https://poetryfromthehart.wordpress.com/2011/08/07/the-yukon-song-bill-watterson/.

Winslow, Kathryn. Big Pan-out. New York: Norton, 1951.

"Women of the Klondike." ExploreNorth.com - Your Gateway to the North. Accessed May 15, 2022. https://www.explorenorth.com/library/yafeatures/klondike_women.html

Zhang, M. "You think 2020 was the year of sourdough? Look back to the gold rush." Salon. Last modified January 20, 2021. https://www.salon.com/2021/01/20/you-think-2020-was-the-year-of-sourdough-look-back-to-the-gold-rush_partner/

Berton, Pierre. War of 1812. First Edition. Canada: Anchor Canada, 2011.

Dickinson, John. Young, Brian. A Short History of Quebec. Fourth Edition. Montreal: McGill-Queen's University Press, 2008.

Gadoury, Lorraine. 1992. La Noblesse de Nouvelle France: Familles et alliances. Montreal: Hurtubise HMH.

Hamelin, Jean. Gagnon, Nicole. 1984. Histoire de catholicisme Quebecois: le xxe sciècle. Vol. I: 1898-1940. Montreal: Boréal Express.

Jones, Richard. 1972. Community in Crisis: French Canadian Nationalism in Perspective. Toronto: McClelland & Stewart.

Lachance, André. 1978. La justice criminelle du roi au Canada au XVIIIe sciècle. Tribunaux et officiers. Quebec: Presses de l'Université Laval.

Langlois, Simon, Jean-Paul Baillargeon, Gary Caldwell, Guy Fréchet, Madeleine Gauthier, and Jean Pierre Simard. 1990. La société Quebecoise en tendances, 1960-1990. Quebec: Institut Quebecois de recherche sur la culture.

Latouche, Daniel. Poliquin-Bourassa, Diane. Bergeron, Gérard. 1979. 1900 à 1959: manifestes Quebecois. Montreal: Boreal.

Pratte, André. Kay, Jonathan. Legacy: How French Canadians Shaped North America. First Edition. Toronto: Penguin Random House, 2016.

Ryan, William F. The Clergy and Economic Growth in Quebec (1896-1914). Quebec: Presses de l'Université Laval, 1966.

Sweeny, Robert. 1978. A Guide to the History and Records of Select Montreal Businesses before 1947. Montreal: Centre de recherche en histoire économique du Canada français.

Tousignant, Pierre. 1973. Problématique pour une novuvelle approche de la constitution de 1791. Revue d'histoire de l'Amérique française 27 (septembre): 181-232.

Printed in the USA
CPSIA information can be obtained
at www.ICGtesting.com
LVHW022340141023
760910LV00006B/119